AF411147

AUSTRALASIAN NATURE PHOTOGRAPHY

ANZANG FIFTH COLLECTION

AUSTRALASIAN NATURE PHOTOGRAPHY

ANZANG FIFTH COLLECTION

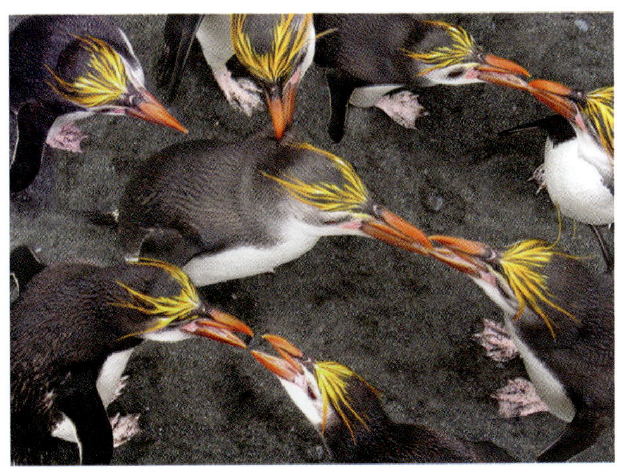

EDITOR: STUART MILLER

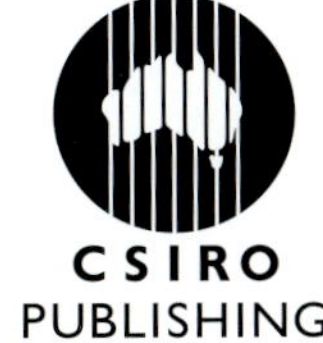

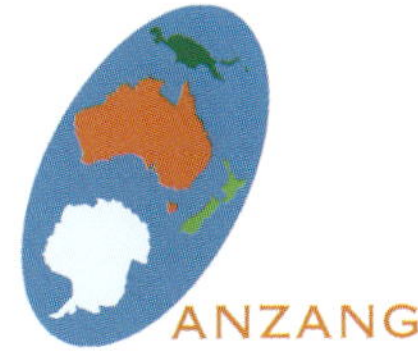

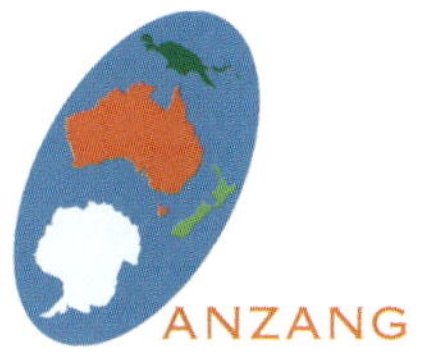

ANZANG Nature
Mailing address:
GPO Box 2828
Perth, Western Australia 6001
Australia

Office address:
51 Colin Street
West Perth, Western Australia 6005
Australia

Telephone: +61 (0)8 9321 3685
Fax: +61 (0)8 9226 3395
Email: compete@anzangnature.com
Website: www.anzangnature.com

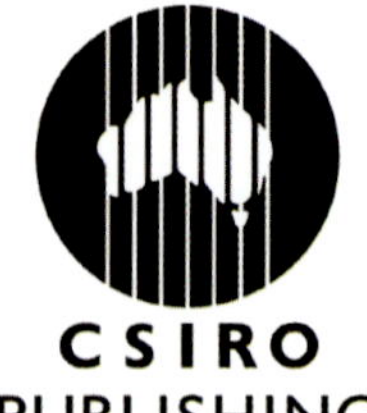

Published by:
CSIRO PUBLISHING
150 Oxford Street
(PO Box 1139)
Collingwood, Victoria 3066
Australia

Telephone: +61 (0)3 9662 7666
Local call: 1300 788 000 (Australia only)
Fax: +61 (0)3 9662 7555
Email: publishing.sales@csiro.au
Website: www.publish.csiro.au

Distributed in Australia by:
Steve Parish Publishing Pty Ltd
PO Box 1058
Archerfield QLD 4108
Australia
Website: www.steveparish.com.au

Text and photographic editing, graphic design: Stuart Miller
Printed in Singapore by Craft Print

Front cover:
ANZANG Nature and Landscape
Photographer of the Year – 2008
Fighting egrets
Allen Peate, Tweed Heads, New South Wales

Most images in this book may be ordered as individual photographic prints. For all details visit the ANZANG website at www.anzangnature.com.

Contents

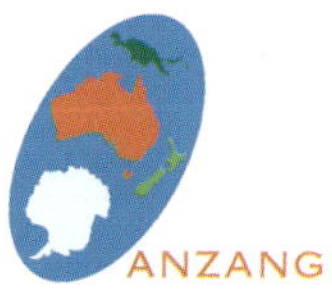

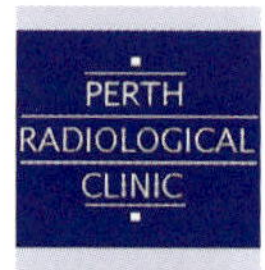

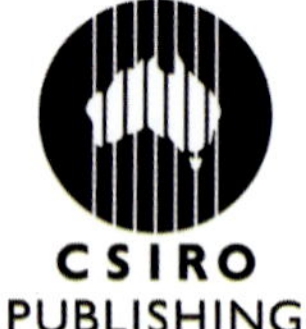

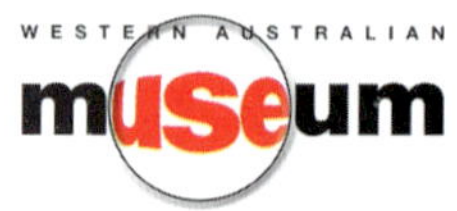

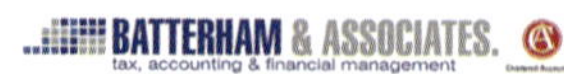

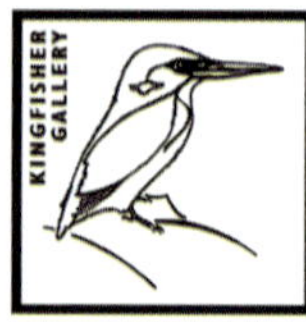

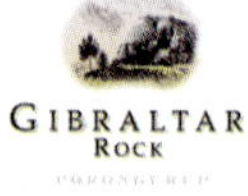

ANZANG Nature would like to thank our sponsors who in 2008 have so generously supported this fifth cycle of competition and exhibition.

Major Sponsors

Perth Radiological Clinic
CSIRO Publishing
The Zimmermann family
Western Australian Museum

Corporate Sponsors

Cameron Batterham and Associates
Colin Street Day Surgery
Gibraltar Rock
Kingfisher Gallery
Medical Audiology Services
Mountain Ocean and Travel Publications P/L
Western Diagnostic Pathology

Individual Sponsors

Mrs Alison Huber and her brother, Dr Stuart Miller, in memory of their parents, Dr Robert and Mrs Clarice Miller, both late of Waikerie, South Australia.

ANZANG Nature
Chairman: Dr Stuart Miller
Secretary: Mr Cameron Batterham
Advisors: Mr Bruno Zimmermann
             Dr Robert Edwards AO
             Prof. Ivan Shearer AM

2008 Competition Judges
Ms Belinda Barnes, Mr Roger Garwood, Dr Stuart Miller,
Mr Steve Moorhouse and Mr Michael Morcombe

Acknowledgements
This annual event requires considerable assistance. I would like to thank
the following:

The photographers who have entered this year's competition; our
board of advisors for their willing and helpful advice; our judges for
awarding prizes and commendations; Wanda Finkle for coordinating
communication with Australasian photographic clubs; Diane Phelps and
Karen Wilson for their administrative assistance; Kathleen Borona and
Irene Morcombe for assistance during the judging; Jennifer Banyard for
her editing assistance; and Jan Miller for her assistance throughout all
phases of this competition and exhibition.

Dr Stuart Miller
Chairman, ANZANG Nature
2008

Australia, New Zealand, Antarctica and New Guinea

Introduction

The ANZANG program has become an established event in the annual calendar for photographers and the viewing public. Now in its fifth year, ANZANG again presents the collection of winning and highly commended images selected by our judges. All of these images with the 'Exhibition' following their code have been further selected for the travelling exhibition.

CSIRO Publishing have again partnered with ANZANG in the publication of 'The Collection'.

Following Steve Parish's enthusiastic involvement with the ANZANG judging panel in 2007, he has committed Steve Parish Publishing to producing the first ANZANG calendar in panoramic format. This is another welcome development giving an even wider audience for the remarkable nature and landscape images that the ANZANG competition attracts.

Dr Stuart Miller,
Chairman, ANZANG Nature, 2008

ANZANG Nature and Landscape
Photographer of the Year – 2008

The overall winner of the competition is the photographer of the image judged the best of all images entered. Judges, when making their selection, considered the photographic technique, and the aesthetic, artistic and unique quality of all images.

Judges' comment: 'A great action shot of the highest technical quality.'

Prize: $5,000

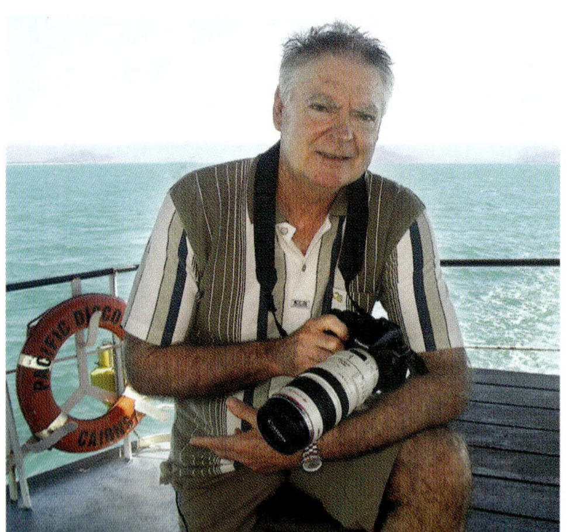

ANZANG Nature and Landscape Photographer of the Year – 2008
Fighting egrets
Allen Peate, Tweed Heads, New South Wales

'Before daylight, I crept into a natural freshwater billabong teaming with birdlife. For about two hours I photographed the birdlife. A small flock of egrets was feeding along the edge of the billabong when a lone egret flew in. A fight broke out just in front of where I was sitting and I was lucky enough to get a series of shots of the fight.'
St Lawrence, Queensland

Canon 20D, 400mm, 1/1600, f5.6
2008 ANZANG Winner, Exhibition

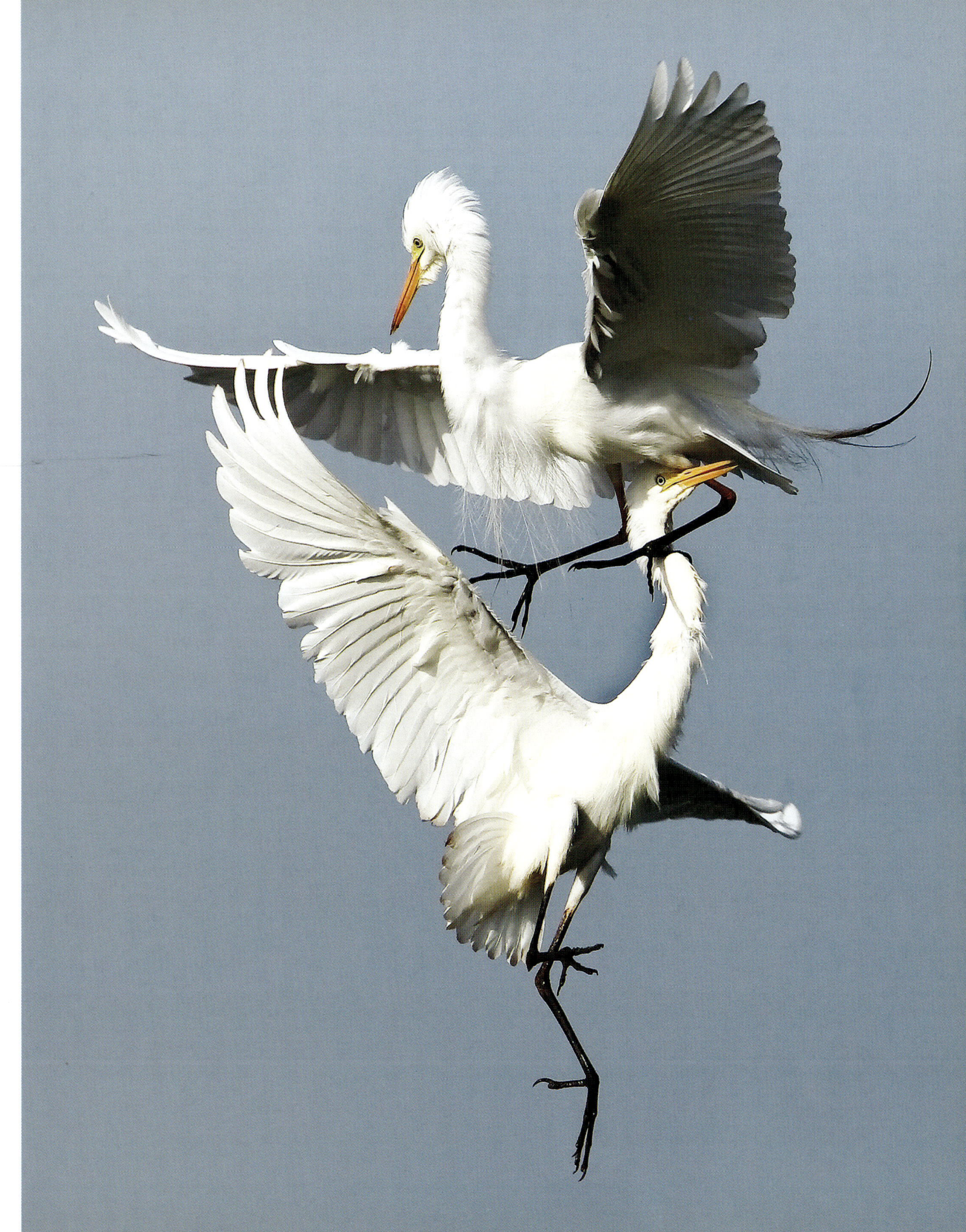

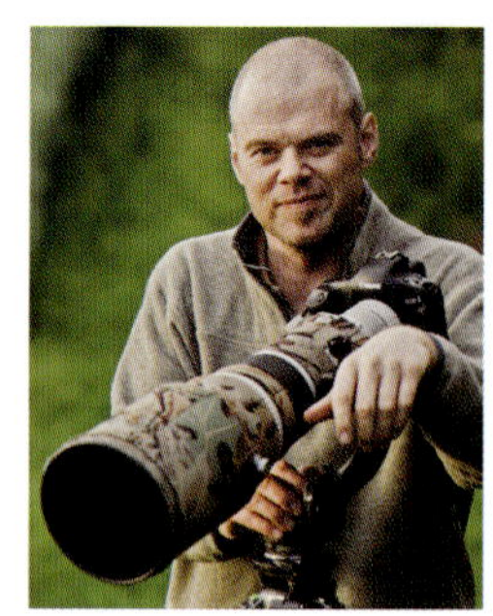

ANZANG Nature and Landscape Photographer of the Year – 2008 Portfolio Prize

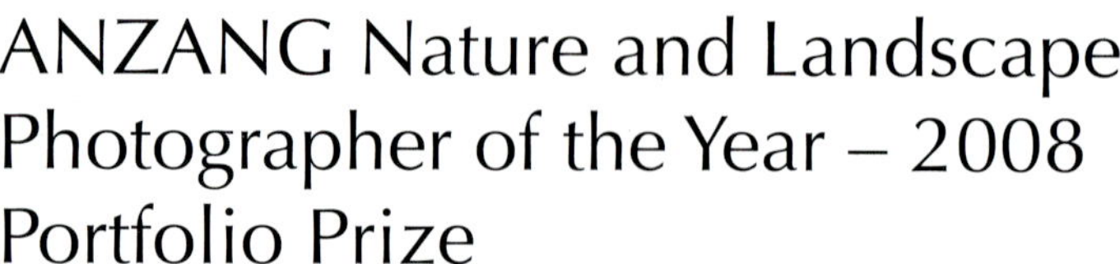

The portfolio prize is awarded to the photographer who enters the best portfolio of six or more entries. Andrew Trowbridge of Christchurch, New Zealand, is the winner of this year's prize.

The images are shown here in small scale but are in full scale in their respective sections.

Judges' comment: 'This is a collection of classic nature and landscape photographs of great quality.'

Prize: $1,000

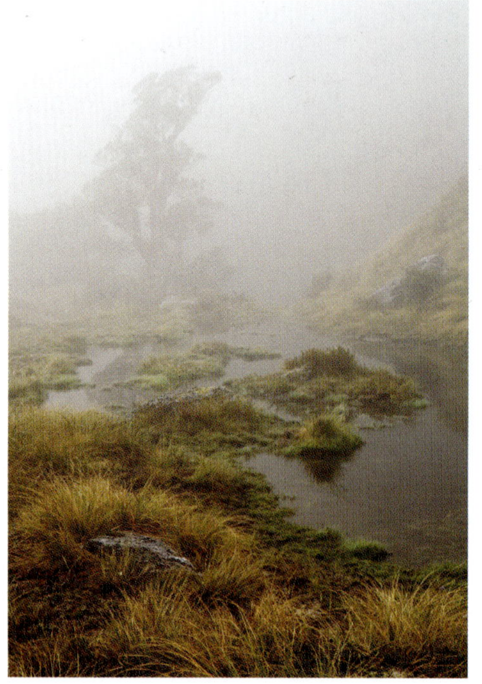

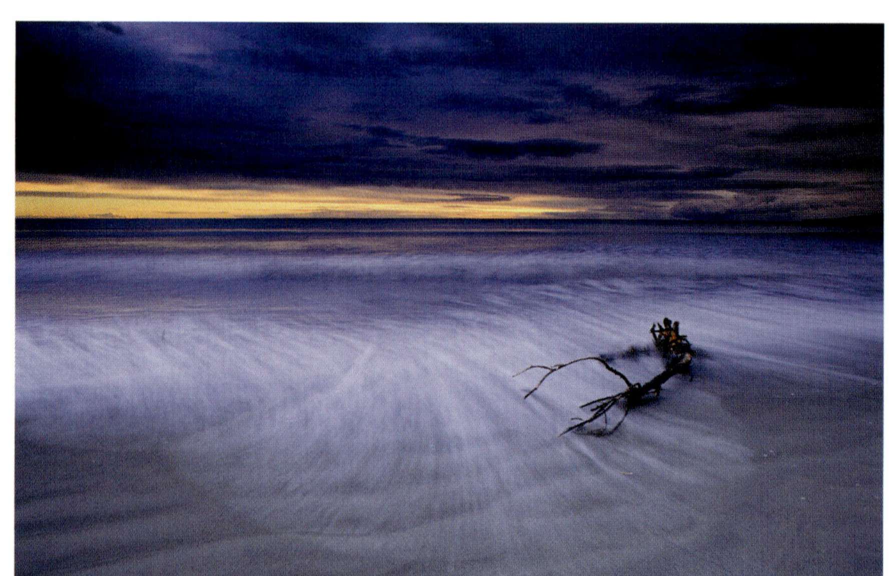

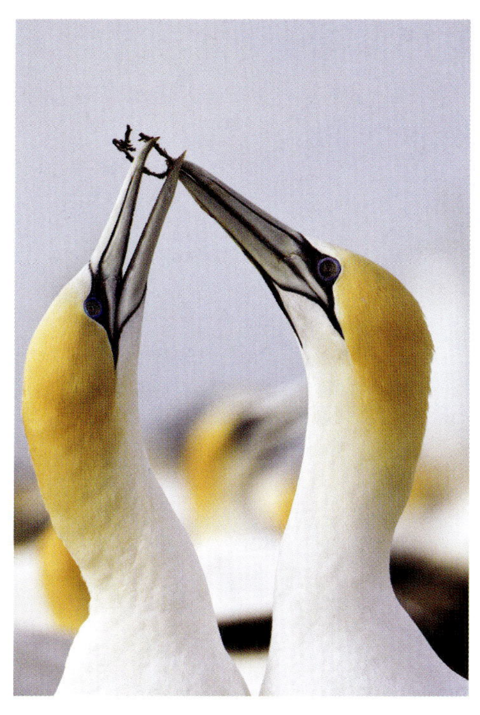
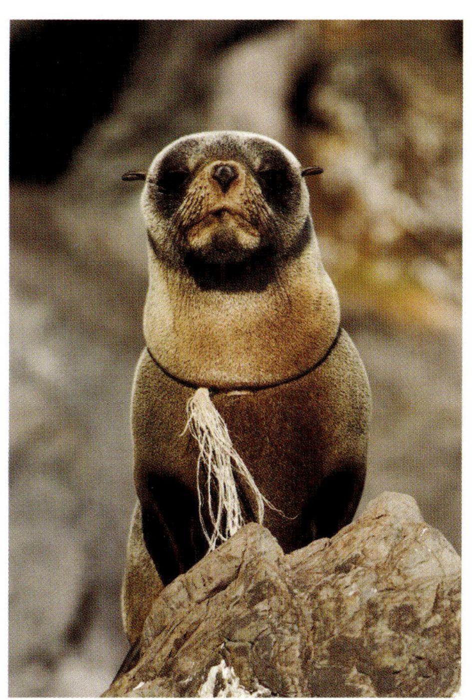
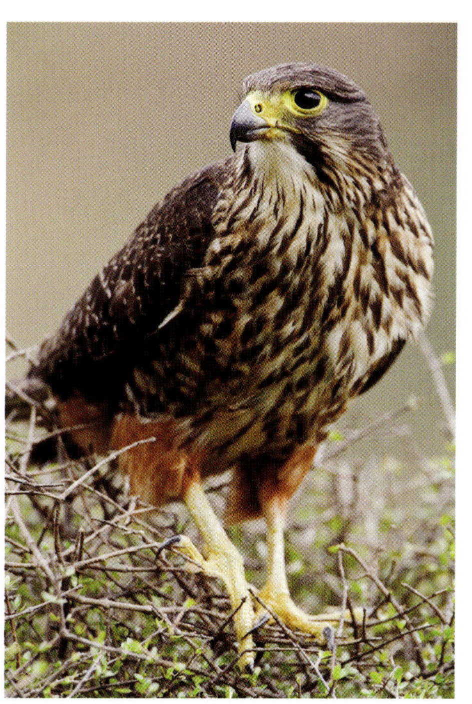
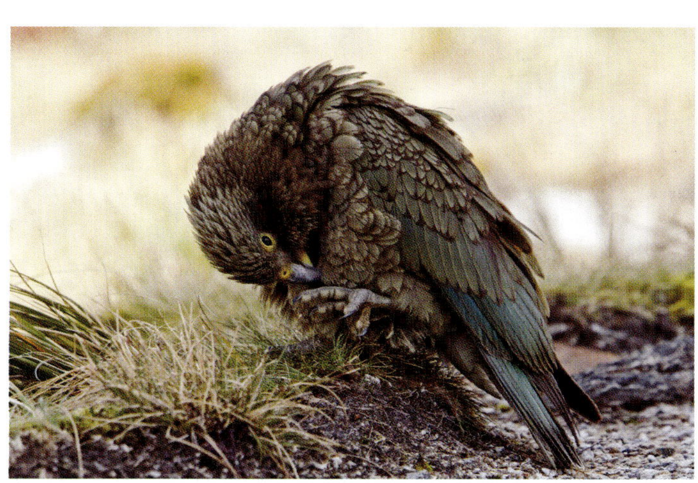
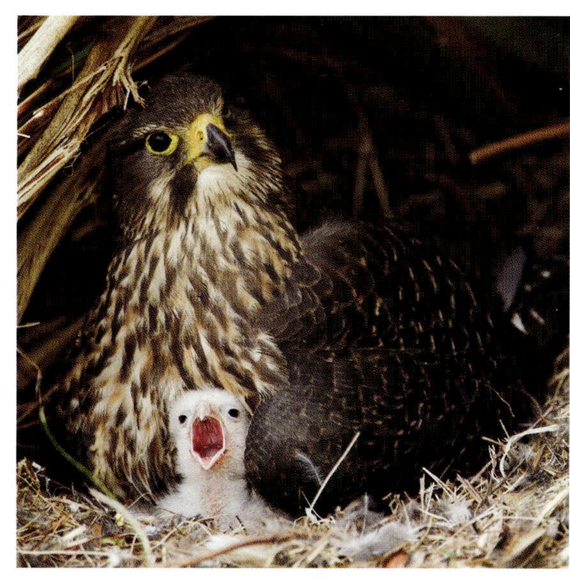

Section 1, Animal Behaviour

The subject or subjects must be engaged in natural activity.

Prize: $1,000

Winner, Animal Behaviour
Crested tern feeding
Graham Morgan, Sussex Inlet, New South Wales

'Small groups of crested terns gather here in the summer. I was
scrambling over rocks and dodging waves when the terns started
plunge feeding. This image was captured as the tern left the water
displaying such acrobatic grace and poise.'
Berrara Cove, New South Wales

Judges' comment: 'This image of a tern's wings frozen at the
height of upbeat is beautiful.'

Canon EOS 1D Mk III, 400mm, 1/4000, f5.6, ISO 200
2008 1-1 Exhibition

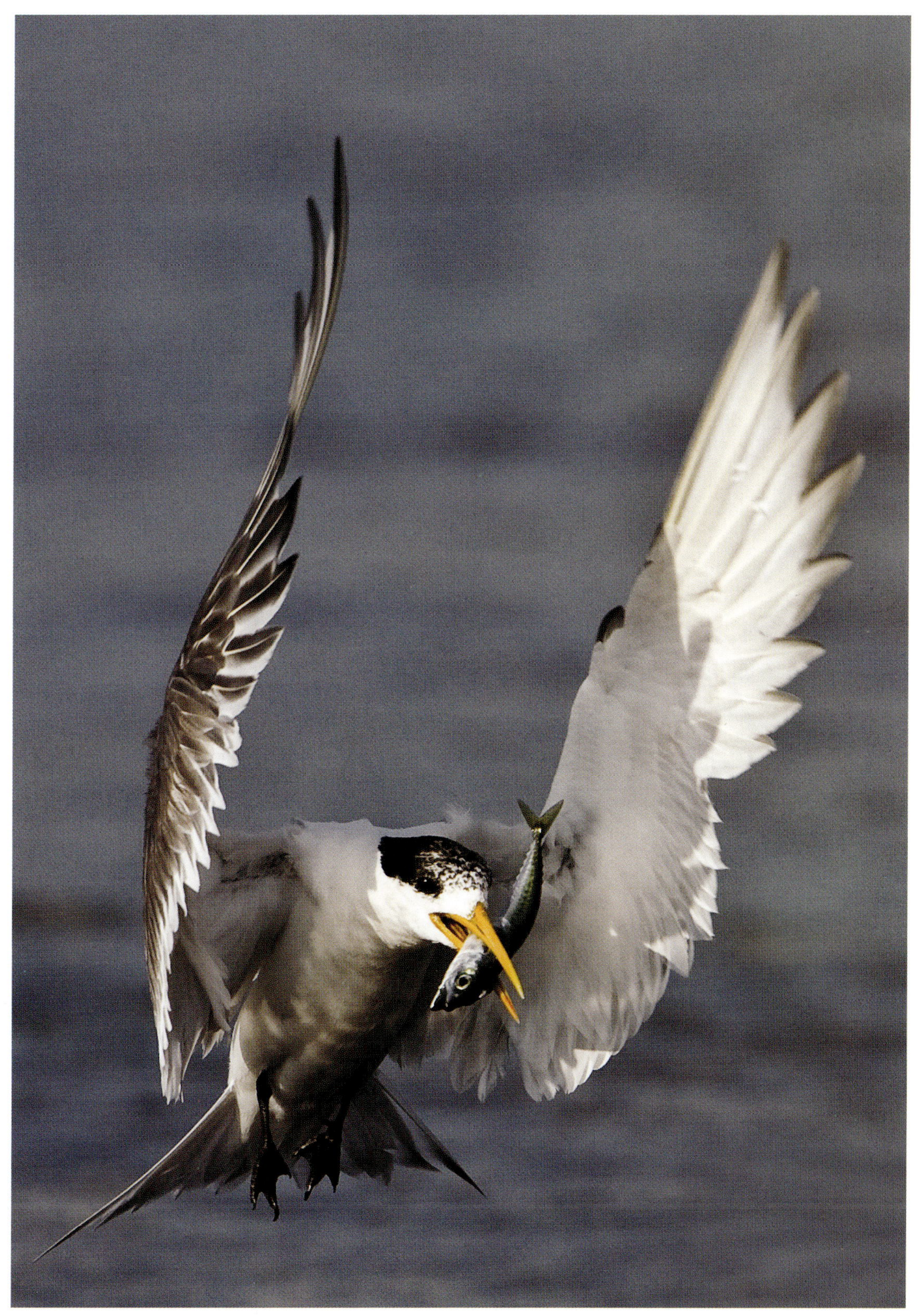

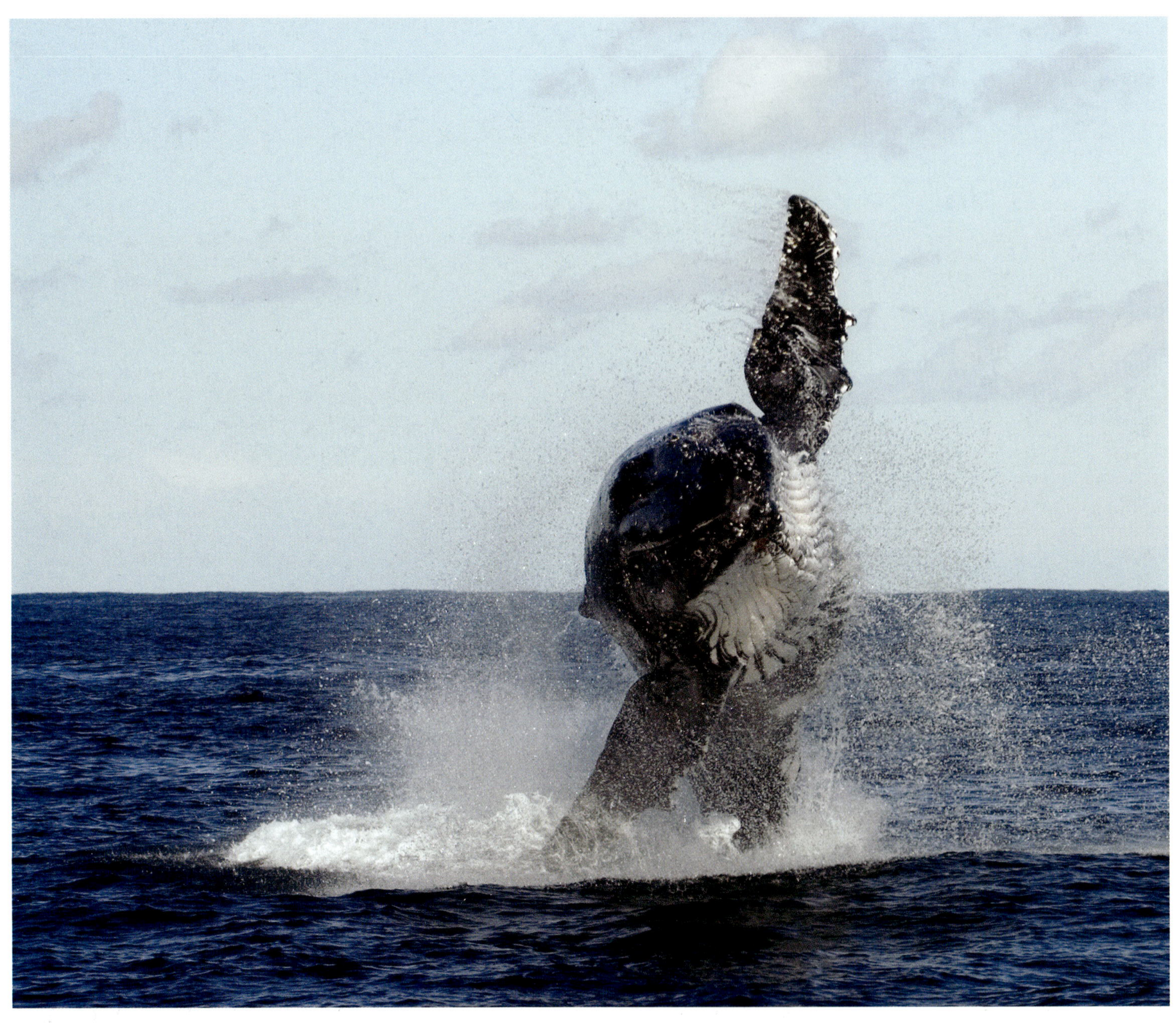

Runner-up, Animal Behaviour
Flying humpback whale
Raymond E. Alley, Anna Bay, New South Wales

'Every time I photograph these magnificent mammals it is special and unique, but this time "Barny" really seemed to want to put on a show. I was sure that he was actually smiling at me when I captured this shot.'
Port Stephens, New South Wales

  Judges' comment: 'One of the best whale action shots we have seen.'
Nikon D2x, 70-200mm, 1/2500, f2.8, ISO 320

Highly Commended, Animal Behaviour
Lunchtime
Judy Kapor, Dongara, Western Australia

'While fishing, we were caught in a strong wind and had to find shelter near an island. I was taking photos while waiting and captured this greedy seagull.'
Onslow, Western Australia

Canon 4000D, 300mm, ISO 400
2008 1-6

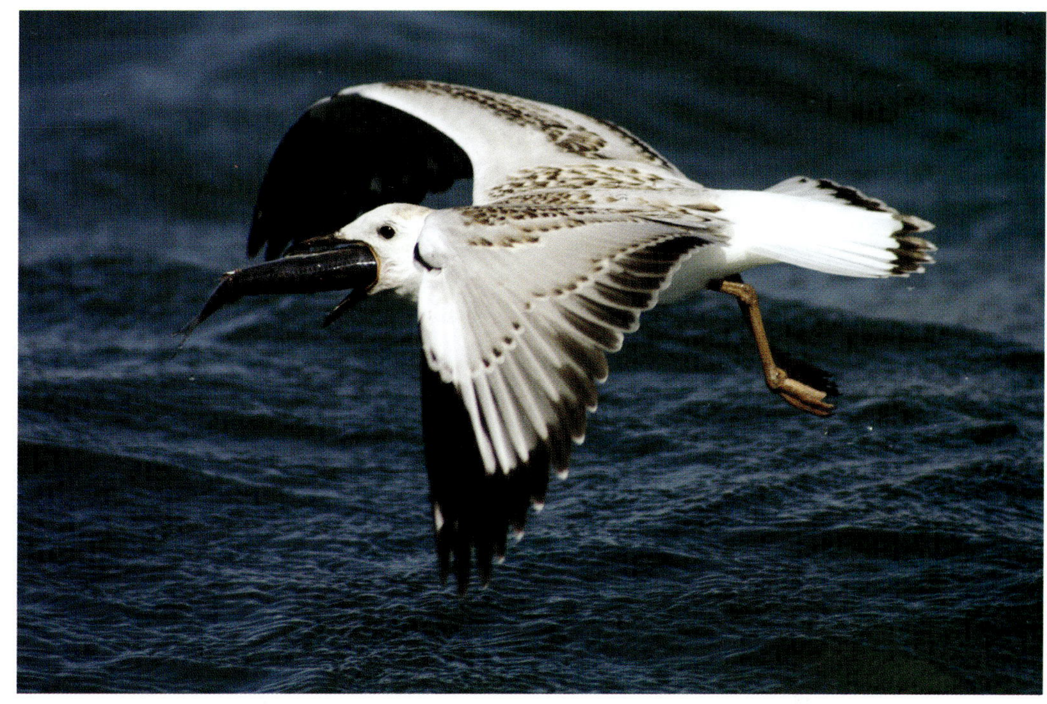

Highly Commended, Animal Behaviour
Common dolphin smile
Vincent Antony, Portland, Victoria

'This photo was taken late afternoon with a pod of about twenty dolphins. I tracked one dolphin instead of eying the pod. The water shadows on the head and the pattern behind the eye captivated me.'
Cape Bridgewater, Victoria

Sony A700, 80-200mm, 1/1250, f4.5, ISO 200
2008 1-7 Exhibition

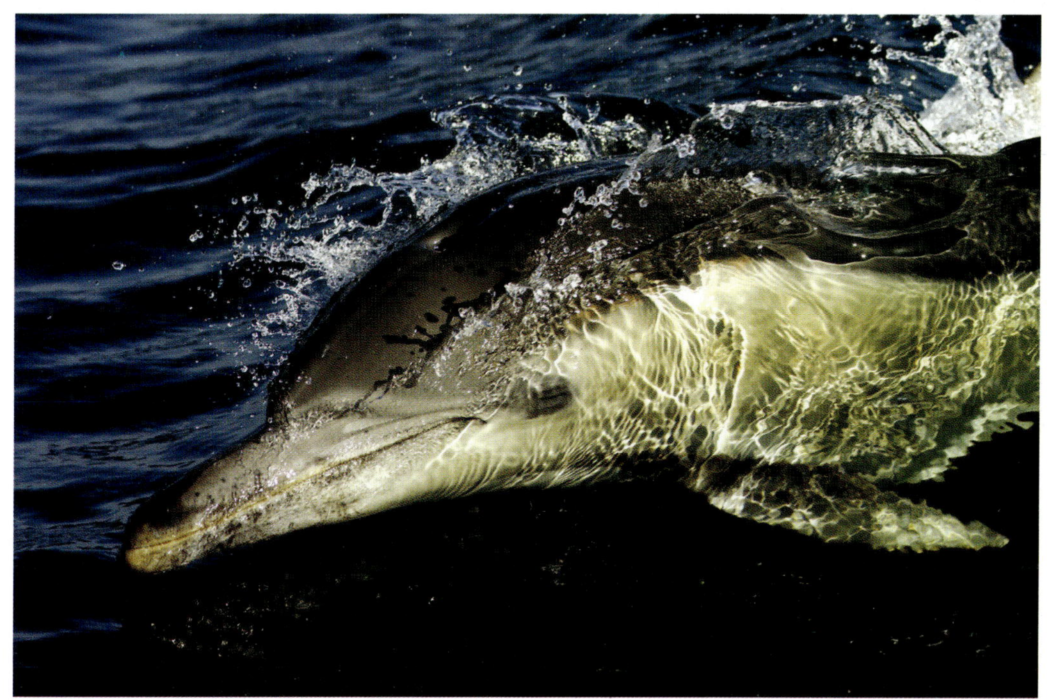

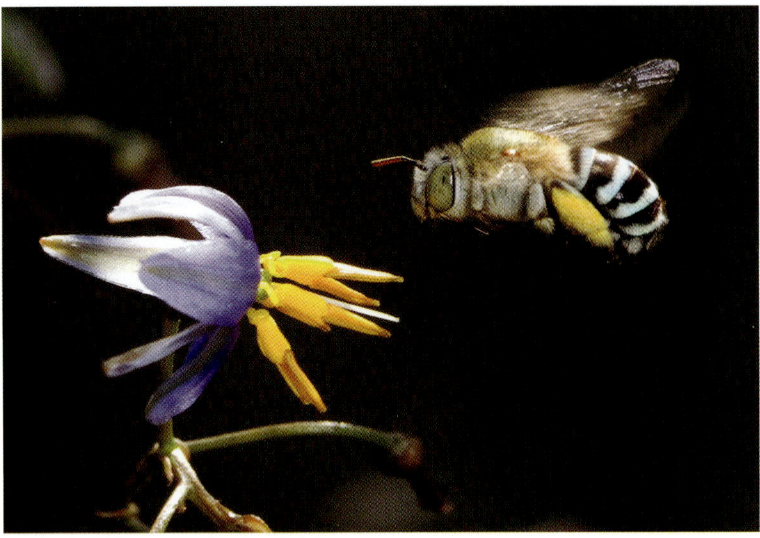

Highly Commended, Animal Behaviour
Blue banded bee at flax lily
Len Stewart, Joondalup, Western Australia

'Observing the native bee around the flax lily presented the challenge to capture the bee in flight. I used a flash duration of 1/32,000, using 1/64th power which was effective in freezing the bee in flight while still showing some motion blur of the wings.'
Joondalup, Western Australia

Nikon D200, 105 micro, 1/125, f16, ISO 400, flash 1/32,000
2008 1-3

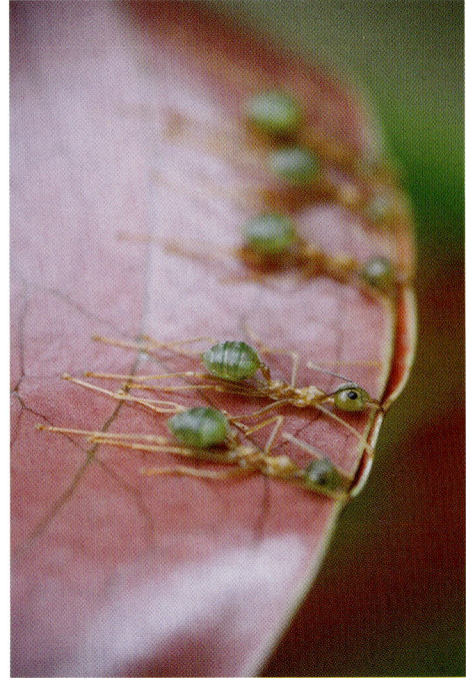

Highly Commended, Animal Behaviour
Green ants
Michael Williams, Newport, Victoria

'These green ants work together by making an ant chain to fold over and bring the edges of the leaf together. This dedicated team lies flat, using their strong jaws to hold the leaf edges in place, while inside the leaf workers seal the edge with silk produced by larvae.'
Behana Gorge, Queensland

Canon 20D, 105mm, 1/4-2/3 exposure compensation, f4.5, ISO 100, flash   2008 1-8 Exhibition

Highly Commended, Animal Behaviour
Hibiscus harlequin beetle protecting eggs
Mark Rayner, Meldale, Queensland

'The bug is tiny, only 10 mm, and moves around her egg cluster on the branch putting her body between her eggs and any perceived threat. I used a white card to reflect light under the front of the beetle.'
Donnybrook, Queensland

Nikon D200, 180mm, 1/6, f16, ISO 100, white card
2008 1-15

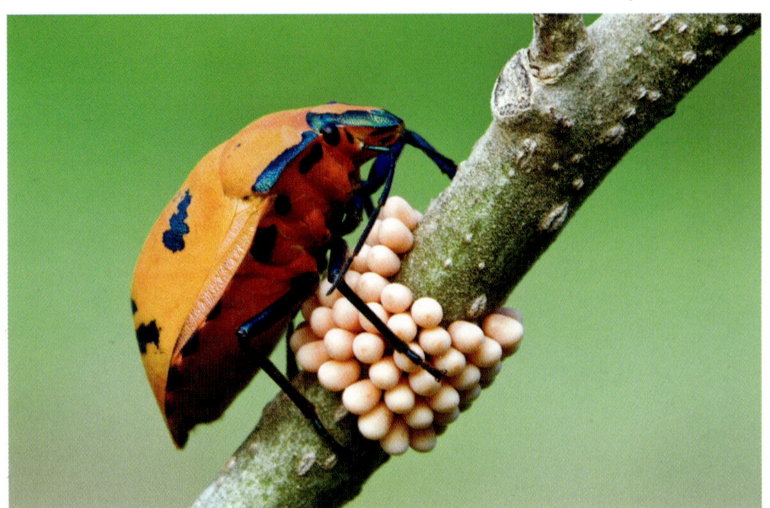

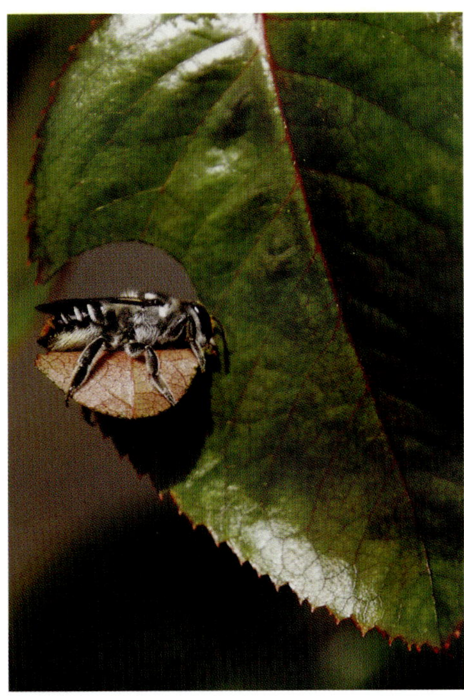

Highly Commended, Animal Behaviour
Leafcutter bee
Gordon Winslade, East Victoria Park, Western Australia

'Leafcutter bees appear to be very selective about the leaves they choose for their nests. Only one rose bush in our garden is used, and this is done infrequently. They only take seconds to cut their little circles, so it is special to capture the moment.'
East Victoria Park, Western Australia

Olympus E330, 12-60mm, 1/8000, f4, ISO 200
2008 1-10 Exhibition

Highly Commended, Animal Behaviour
Communication!
Christian Geyer, Mossman, Queensland

'The green ants are standing on the ridge line of a buttress root. At first look you would assume the behaviour was aggressive. However, it was a gentle expression of sharing information.'
Daintree Rainforest, Queensland

Canon 20D, 90mm macro, 1/8, f15, flash
2008 1-9

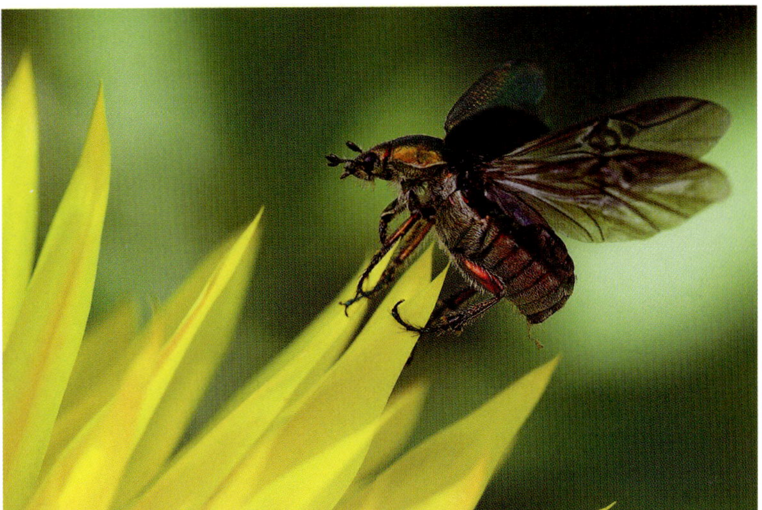

Highly Commended, Animal Behaviour
Beetle lift-off
Shane Howlett, Canning Vale, Western Australia

'Despite living in a beautiful country that I love to explore, it remains amazing what can be found in your own backyard.'
Canning Vale, Western Australia

Canon EOS-5D, 90mm, 1/125, f8, ISO 400
2008 1-11

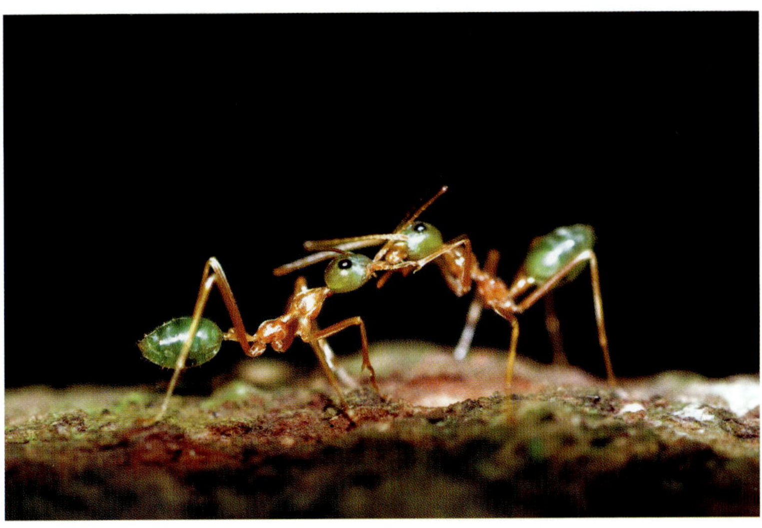

Highly Commended, Animal Behaviour
Double trouble – New Zealand seal pups
Vincent Antony, Portland, Victoria

'The colony is at the base of a 50-metre basalt cliff,
among the basalt boulders. Getting there is tough,
then getting two pups to stay still long enough to
capture a photo in low light conditions is equally
tough. This is a break between play.'
Cape Bridgewater, Victoria

Sony A700, 80-200mm, 1/200, f5, ISO 200
2008 1-12

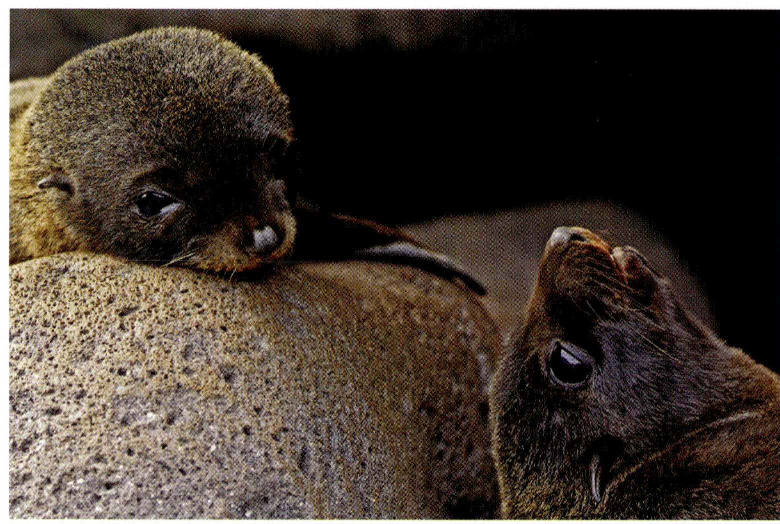

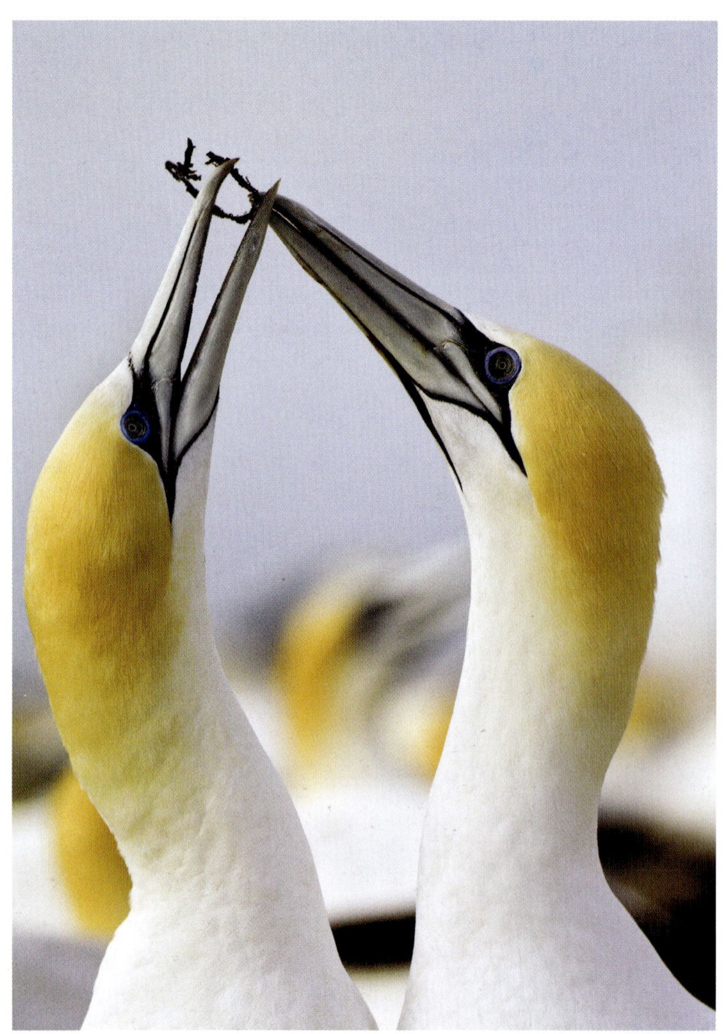

Highly Commended, Animal Behaviour
Gannet courtship display
Andrew Trowbridge, Halswell, Christchurch

'The activity is quite overwhelming at times, and
I kept missing shots because I was constantly
changing lenses to capture everything. I then
realised I needed to concentrate on one thing. They
were very active in their courtship display and I
spent more than 30 minutes with them and came
away with the image I was after.'
Cape Kidnappers, New Zealand

Canon 5D, 400mm, 1/1000, f8, ISO 200
2008 1-16

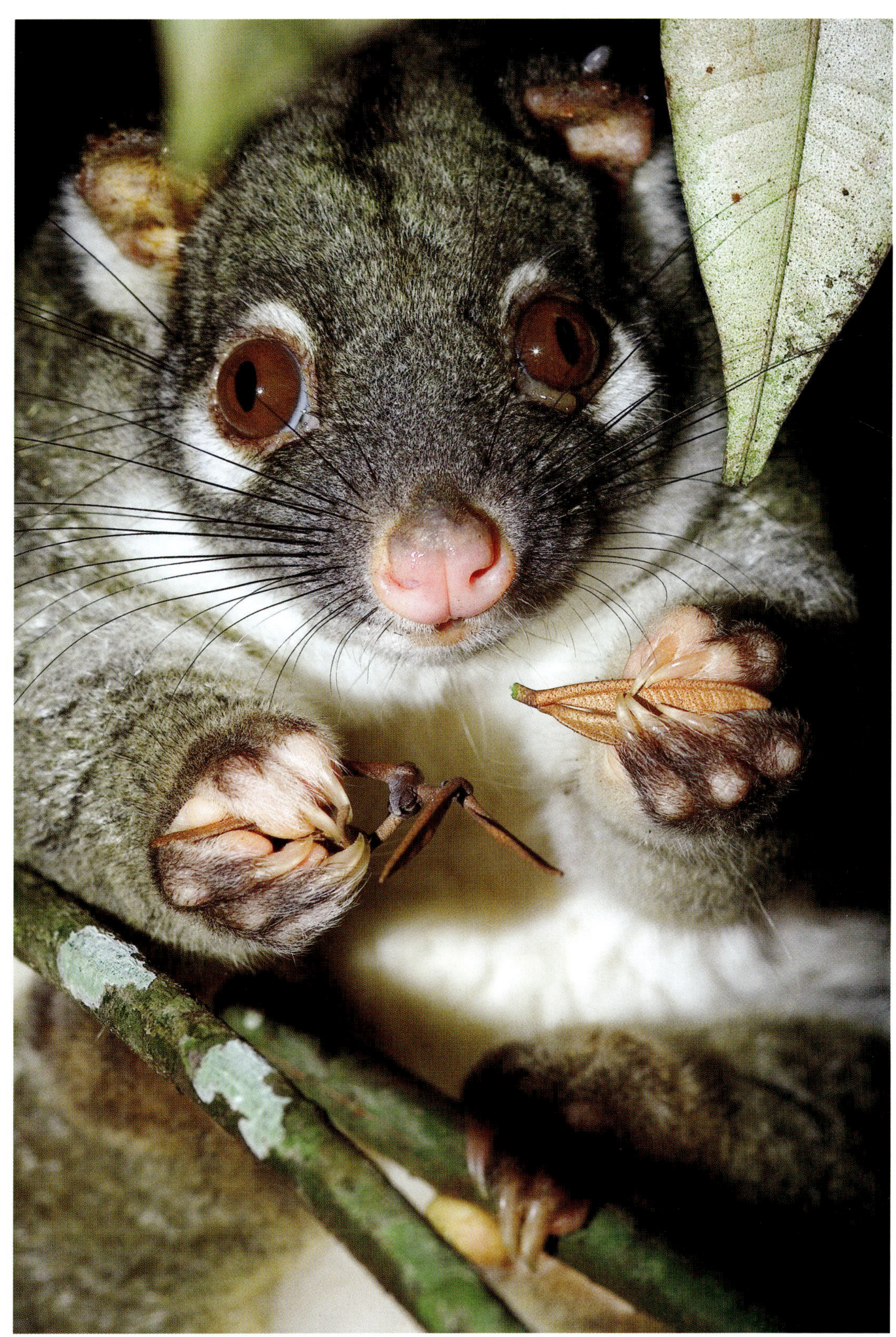

Highly Commended, Animal Behaviour
Green ringtail possum
Michael Williams, Newport, Victoria

'While photographing nocturnal animals we came across this beautiful possum feeding in a fig tree. It paused briefly to check out the disturbance below.'
Curtain Fig NP, Queensland

Canon 20D, 105mm Macro, f7.1, ISO 100, flash
2008 1-13 Exhibition

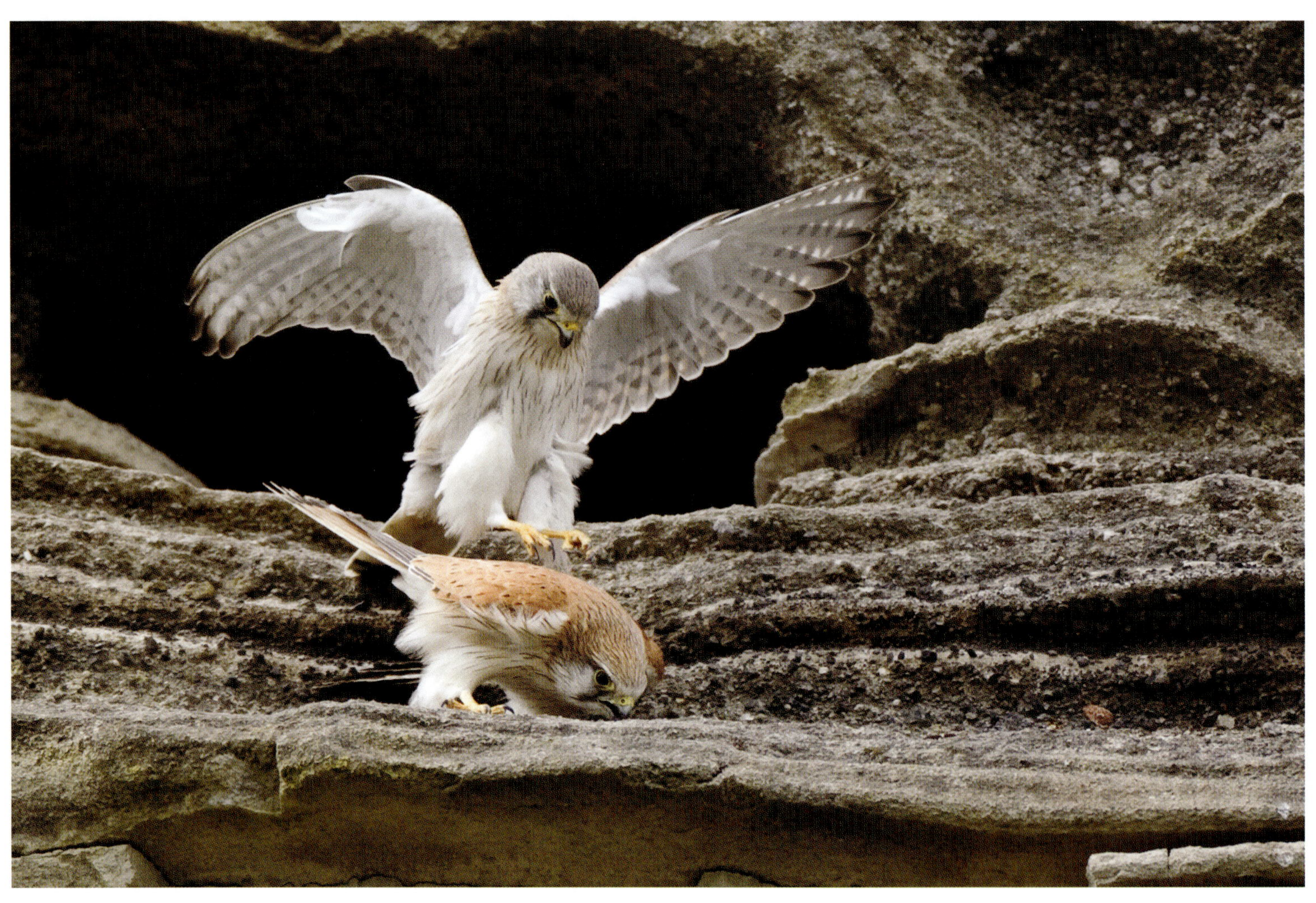

Highly Commended, Animal Behaviour
Mating call
Perry Cho, Warrnambool, Victoria

'I captured this sequence on the cliff edge of this
extinct volcano. My initial reaction was that I had
captured two birds fighting as the action took less
than two seconds. When reviewing the files I was
delighted to see that I had captured a pair of
nankeen kestrels mating.'
Tower Hill Reserve, Warrnambool, Victoria

Canon EOS 1D Mk lll, 600mm, 1/2500, f4, ISO 1000
2008 1-14 Exhibition

Royals gone wild
Mindy Oberne, Grass Valley, USA

'I was suddenly aware of a great cacophony of penguin sounds at my feet. I was able to capture the wonderful reds and yellows of the crests of these royal penguins.'
Macquarie Island, Australia

Canon Power Shot S400, 1/640, f7
2008 1-17 Exhibition

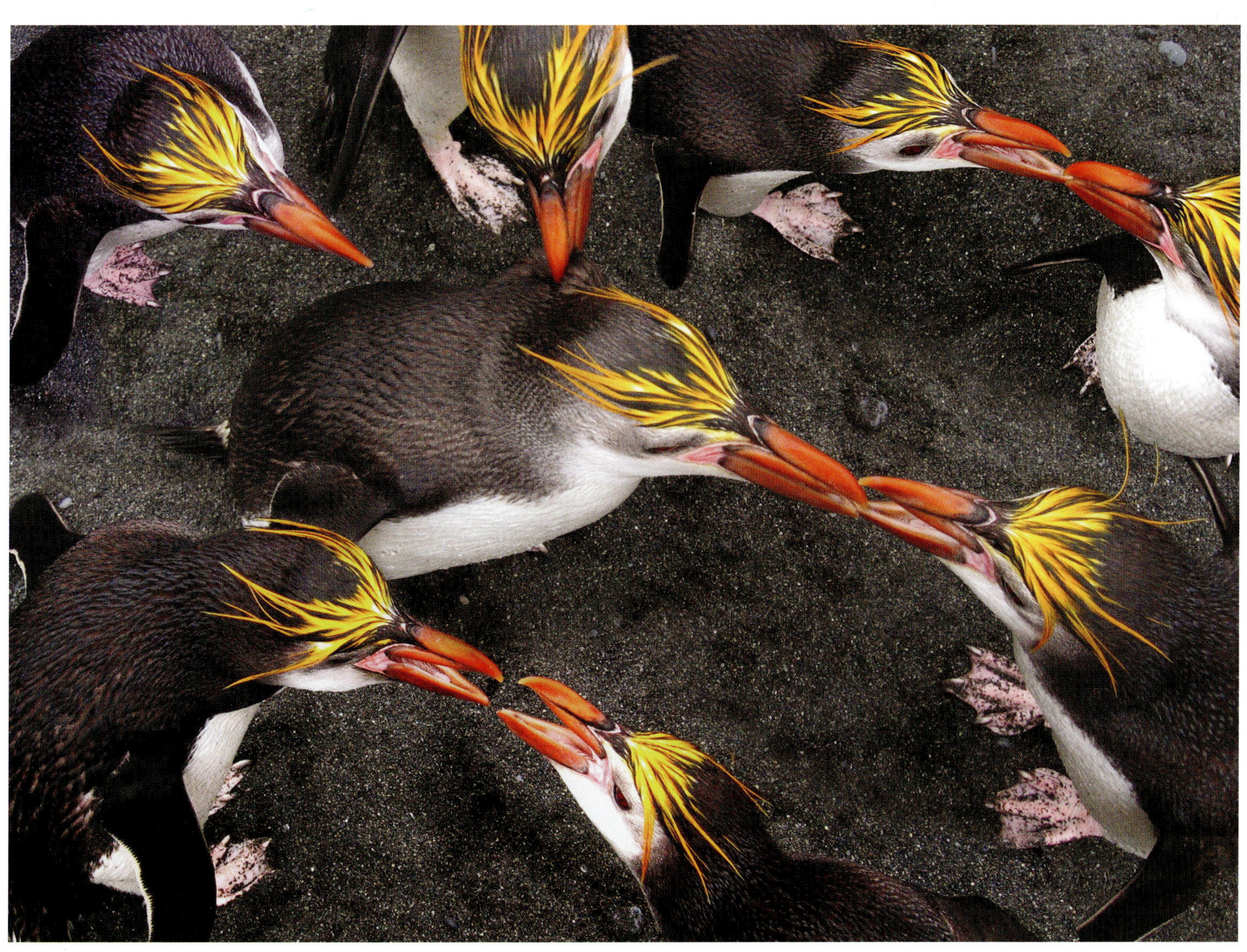

Section 2, Animal Portrait

The subject must be photographed close up, occupying at least 30 per cent of the frame.

Prize: $1,000

Winner, Animal Portrait
Elephant seal scratching
David Burren, Middle Camberwell, Victoria

'This young southern elephant seal, known to the locals as Henry, regularly visits the area for his annual moult. He spends a lot of time lazing around on the beach. I am part of the volunteer group that looks after him.'
Geelong, Victoria

Judges' comment: 'A humorous portrait.'

Canon EOS 10D, 100-400mm, 1/200, f9, ISO 200
2008 2-1 Exhibition

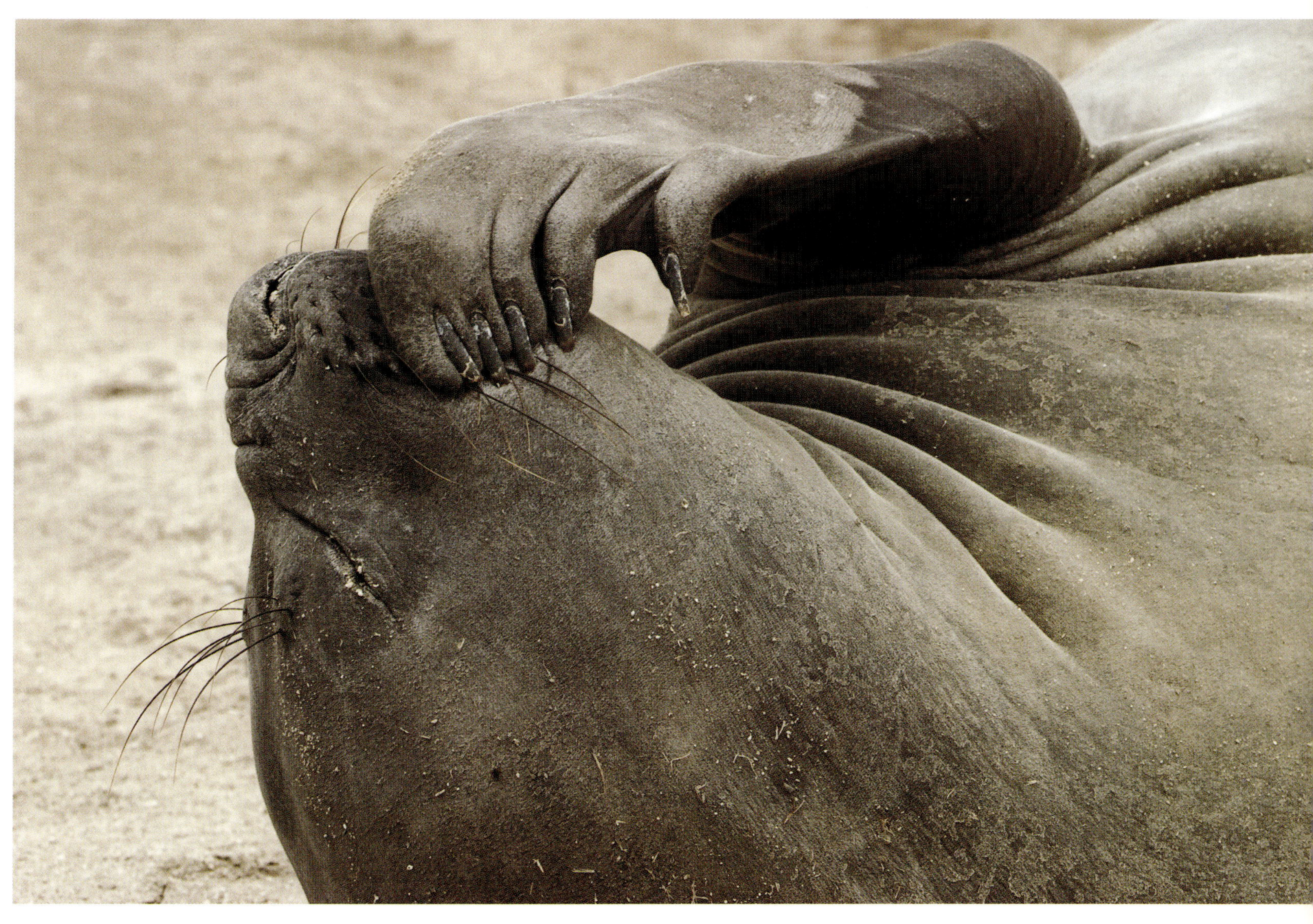

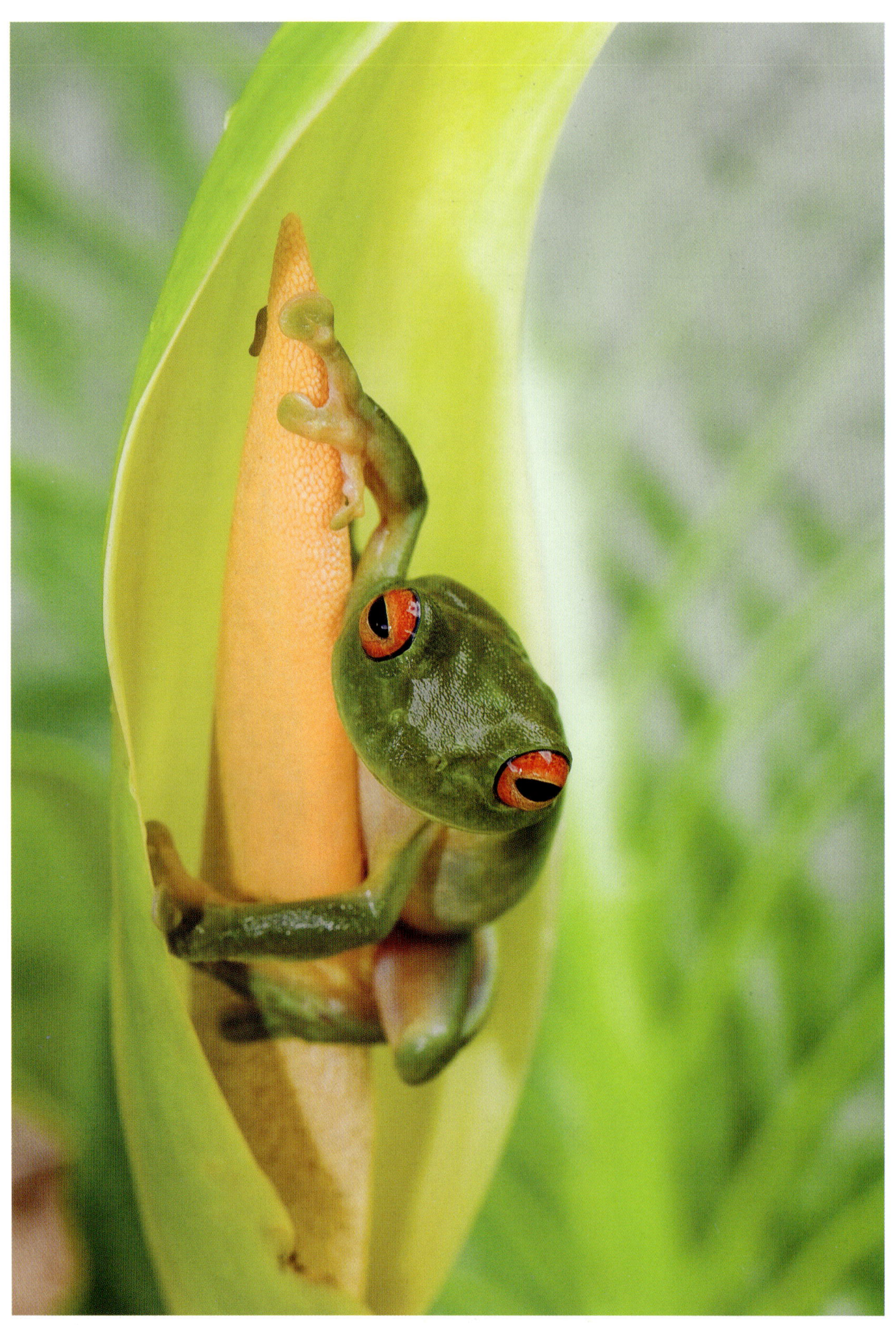

Runner-up, Animal Portrait
You found me! Red-eyed tree frog on flower
Darran Leal, Coolum Beach, Queensland

'Red-eyed tree frogs are perhaps one of Australia's prettiest frogs. Lots of rain flushes them out, and at times you can find them in the dozens. The cunjevoi plant is a perfect hunting platform for them.'
Lamington NP, Queensland

Judges' comment: 'The viewer is engaged through the eyes of the subject, the essence of a portrait.'

Canon EOS5, 100mm Macro, 1/60, f9.5, ISO 100, fill flash
2008 2-2 Exhibition

Highly Commended, Animal
Portrait
Mr Potato Cod
Justin Gilligan, Anna Bay,
New South Wales

'Divers can have intimate
encounters with this group of
potato cod that have become
accustomed to humans. This
particular one took a great
interest in its reflection in the
dome port of the camera.'
Cod Hole, Great Barrier Reef,
Queensland

Nikon D80, 105mm, f4.5,
ISO 100, flash
2008 2-4 Exhibition

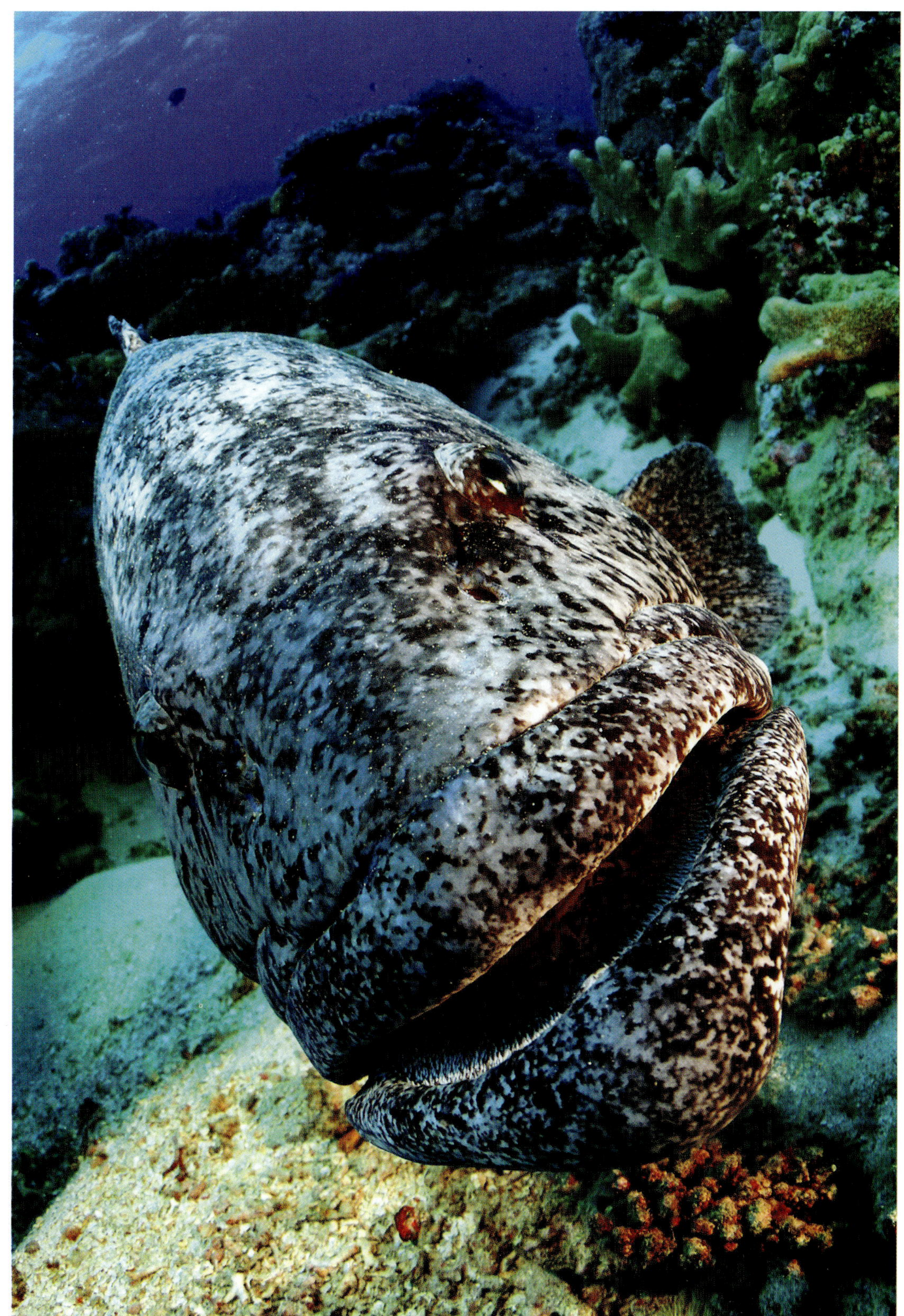

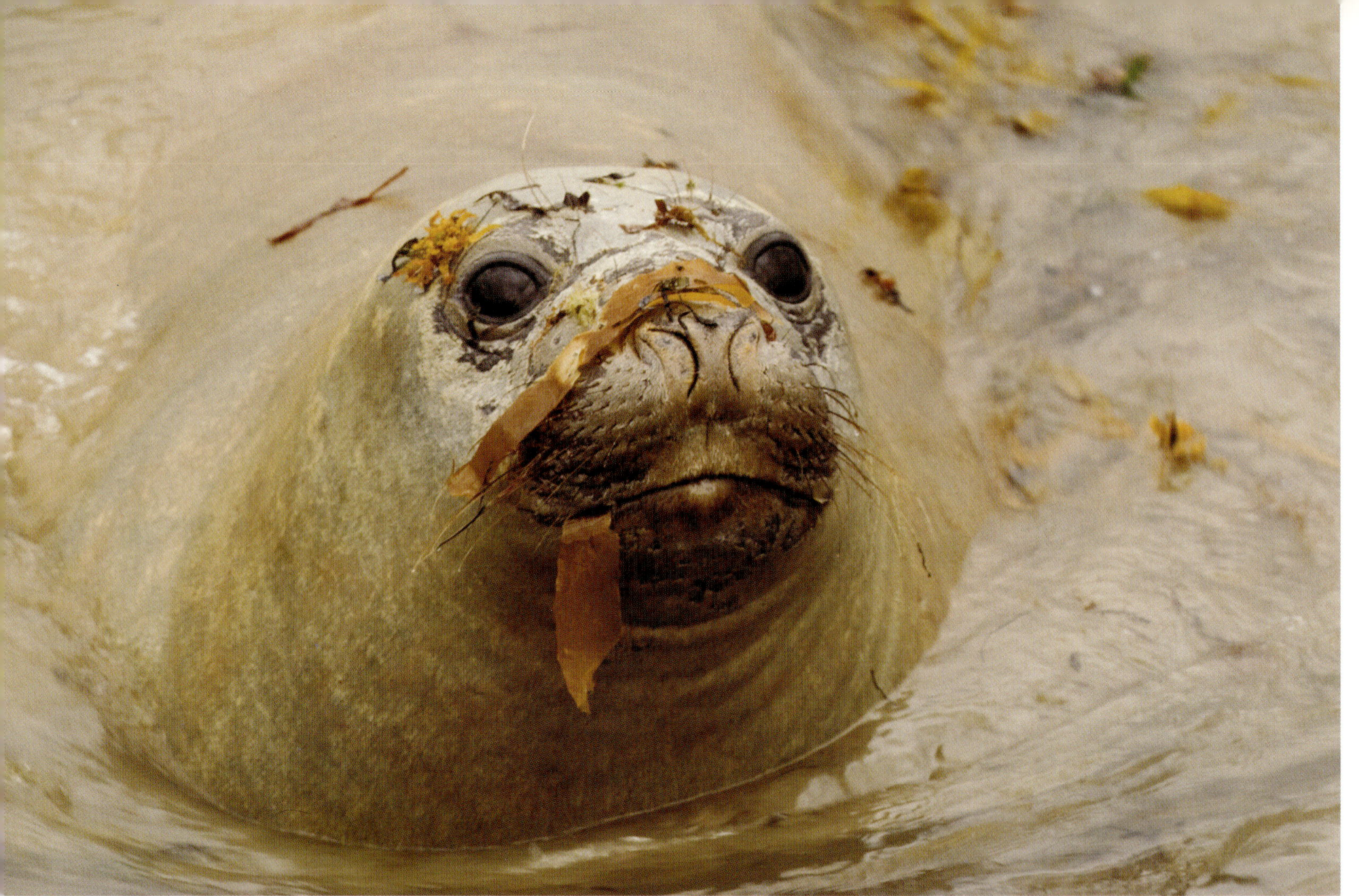

Highly Commended, Animal Portrait
Elephant seal and seaweed
David Burren, Middle Camberwell, Victoria

'Over the years I have spent a lot of time with this
gentle giant called Henry.'
Victoria

Canon EOS 20D, 100-400mm, 1/60, f8, ISO 100
2008 2-3

Highly Commended, Animal Portrait
White-lipped tree frog
Stanley and Kaisa Breeden, Malanda, Queensland

'It had been raining for two days, after a long dry
spell. The males called fervently all night and even
into the early morning. This male was the last
to retire, giving us a rare opportunity for a close
photograph.'
Daintree, Queensland

Canon 1Ds Mk ll, 100mm Macro, 0.6sec, f16
2008 2-5 Exhibition

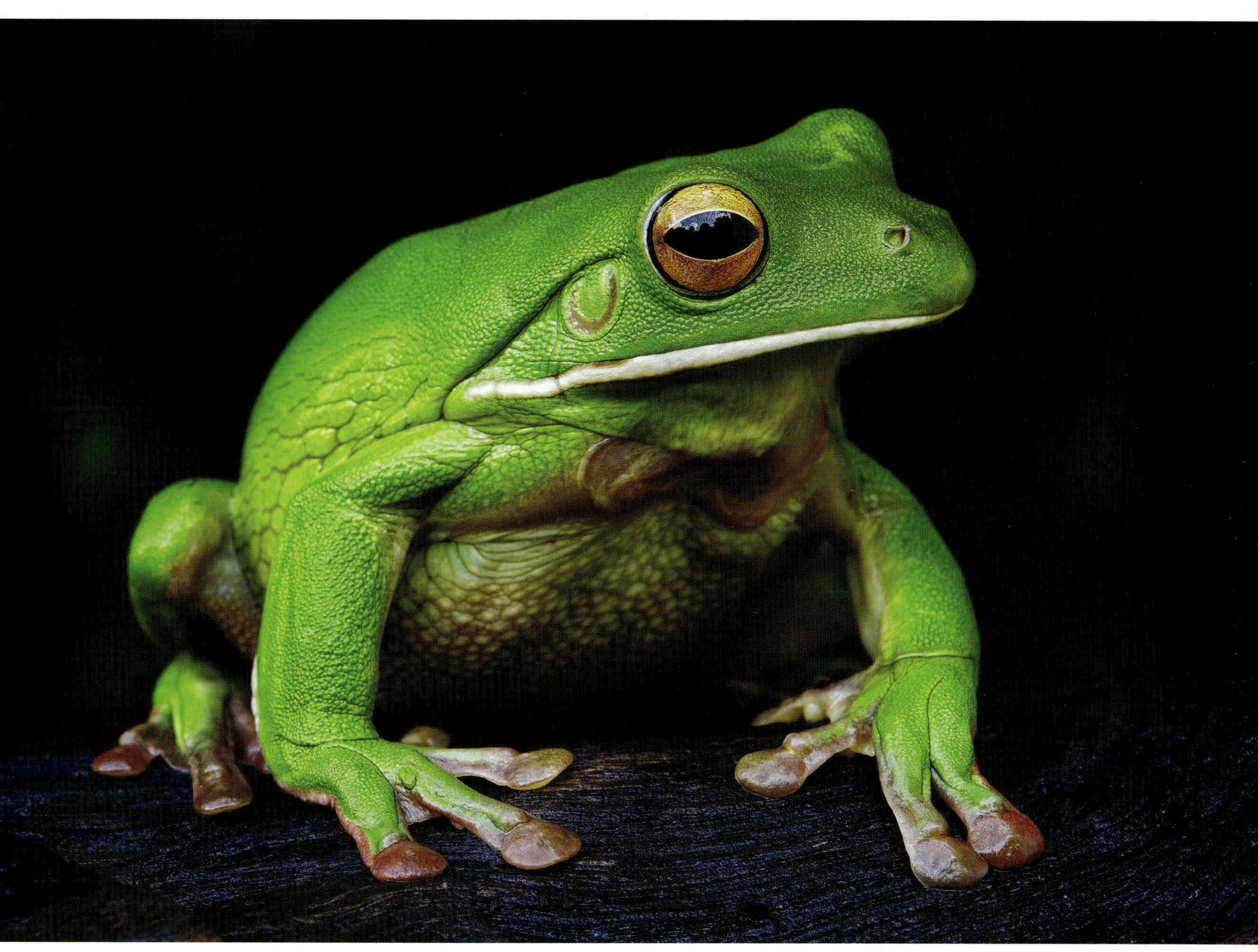

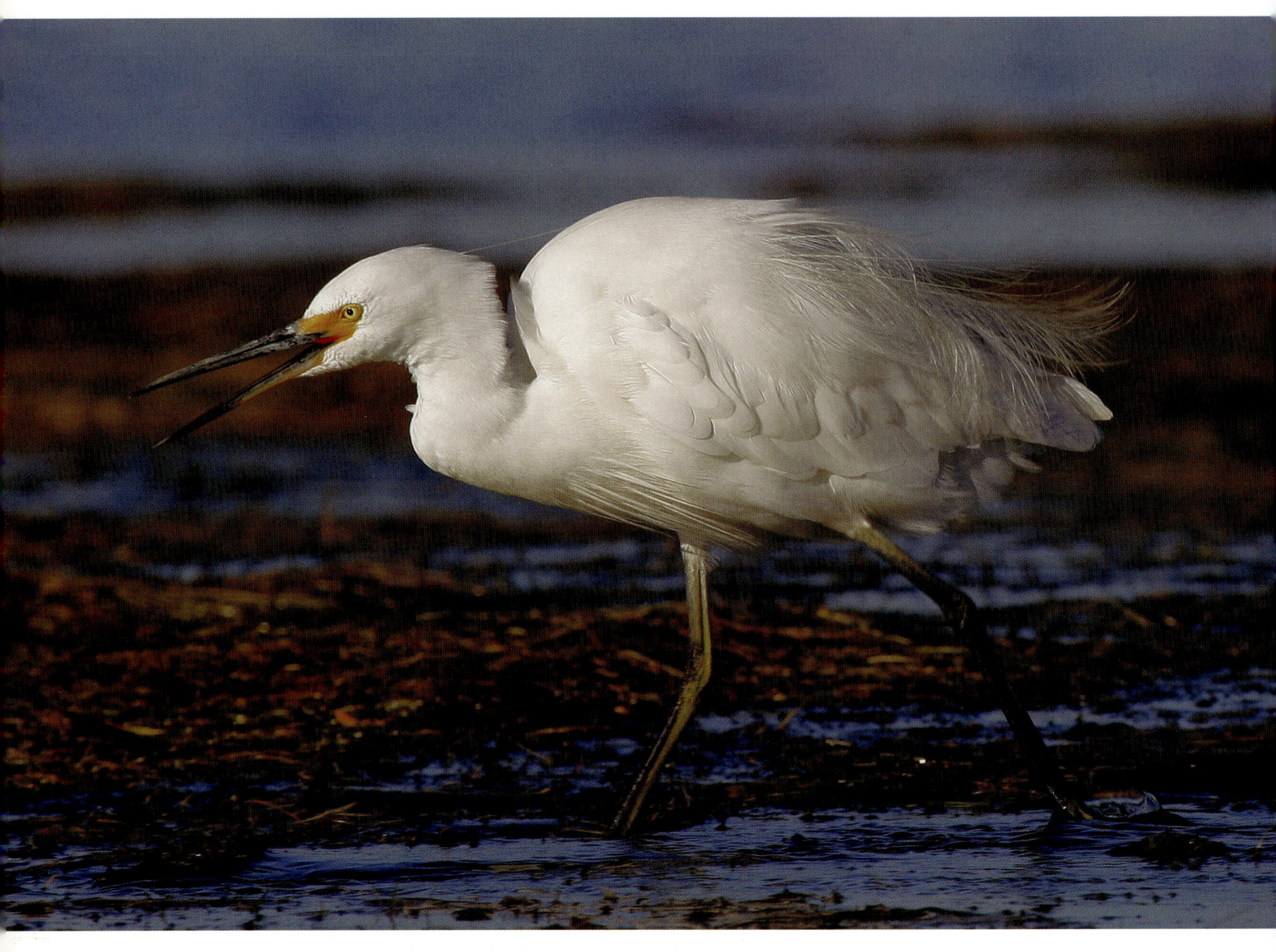

Highly Commended, Animal Portrait
On the prowl
David Rennie, Ravenswood, Western Australia

'After several hours of waiting I had the opportunity to take this shot of the little egret. They are hard to shoot, because when they feed they jump around, never still.'
Mandurah wetlands, Western Australia

Canon 1D MKlll, 100-400mm, 1/250, f10, ISO 100
2008 2-7 Exhibition

Highly Commended, Animal Portrait
Fledgling nankeen kestrel
Pam Osborn, Applecross, Western Australia

'I had been watching this fledgling preparing to leave the nest for five days. Then the nest was empty and I found it close by in the bushes. It had made it! Its mother was still supplementing its diet.'
Ningaloo Reef National Park, Western Australia

Nikon D200, 300mm, 1/1000, f7.1, ISO 320
2008 2-8 Exhibition

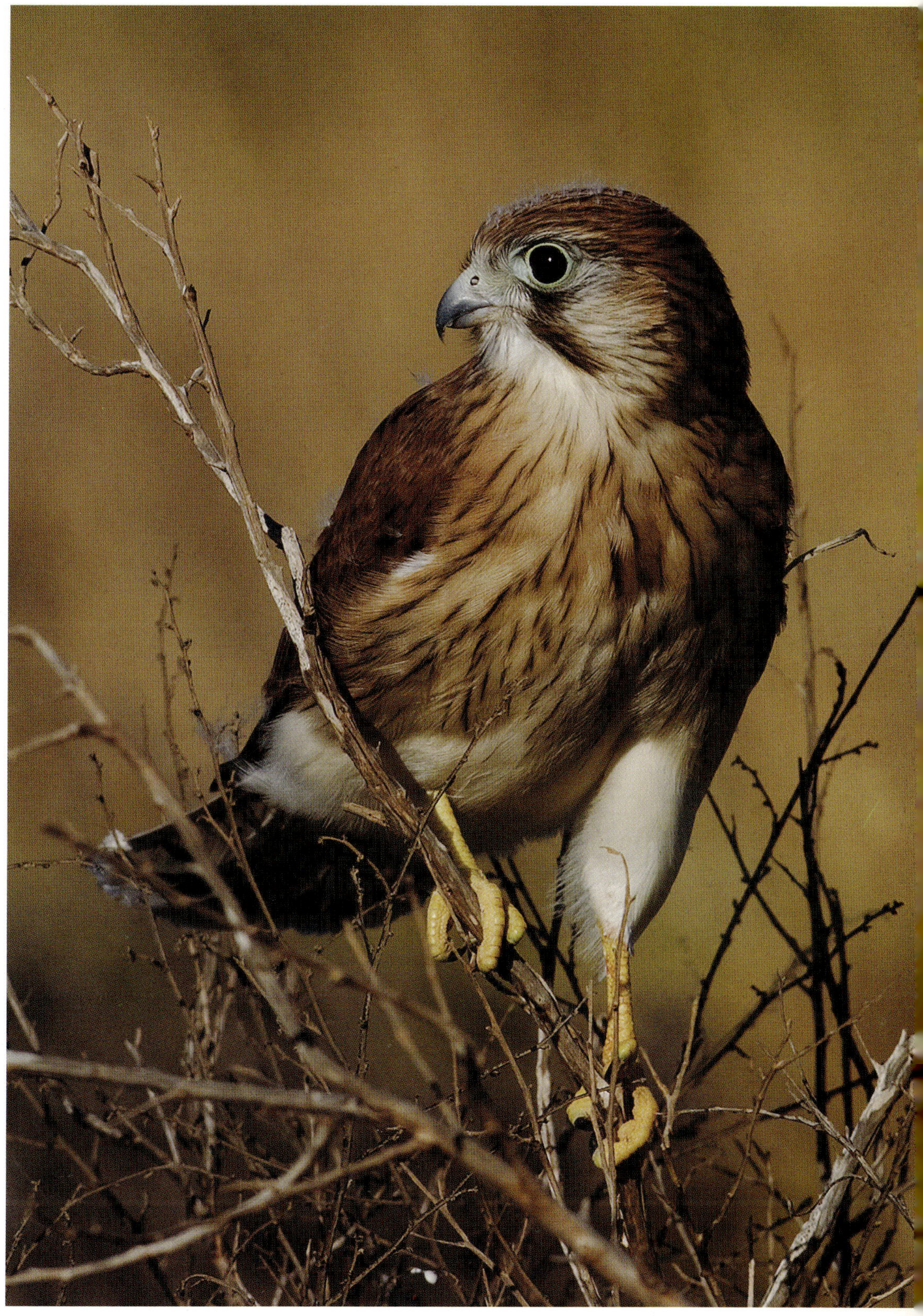

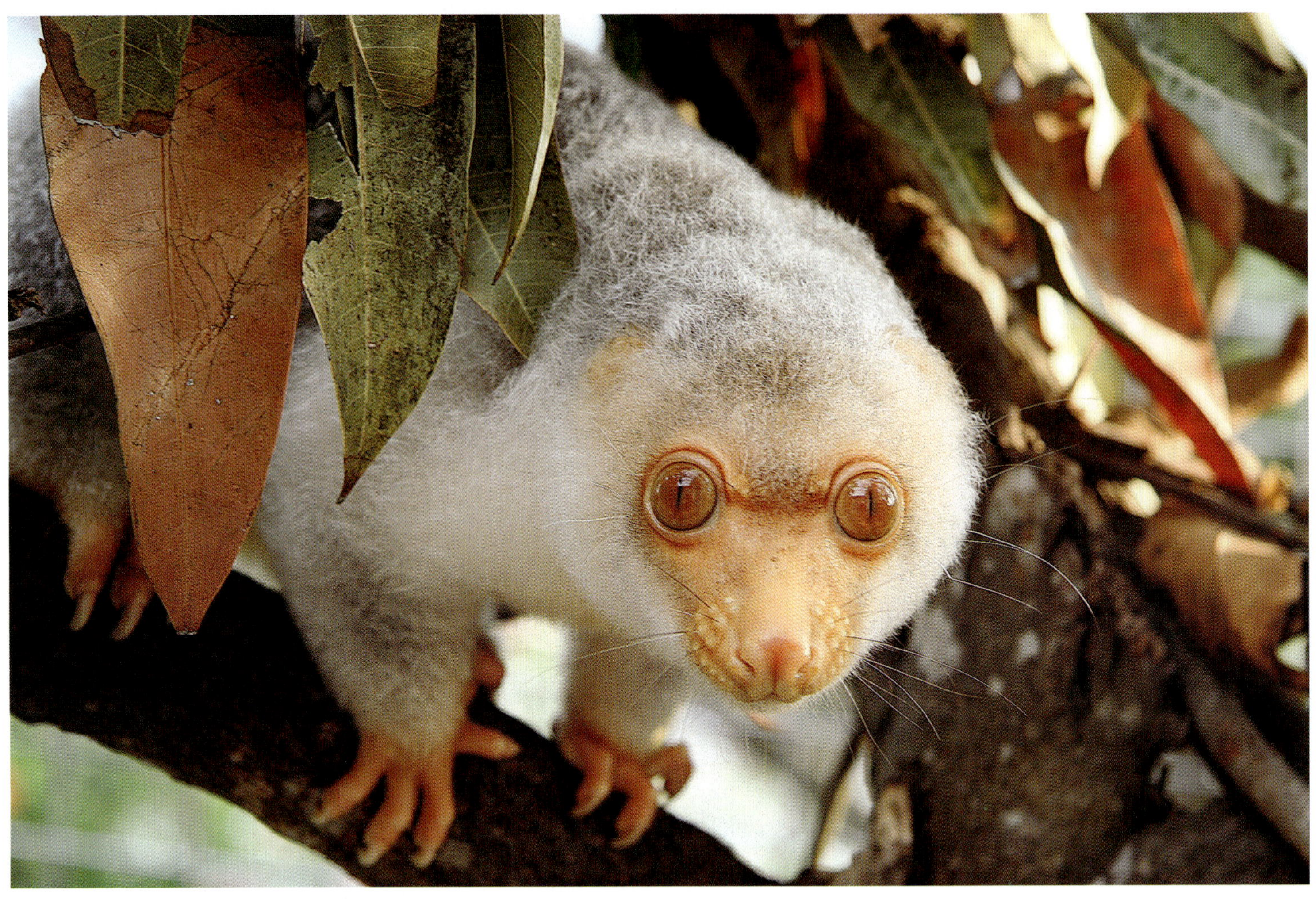

Highly Commended, Animal Portrait
Young cuscus rescued from dead mother
Julie Archer, Stanwell Park, New South Wales

'A friend had rescued this baby cuscus after the mother had been hit by a truck and was caring for it until it could be released. It wasn't tame and had a good bite, but was not too scared of people, as her providers. This was taken through her cage.'
Port Moresby, Papua New Guinea

Canon 350D, 1/100, f5.6, ISO 400, flash
2008 2-10 Exhibition

Highly Commended, Animal Portrait
Western grey kangaroo
Melyssa Parker, Armadale, Western Australia

'This is a common place for tourists, and the kangaroos hang around the picnic spots, not at all shy. This allows for good photo opportunities.'
John Forrest NP, Western Australia

Canon 300D, 75-300mm, 1/250, f5.6, ISO 200
2008 2-9

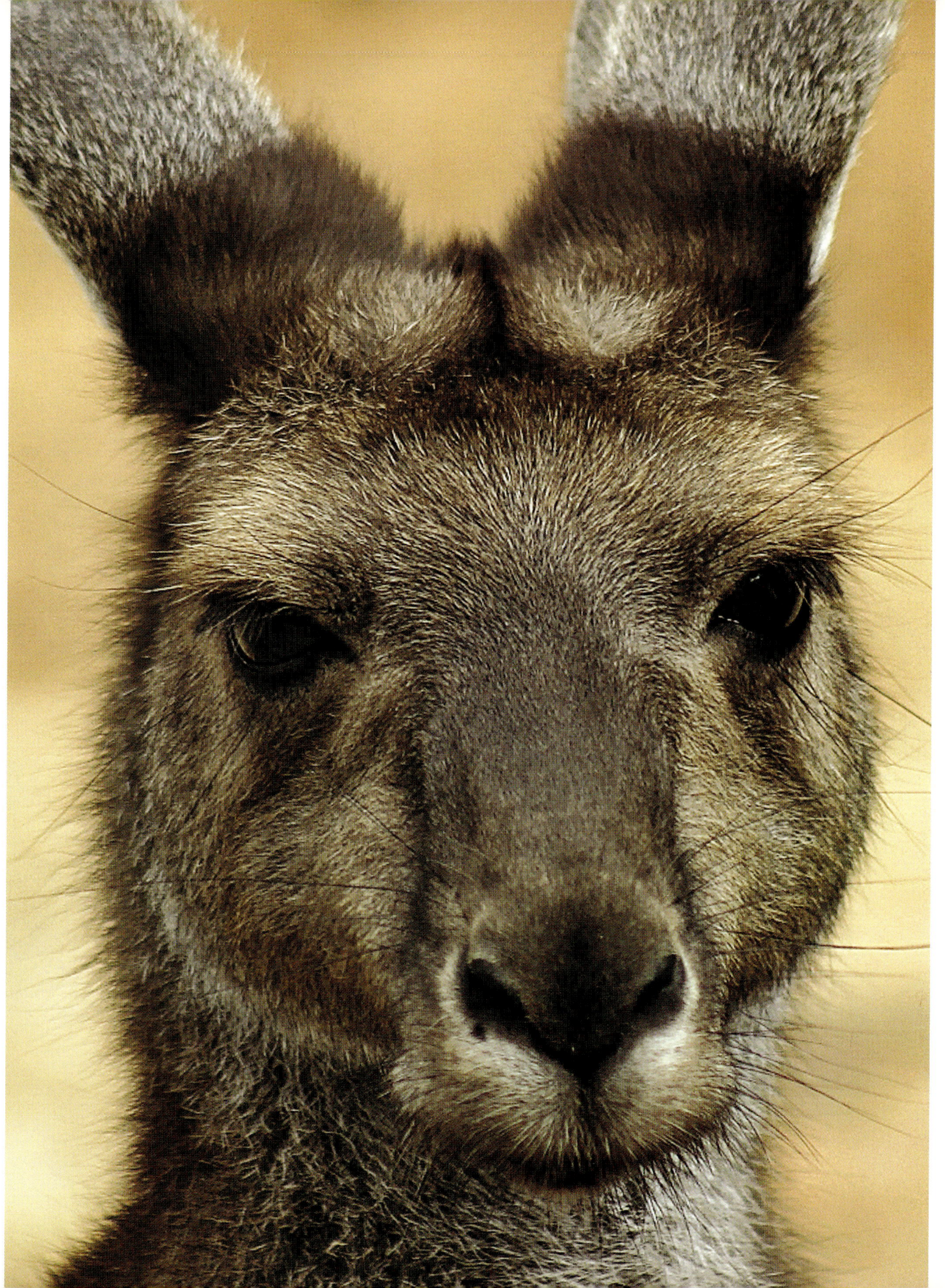

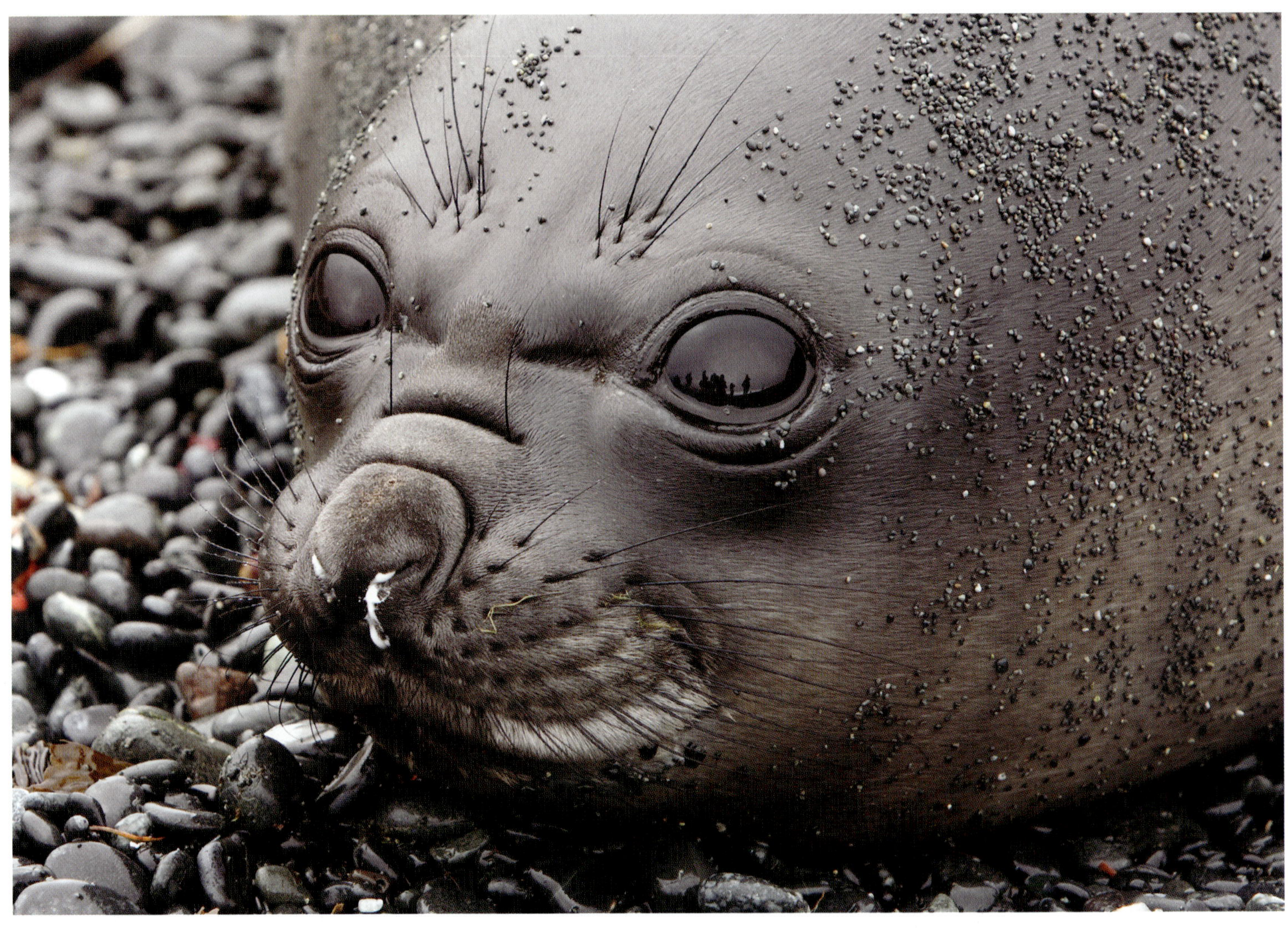

Highly Commended, Animal Portrait
Southern elephant seal pup in portrait
Michael Todd, Huonville, Tasmania

'The pups are extremely engaging, cute and curious.
They are unafraid of humans, bringing home our
responsibility to protect the island and its residents.
If you look closely you can see the reflection of the
photographer in the eyes.'
Macquarie Island, Australia

Canon EOS 40D, 70-200mm, 1/40, f2.8, ISO 200
2008 2-15

Highly Commended, Animal Portrait
Orange dart skipper
Jacqueline Hammer, Redlynch, Queensland

'This skipper was perfectly positioned on a dew-
laden leaf in my garden and not bothered at all by
my presence.'
Redlynch, Queensland

Canon 300D, 100mm macro, 1/5, f10, ISO 200
2008 2-11

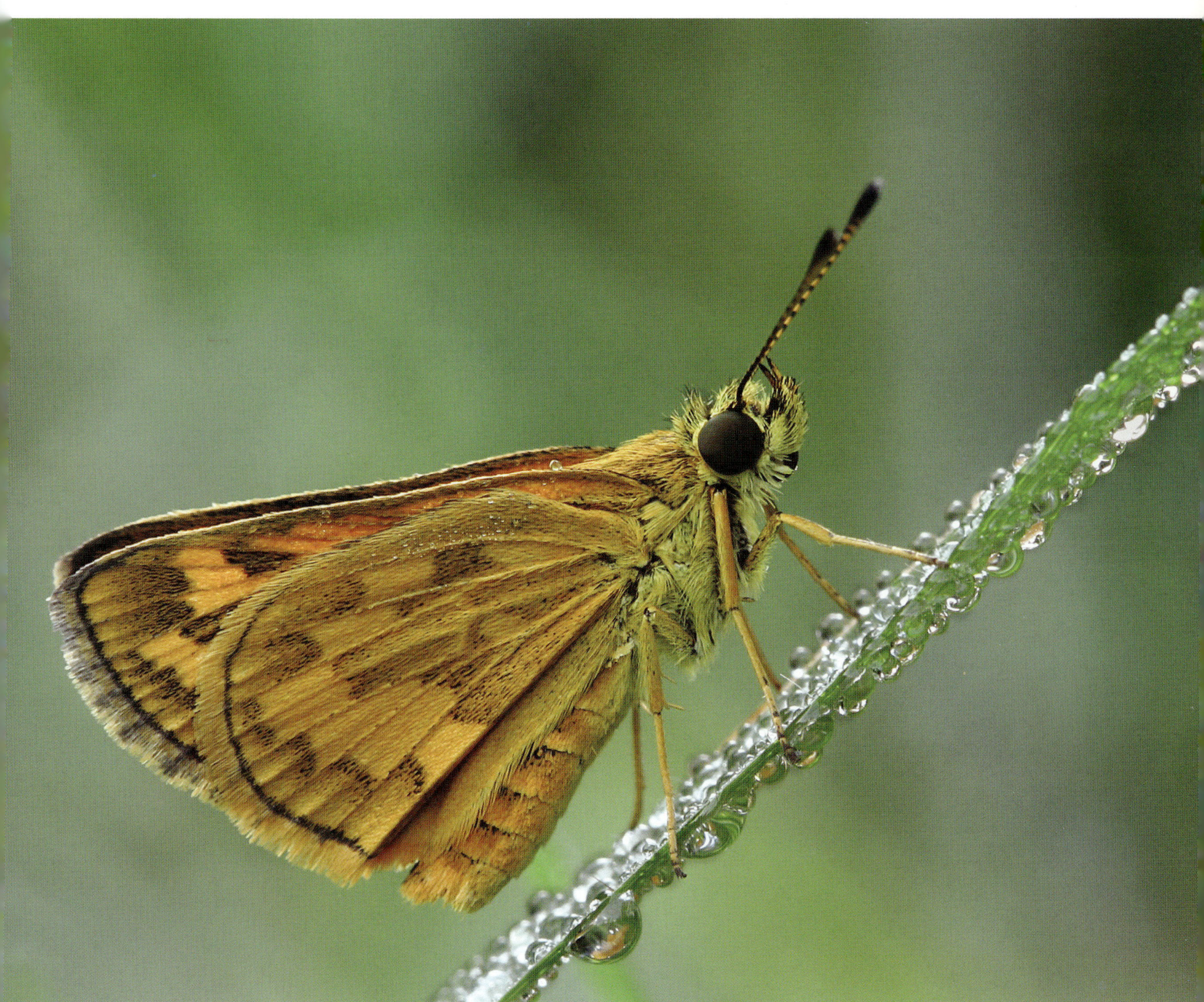

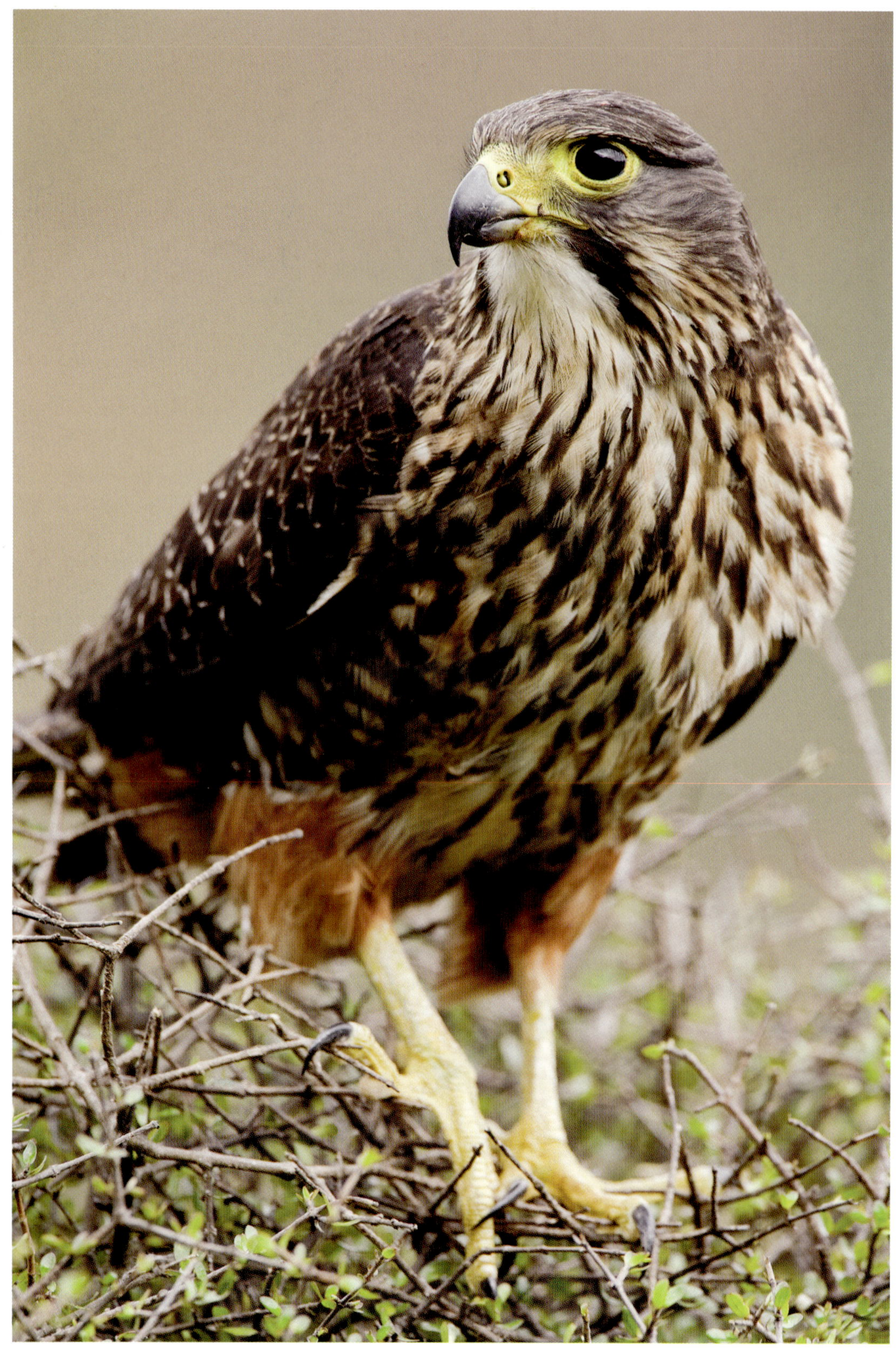

Highly Commended, Animal
Portrait
Female New Zealand falcon
Andrew Trowbridge,
Halswell, Christchurch

'This is the female on top
of a bush waiting for the
male to return with food
for the chicks. The chicks
were about twenty days old
and were left in the nest by
themselves, with one bird
keeping a lookout for danger
from a nearby tree.'
Oreti River, Southland, New
Zealand

Canon 5D, 500mm, 1/200,
f8, ISO 400
2008 2-12 Exhibition

Highly Commended, Animal Portrait
Male king parrot
Sandy Carroll, Malanda, Queensland

'This was a memorable moment shared with this
parrot as he peered around to look at me with those
shy and gentle eyes. He let me take two shots before
taking off, his vibrant red feathers flashing through
the forest canopy.'
Lake Eacham, Queensland

Canon 30D, 100-400mm, 1/320, f5.6, ISO 400
2008 2-14

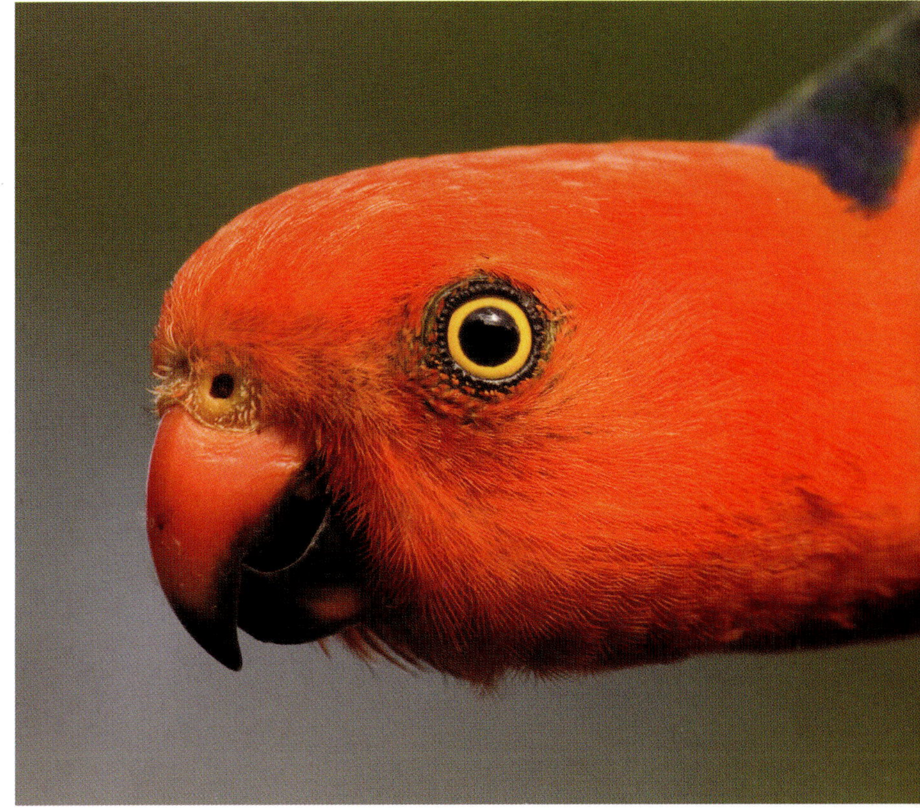

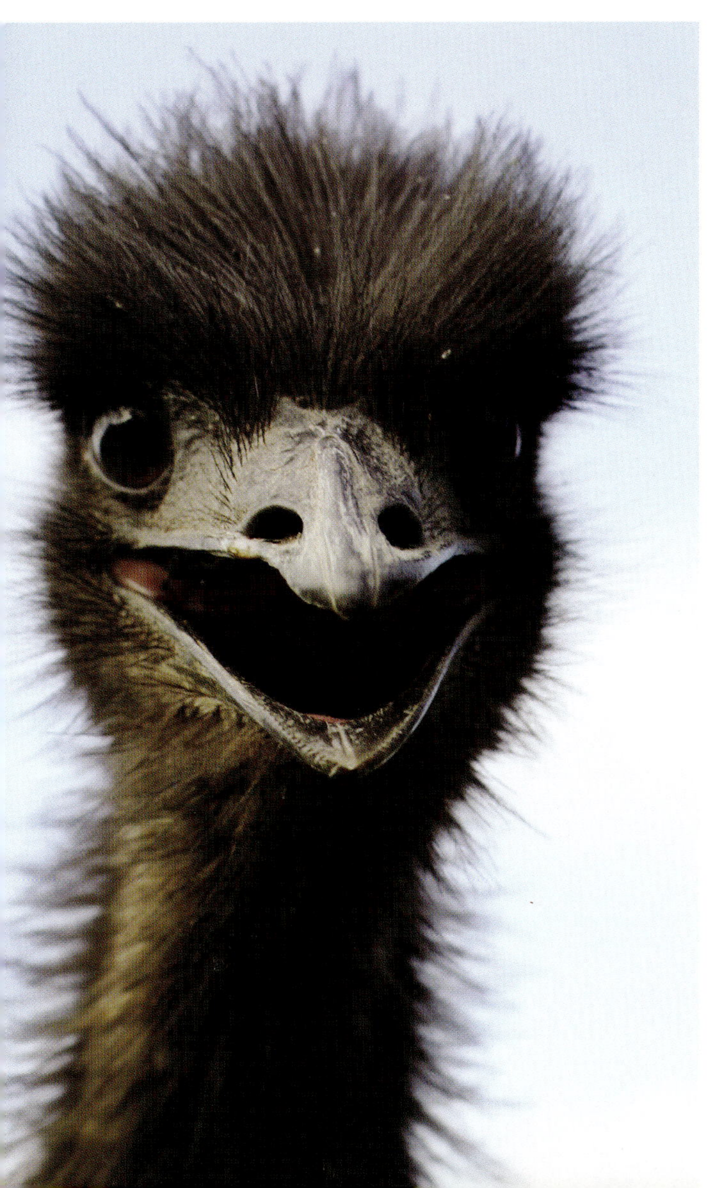

Highly Commended, Animal Portrait
An inquisitive emu
Mark Kolbe, Bexley, New South Wales

'This image captures the comical aspects of an
inquisitive young emu. The look of surprise occurred
when it found me in the long grass. It came and
stood over me, interested to see why I was lying on
my back with my camera.'
Boambee, New South Wales

Canon EOS-1D Mk ll, 50mm, 1/125, f6.3, ISO 200
2008 2-13

Section 3, Botanical Subject

This may be a portrait or habitat shot.

Prize: $1,000

Winner, Botanical Subject
Helix – opened pod of the scarlet bean
Stanley & Kaisa Breeden, Malanda, Queensland

'The scarlet bean seed pods, as their name suggests, are bright red. Usually we find them unopened. So when we saw this one, with its outrageous yellow and blue apparition glowing in the dark forest, we did a double take. The perfection of it is overwhelming – not one seed missing.'
Cairns, Queensland

Judges' comment: 'A beautiful and dramatic shot with intense colour and strong form.'

Canon 1Ds Mk ll, 100mm macro, 3.2sec, f16
2008 3-1 Exhibition

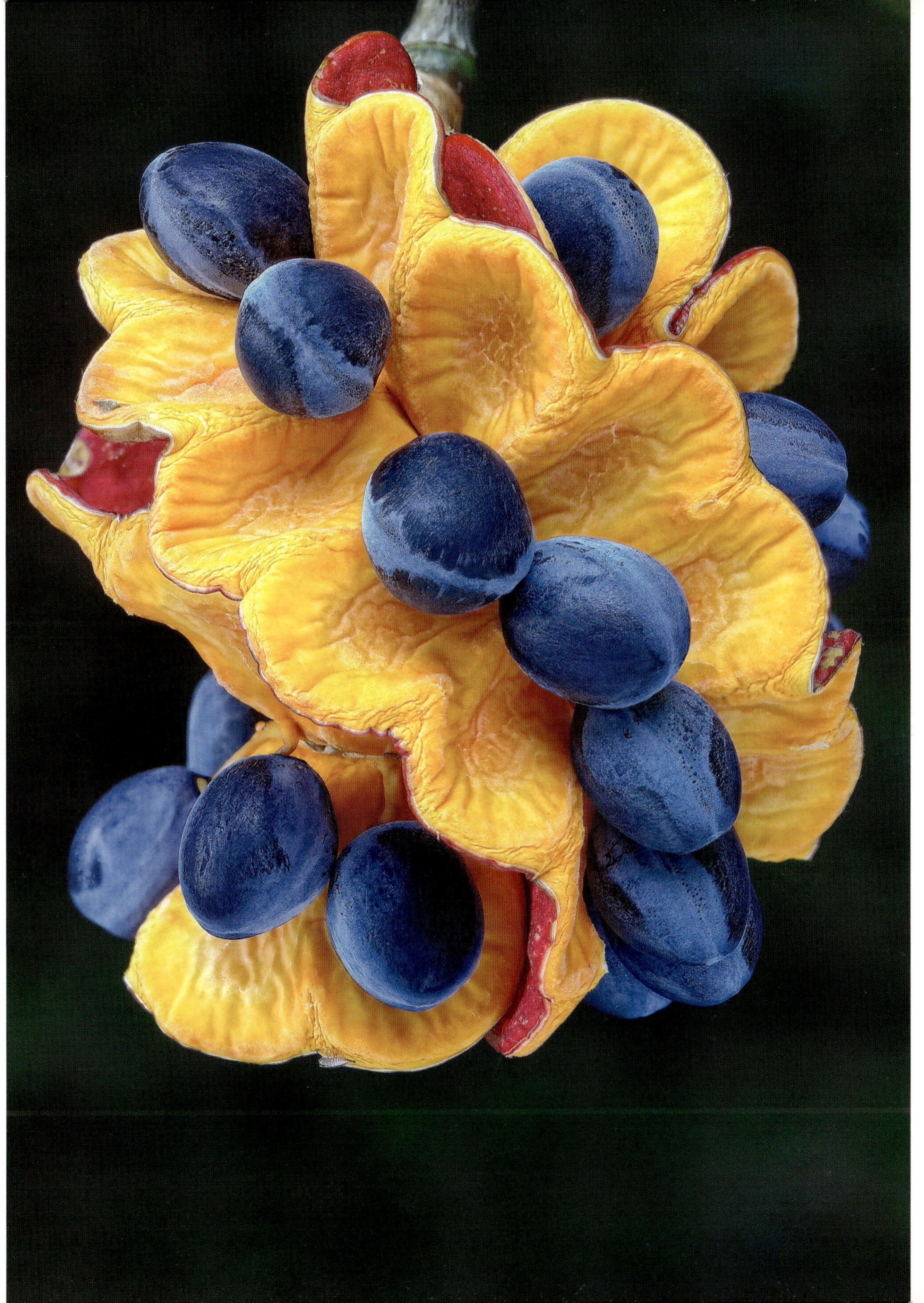

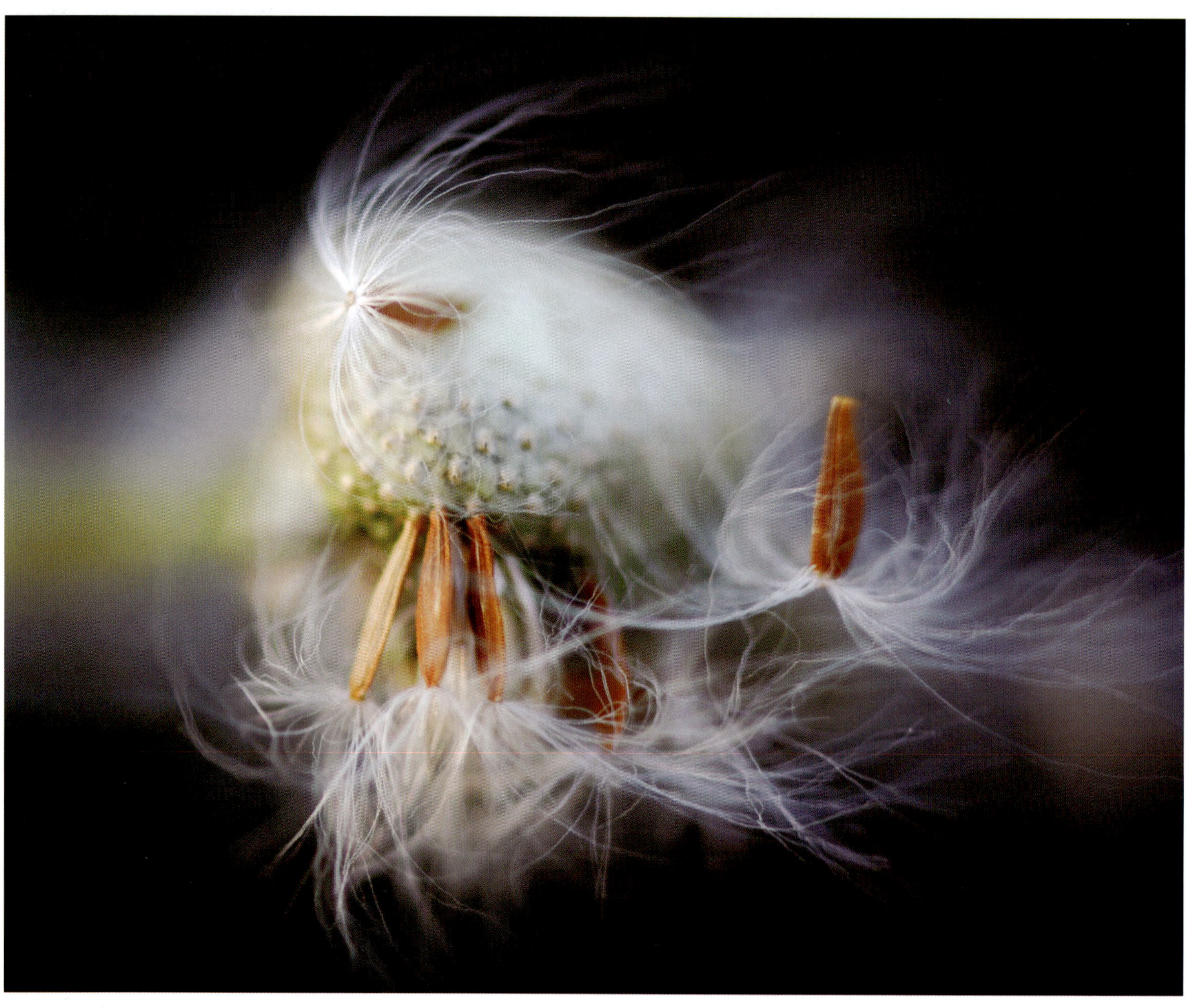

Runner-up, Botanical Subject
Dandelion caught in the breeze
Kate Miners, Bassendean,
Western Australia

'The dandelion is small, delicate
and has the most incredible
texture, but is often overlooked
by everyone except small
children, who simply delight in
blowing the seeds far and wide.
For me dandelions represent the
beauty of macro photography.'

Judges' comment: 'A well
constructed macro shot with a
strong dynamic element.'

Nikon D40x, 105mm, 1/125,
f4.8, ISO 220
2008 3-2 Exhibition

Highly Commended, Botanical
Subject
Reach for the sky
Louise Wolfers, Ringwood East,
Victoria

'This fungus was growing on the
end of a fallen branch. I liked
the way you could see its base
hairs and long slender stems.
I placed the branch up off the
ground and photographed it
looking into the dark shadowy
background. I replaced the
branch on the ground so that it
will grow again next year.'
Mt Donna Buang, Victoria

Canon 400D, 100mm, 1.6 sec,
f9, ISO 200
2008 3-3 Exhibition

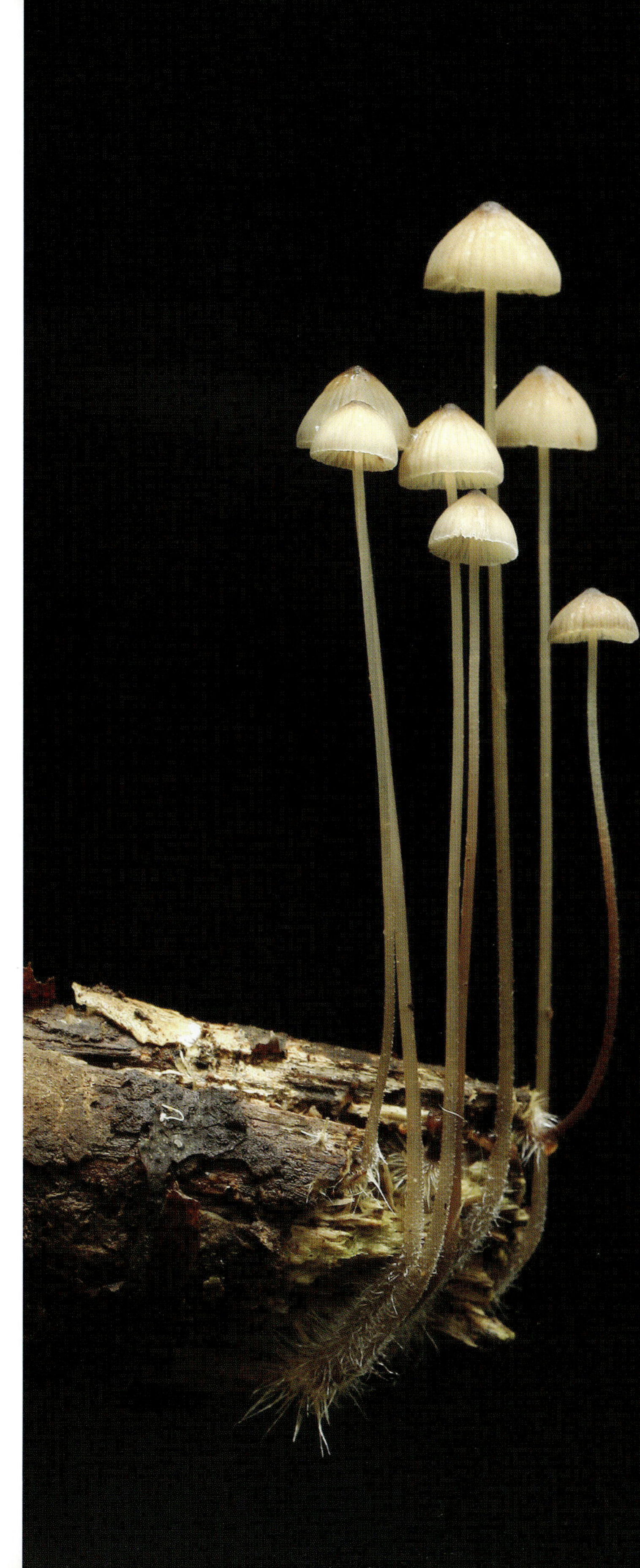

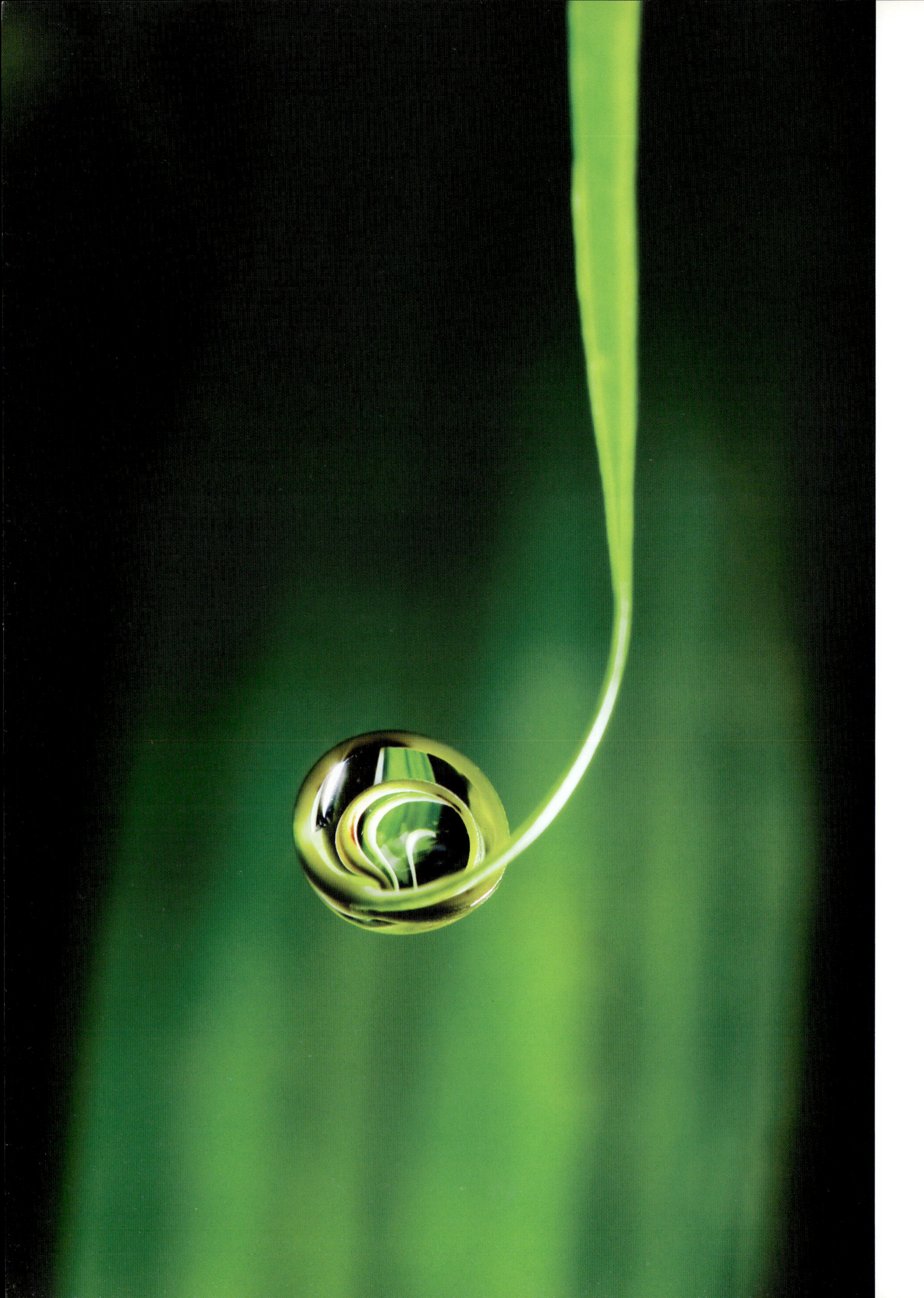

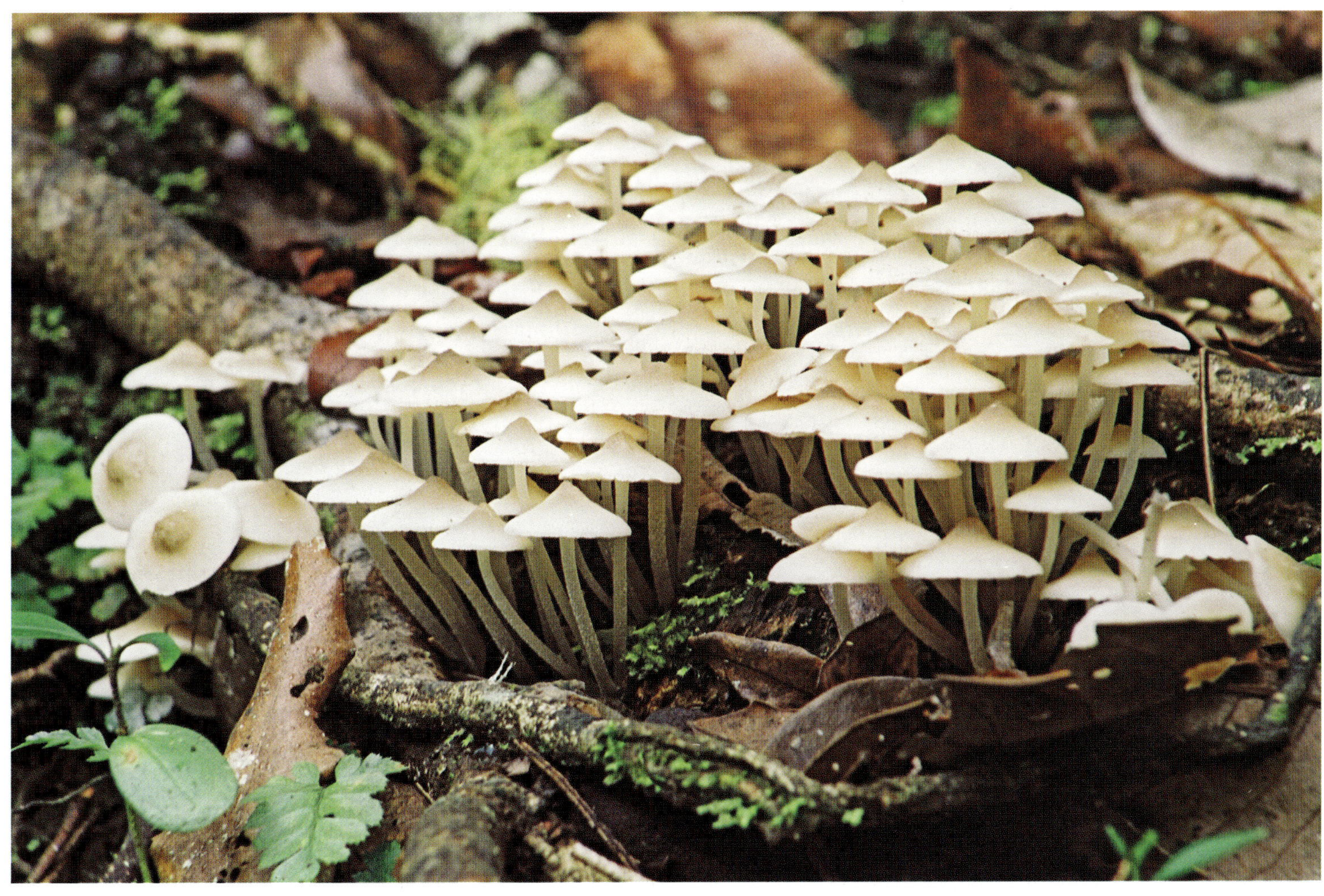

Highly Commended, Botanical Subject
New life – leaf frond
Darran Leal, Coolum Beach, Queensland

'I was walking through the devastation left by Cyclone
Larry. It was like a bomb had gone off – trees down,
no vines, mosses gone. Then I discovered this new
shoot. For me it showed endurance, rebirth, that our
natural world can recover.'
Cairns, Queensland

Canon EOS 5, 100mm Macro, 1/125, f22, ISO 100,
fill flash
2008 3-4 Exhibition

Highly Commended, Botanical Subject
Rainforest fungi
Sandy Carroll, Malanda, Queensland

'These magical fungi were growing near a walking
track at ground level. In order to photograph the
delicate stalks I needed to get as low to the ground
as possible, the tripod legs stretched out to the
maximum. I went back a few days later and they
had disappeared totally.'
Mt Hypipamee NP, Queensland

Fuji Superia Film, f22, ISO 200
2008 3-5

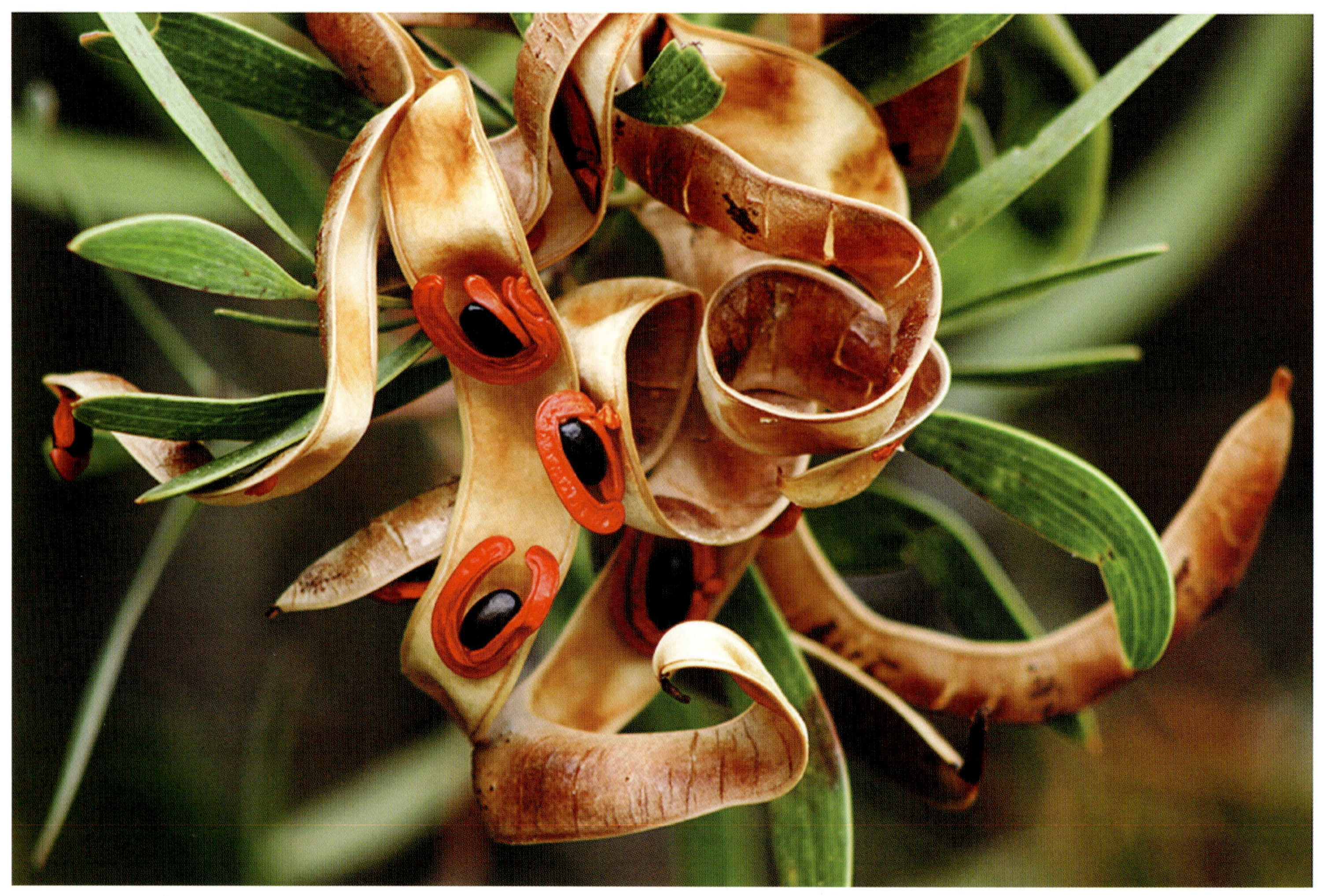

Highly Commended, Botanical Subject
Seeds of wattle genus
Keri Heart, Kingston Beach, Tasmania

'We came across many shrub wattles with their
pods bursting open. The shiny black seeds were
surrounded by these lovely red horseshoe shapes.'
Eyre Bird Observatory, Western Australia

Canon 400D, 230mm, f7.1, 1/1400, ISO 400
2008 3-6 Exhibition

Highly Commended, Botanical Subject
**Grass tree (*Xanthorrhoea pressii*) regeneration after
bushfire**
Len Stewart, Joondalup, Western Australia

'I was attracted to the graduation of colour, as the
plant begins to regenerate after a summer bushfire.
The burnt tips of the fronds add pathos to the
subject.'
Joondalup, Western Australia

Nikon D200, 105mm Micro, f16, 1/125, ISO 100
2008 3-7 Exhibition

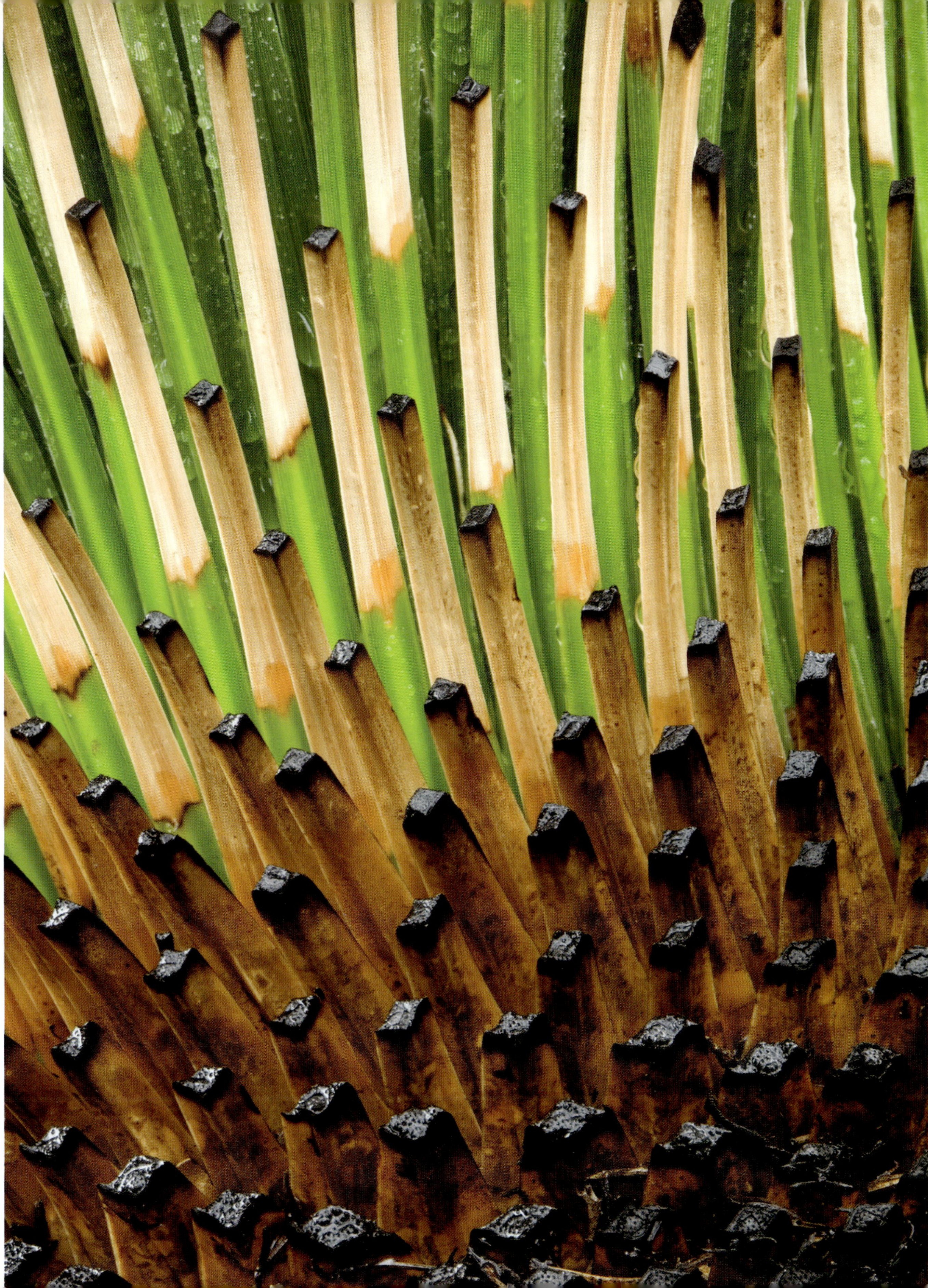

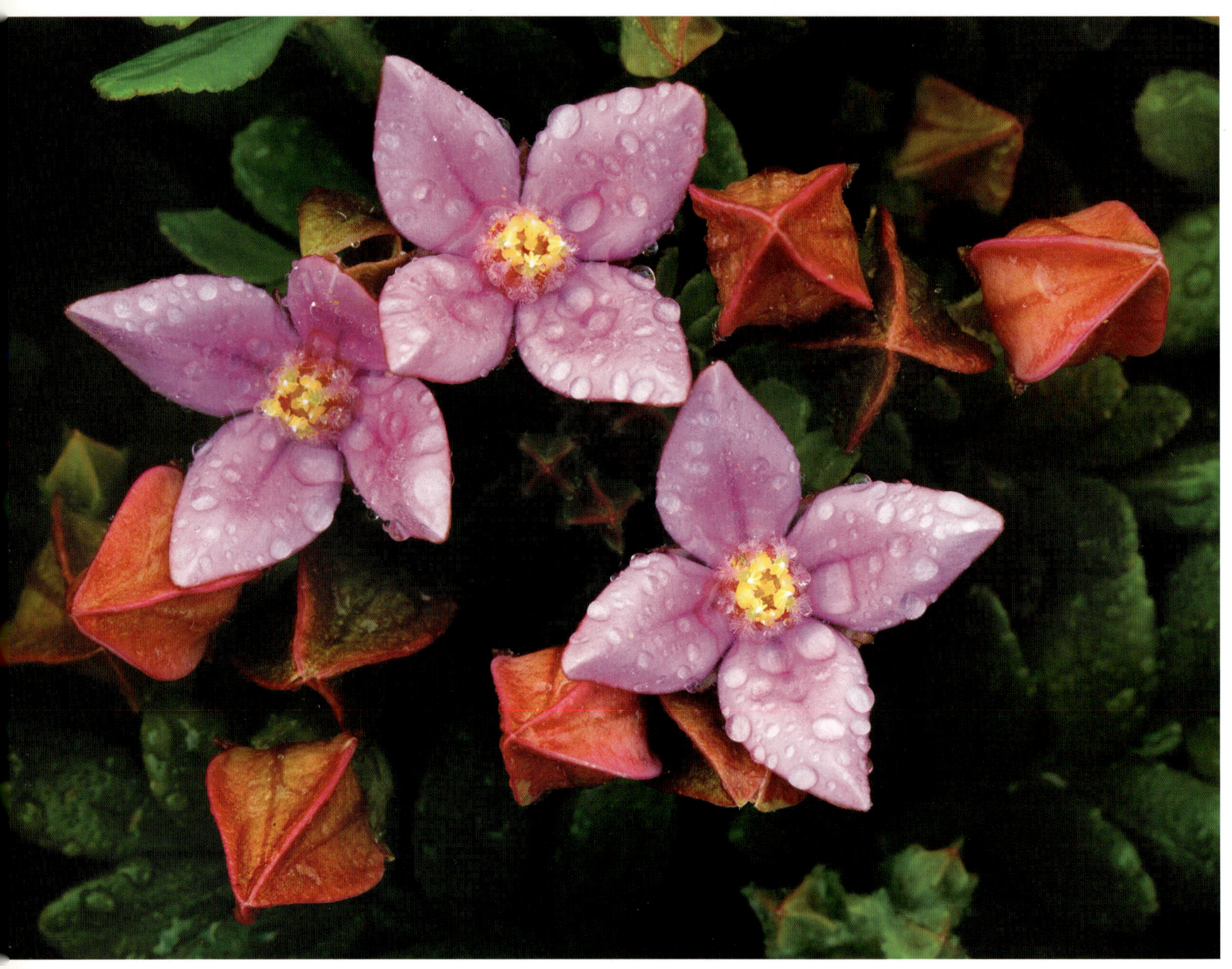

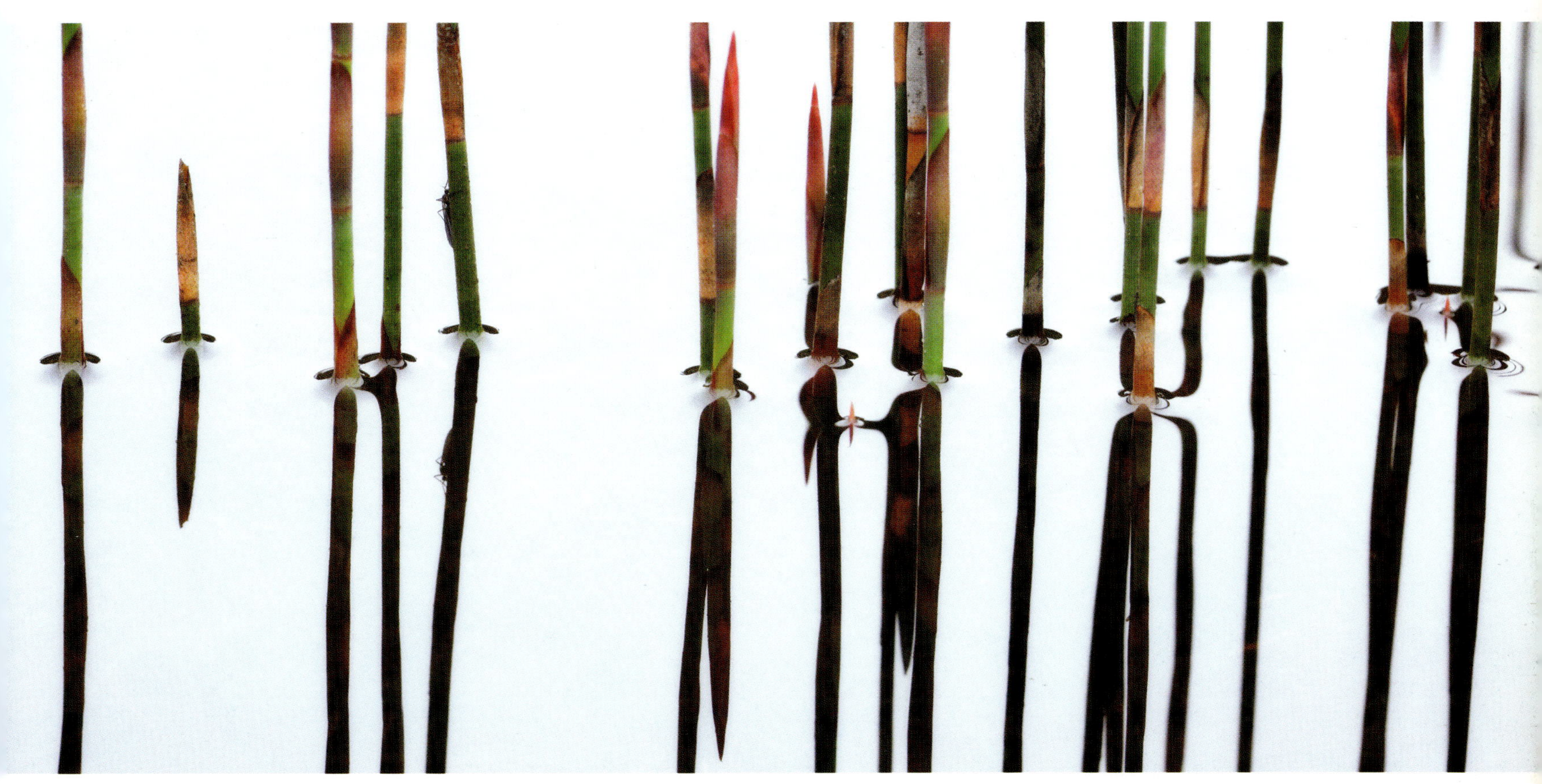

Highly Commended, Botanical Subject
Winged boronia (*Boronia alata*) after rain
Jeremy Turner, Stirling, Australian Capital Territory

'While hiking, the weather was stormy. I was heading back to camp during passing squalls when I noticed the winged boronia bush, the flowers covered in drops of rain. I had to keep my whole body over the camera to keep it dry.'
Leeuwin–Naturaliste NP, Western Australia

Pentax 645, 120mm, 4sec, f32, Fujichrome Velvia 50
2008 3-8 Exhibition

Highly Commended, Botanical Subject
Reed reflection at Cradle Mountain
Wolfgang Glowacki, Sandy Bay, Tasmania

'It was a broody kind of day – low clouds and heavy thunderstorms. After sheltering from the storm I noticed the small reeds perfectly reflected in the water.'
Cradle Mountain, Tasmania

Canon 5D, 2 sec, f5.6
2008 3-9

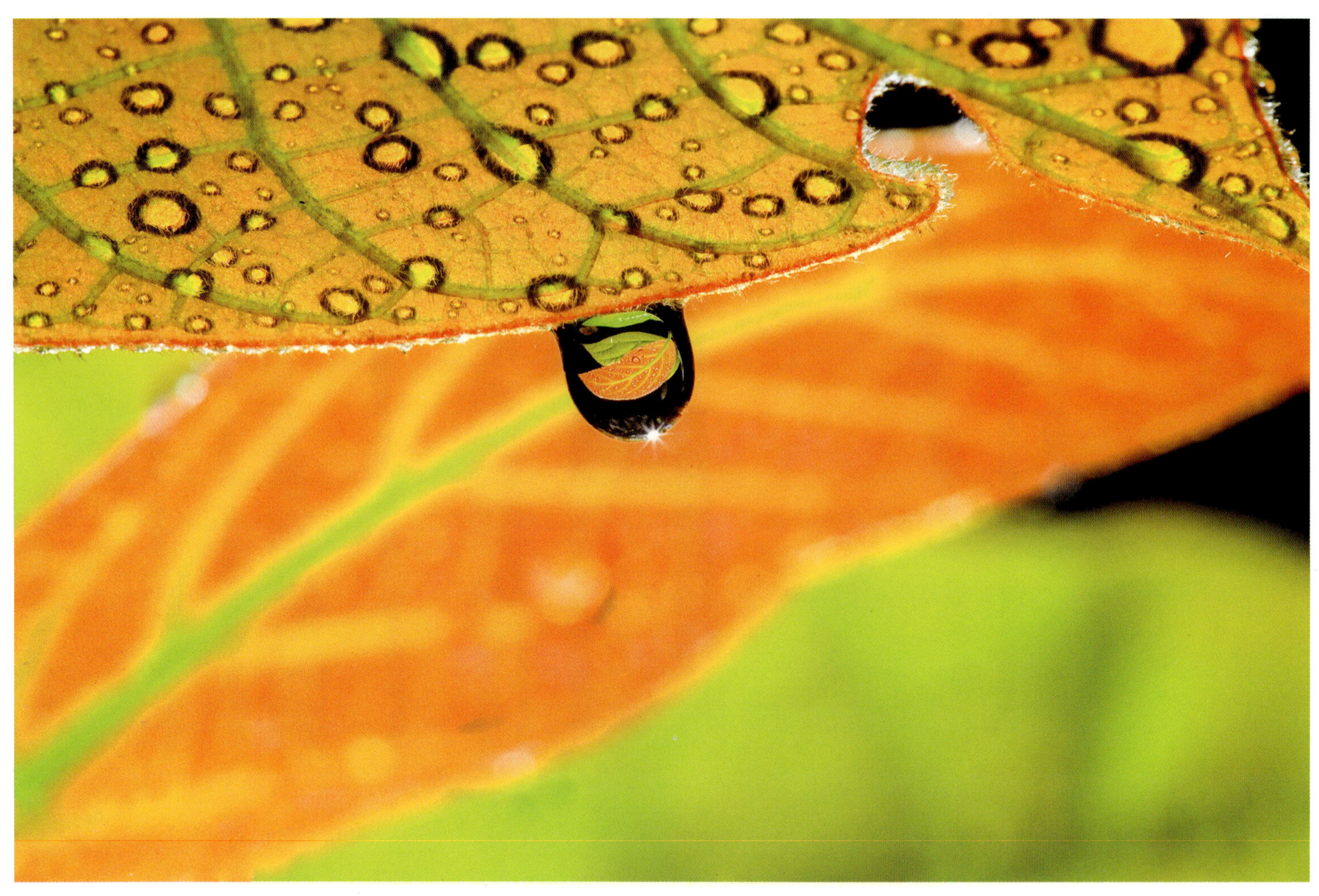

Highly Commended, Botanical Subject
Leaf after rain in rainforest
Darran Leal, Coolum Beach, Queensland

'A shower of rain was the difference when I went
looking for unusual subjects. I was very excited
when I discovered the lone drop with reflection. Just
a few seconds after I had taken the shot the wind
blew it away.'
Cairns, Queensland

Canon EOS 5, 100mm macro, 1/125, f22, ISO 100,
fill flash

 2008 3-10 Exhibition

Highly Commended, Botanical Subject
Spider orchid
Lynne McMahon, Oura, New South Wales

'I was fortunate enough to find this beautiful spider
orchid growing in leaf litter beneath the eucalyptus.
I took photos of it from various angles but decided it
looked best from above, especially with the visiting
insect.'
Beechworth, Victoria

Nikon D50, 105mm Macro, 1/800, f4.5, ISO 400
2008-3-11

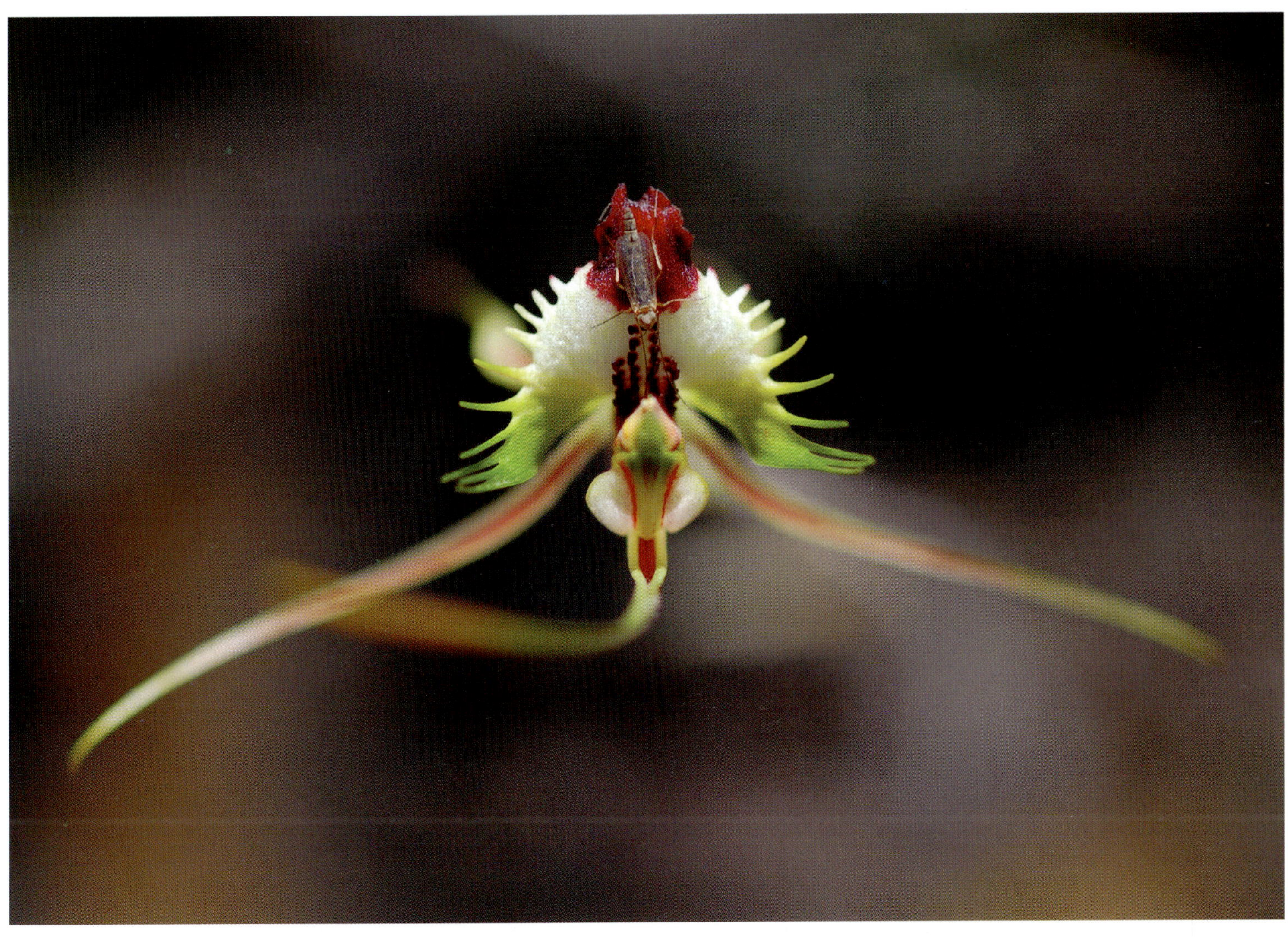

Section 4, Underwater Subject

This may be a portrait of an animal or plant, or a habitat shot.

Prize: $1,000

Winner, Underwater Subject
Leafy sea-dragon portrait
Shannon Conway, South Fremantle, Western Australia

'Gaining their trust is the secret of getting close to most animals.
Over two days I spent four hours finding this particular sea-dragon
and gaining its trust. It became inquisitive about me as time went
on. I particularly like the eye contact.'
Rapid Bay Jetty, Yorke Peninsula, South Australia

Judges' comment: 'A remarkable creature rendered well as a
portrait.'

Nikon Dx, Subal Housing, 60mm macro, 1/250, f13, ISO 100,
flash
2008 4-1 Exhibition

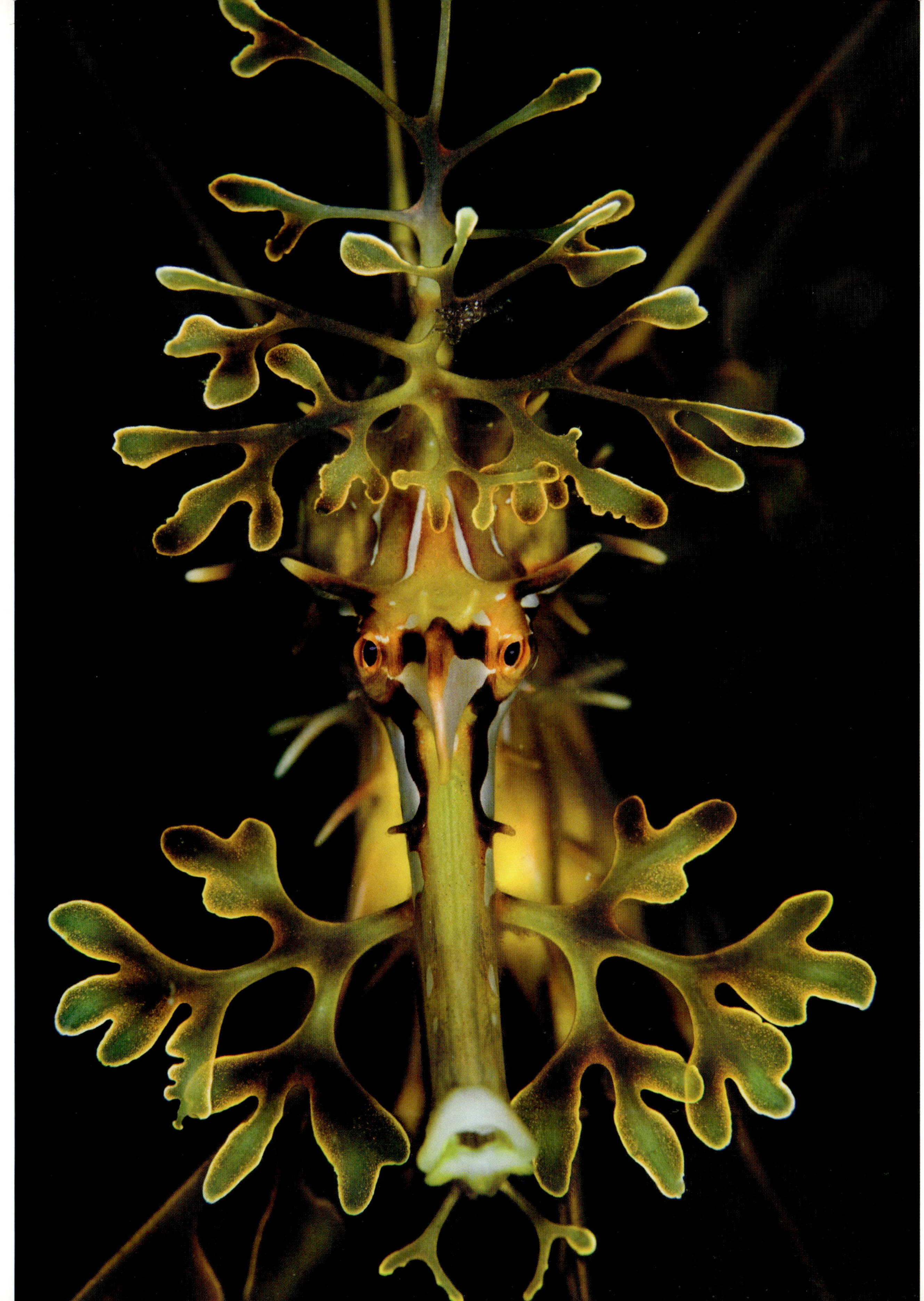

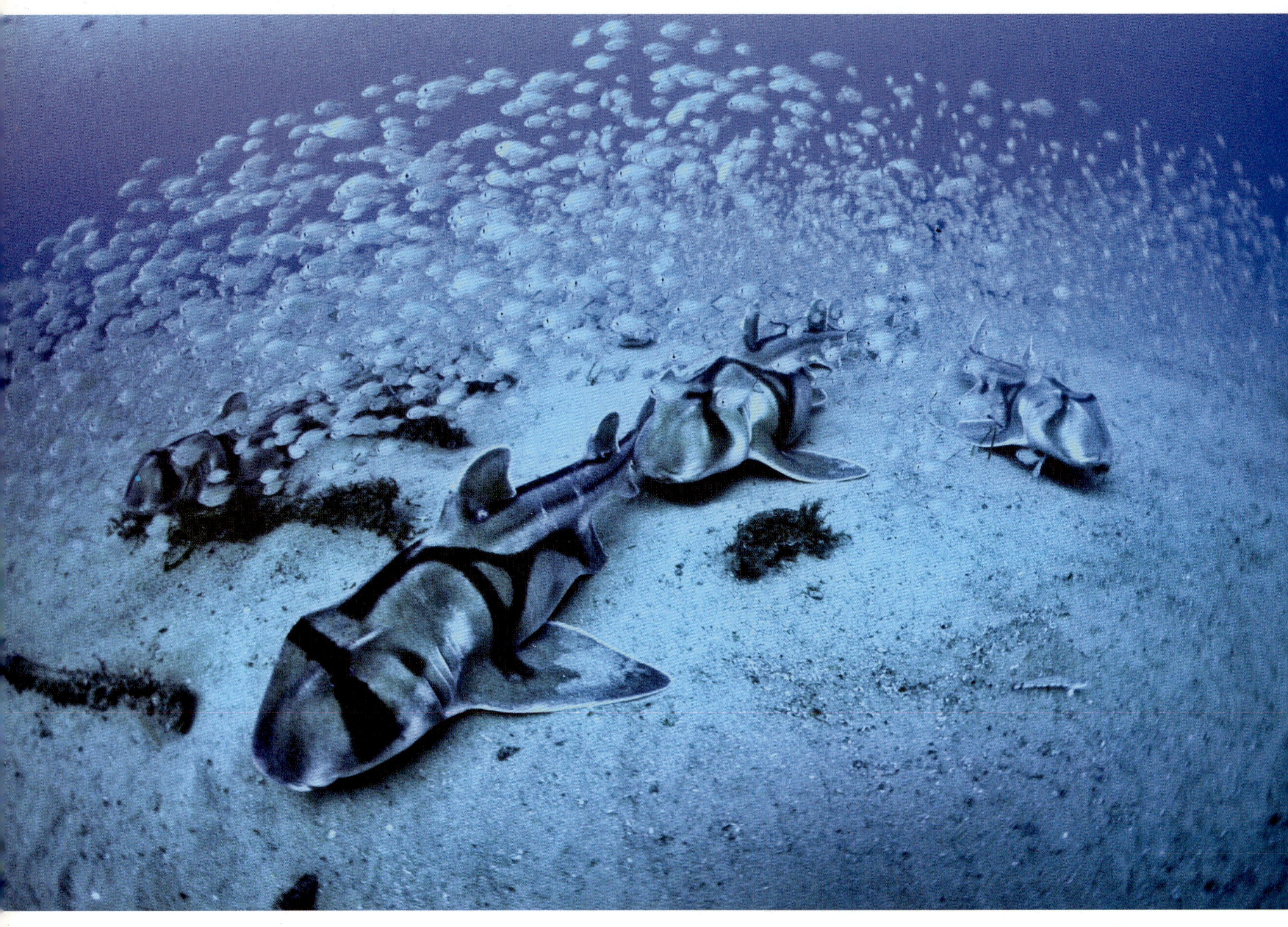

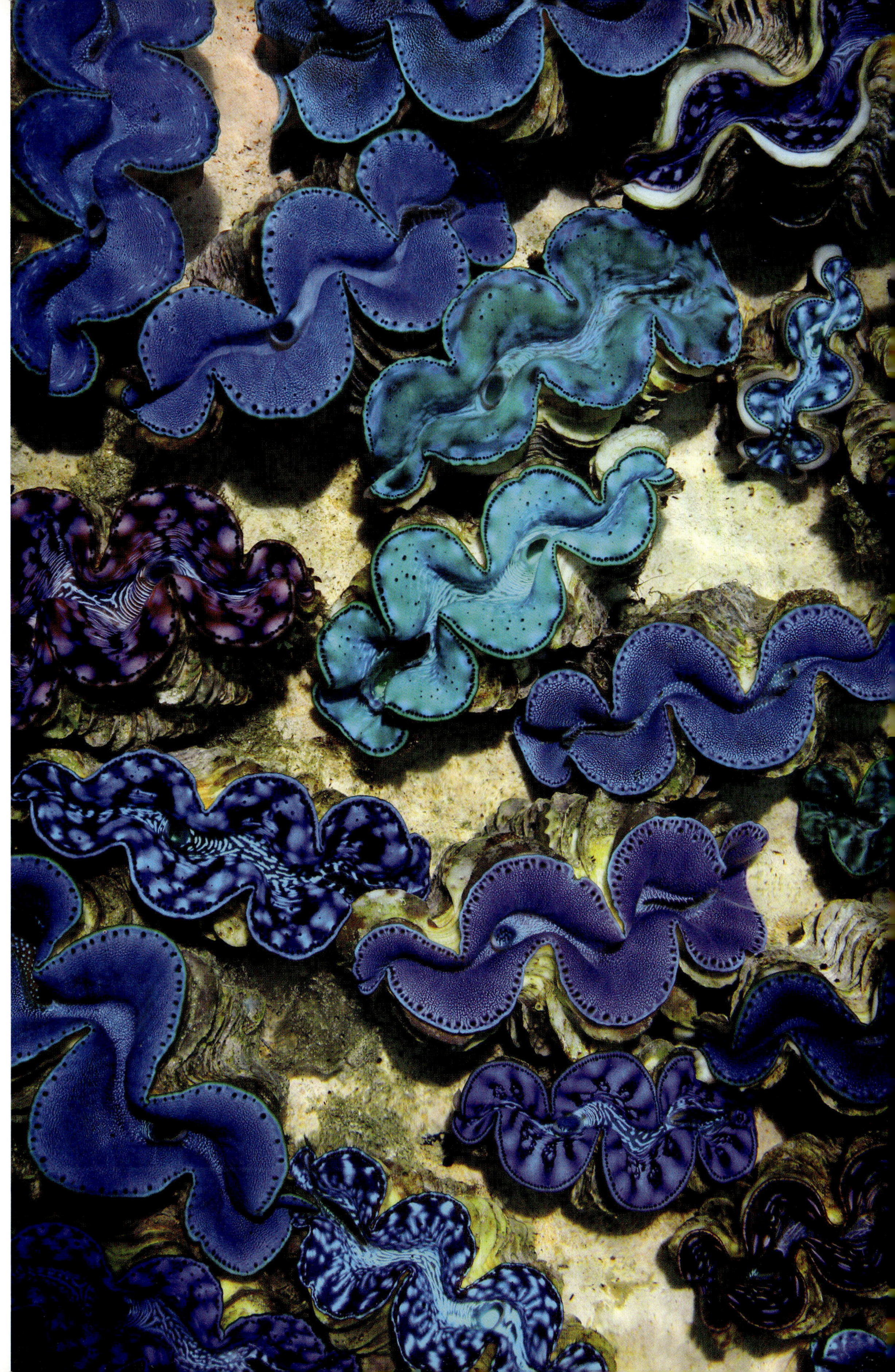

Runner-up, Underwater
Subject
Port Jackson sharks
Mark Spencer, Boambee,
New South Wales

'This aggregate was
found while exploring a
shipwreck. The sharks were
photographed using the
ambient light atmosphere
of this relatively deep
habitat. Port Jackson sharks
are bottom-dwelling small
sharks sometimes found
aggregating.'
Off Sydney, New South
Wales

Judges' comment: 'The use
of ambient light gives the
viewer a strong sense of
place.'

Nikon F4, 16mm fish-eye,
Provia 400F
2008 4-2 Exhibition

Highly Commended,
Underwater Subject
Blue clams
Alex Cearns, North Perth,
Western Australia

'These clams are reared from
larvae in large saltwater
tanks. Once they reach an
adequate size they are released into the lagoon. As my
shadow fell over the clams
they retreated into their shells
and I had to remain very still
for several minutes before
they opened up again.'
Cocos (Keeling) Islands,
Western Australia

Canon 5D, 24-105mm, f8,
ISO 400
2008 4-3 Exhibition

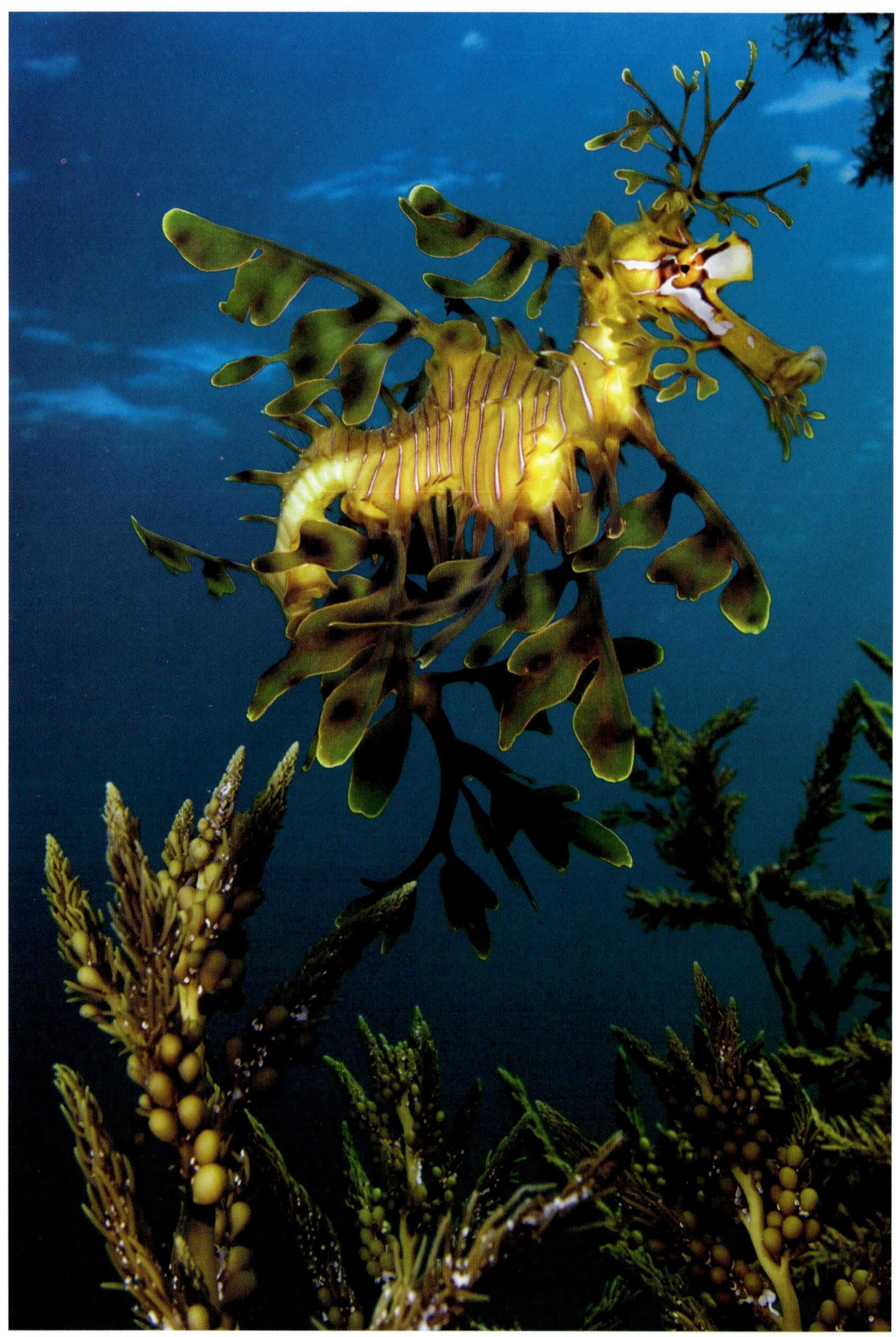

Highly Commended,
Underwater Subject
Leafy sea-dragon
Shannon Conway, South
Fremantle, Western Australia

'Over five days, in between
low tides and challenging
sea conditions, I spent over
fourteen hours in the water.
We found seven different
sea-dragons, some of the
males carrying eggs. I liked
the composition of this image
as it shows the subject in
its weed environment with
separation and eye contact.'
Rapid Bay Jetty, Yorke
Peninsula, South Australia

Nikon D2x, Subal Housing,
12-24mm, 1/80, f10,
ISO 100, flash
2008 4-4

Highly Commended,
Underwater Subject
Lace scorpionfish
Dominic Barrington,
Mollymook, New South Wales

'These fish are masters of
disguise. This image shows a
rarely caught glimpse of the fish
in mid yawn.'
Loloata Island, Papua New
Guinea

Nikon D200, 60mm, f8, 1/60,
ISO 100
2008 4-5

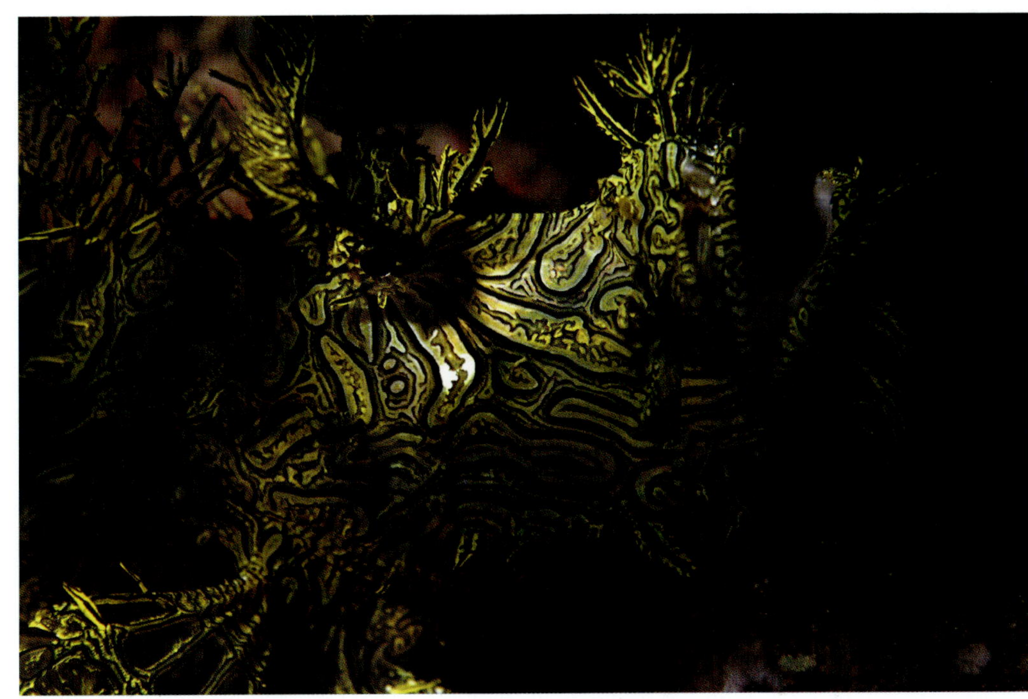

Highly Commended,
Underwater Subject
Anglerfish
David Fagan, Chipping Norton,
New South Wales

'Returning to shore at the end
of a night dive, the anglerfish
was in less than three metres of
water amongst kelp and I only
had two frames left on my film.
Quite a challenge.'
Nelson Bay, New South Wales

Nikon F100, 60mm, Fuji Velvia
2008 4-12

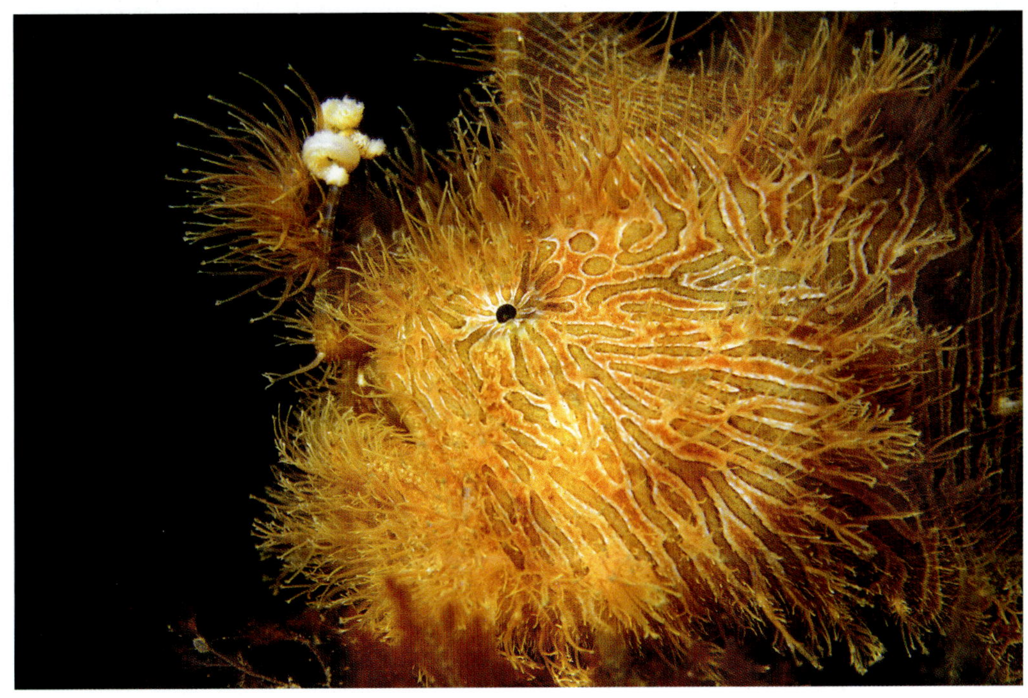

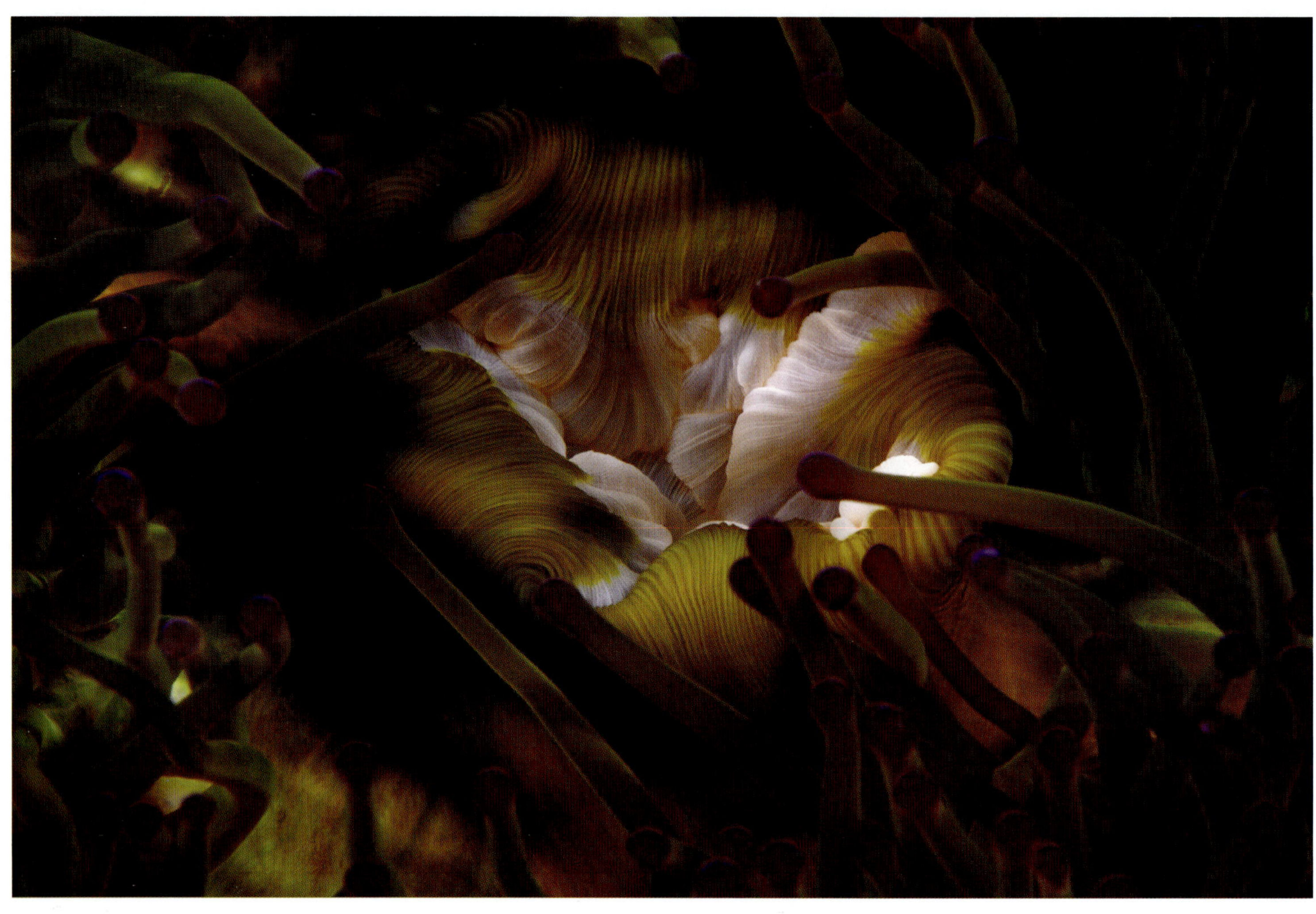

Highly Commended, Underwater Subject
Anemone mouth
Dominic Barrington, Mollymook, New South Wales

'The beauty of the colours and textures of this anemone struck me. It is relatively unusual to see an anemone as open and spread out and exhibiting its mouth as freely. Its mouth is normally hidden by tentacles and anemone fish.'
Loloata Island, Papua New Guinea

Nikon D200, 60mm, 1/125, f22, ISO 100
2008 4-6 Exhibition

Highly Commended, Underwater Subject
Nautilus
Mark Spencer, Boambee, New South Wales

'It is unusual to encounter these bizarre creatures
in the wild. I was part of a special expedition with
staff and scientists associated with WWF to promote
the Coral Sea as a marine park, and had the special
opportunity to examine the creatures.'
Coral Sea, Australia

Nikon D200, Seacam Housing, 10-20mm, 1/30, f18,
ISO 200, flash
2008 4-7

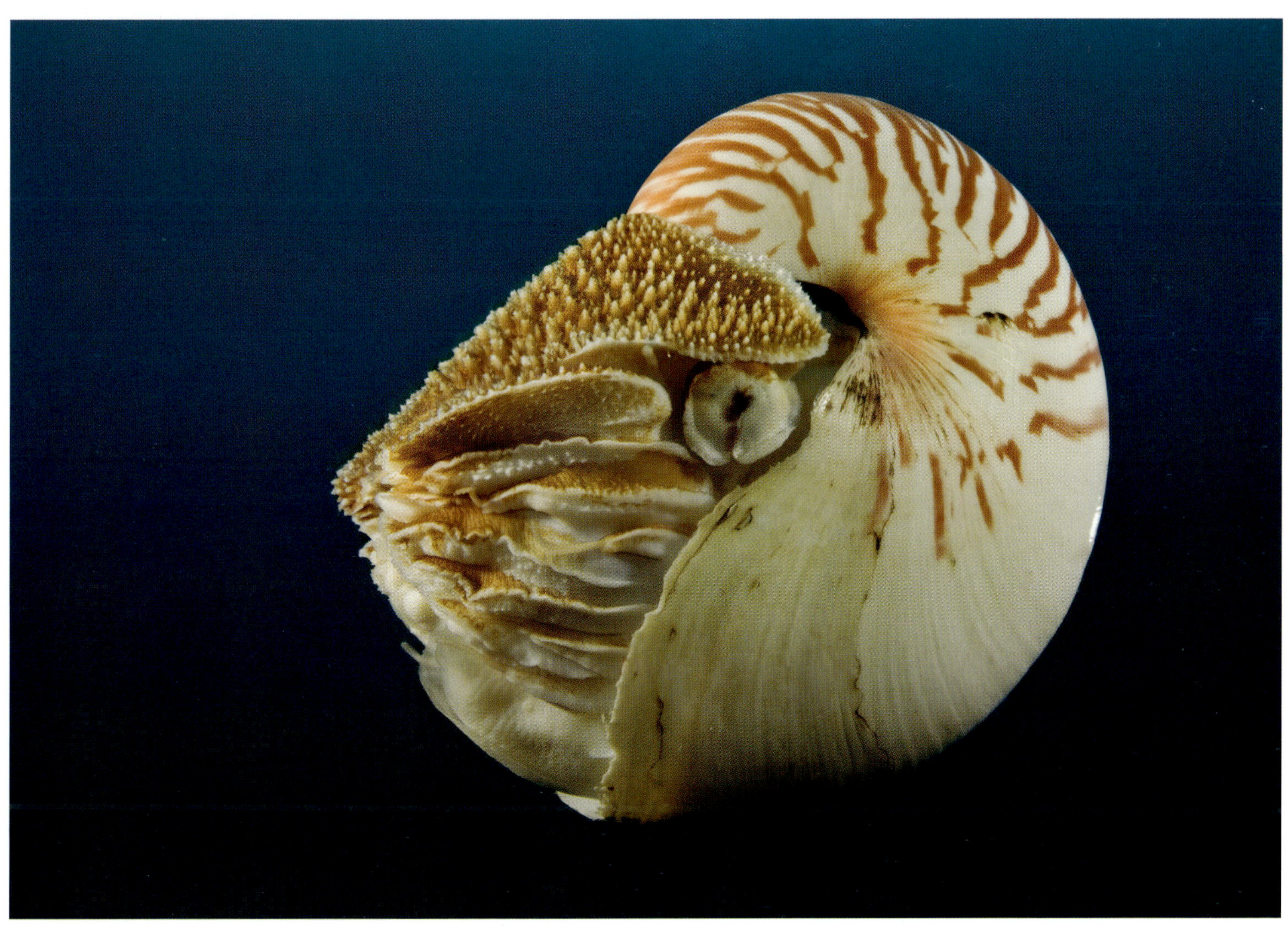

Highly Commended,
Underwater Subject
Crocodile fish eye
David Fagan, Chipping
Norton, New South Wales

'This image joins the
underwater world to the
surface, as the reflection of
the sky can be seen in the
fish's eye.'
Uepi Island, Solomon Islands

Nikon F100, Subal Housing,
flash
2008 4-10

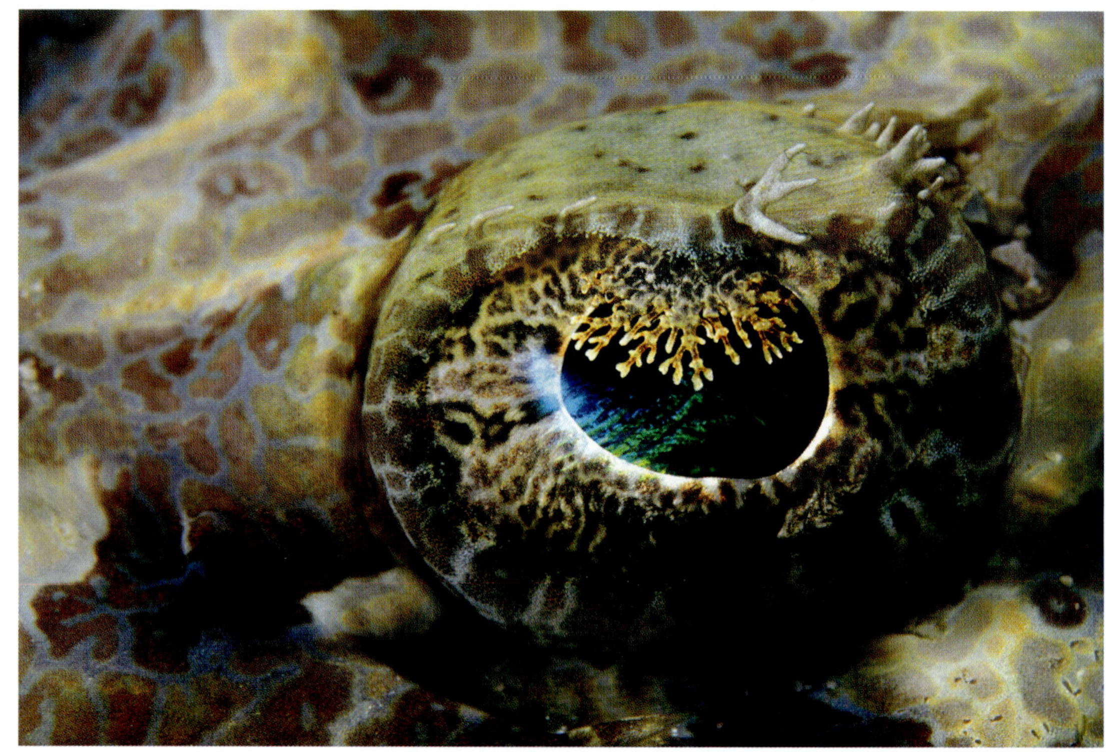

Highly Commended,
Underwater Subject
**Surrounded by food –
flathead on the prowl**
Darran Leal, Coolum Beach,
Queensland

'I came across this unusual
scene. The flathead was
simply cruising through the
school of herring to a new
hiding spot, while the herring
kept to a safe distance.'
Fraser Island, Queensland

Canon EOS 5, 100-400mm,
1/350, f4.5, ISO 400
2008 4-9

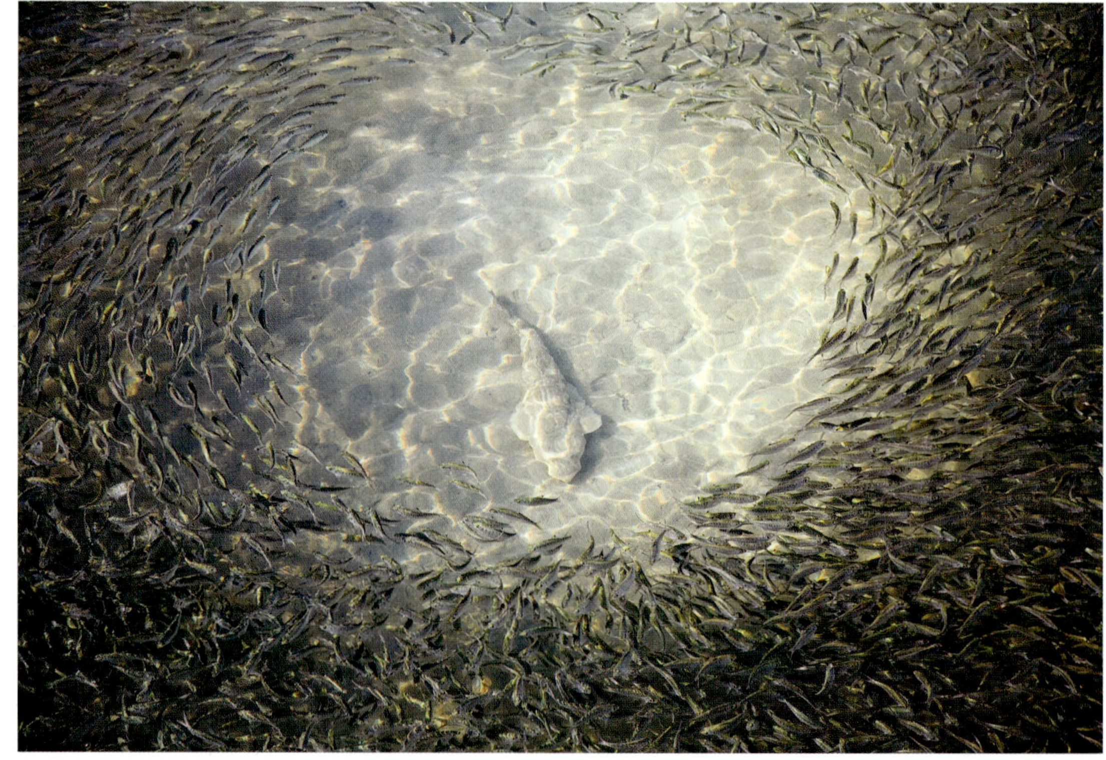

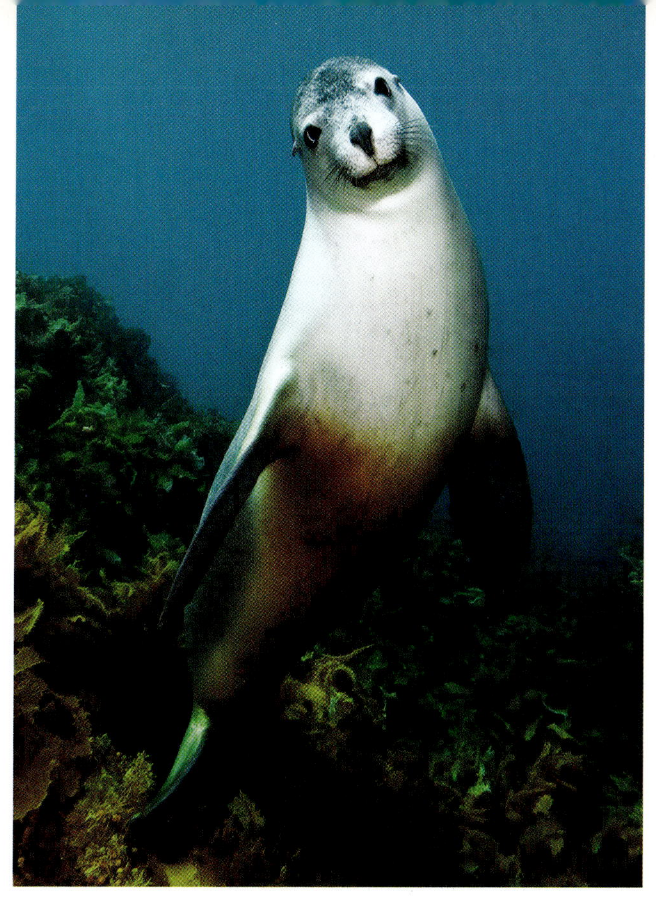

Highly Commended,
Underwater Subject
Australian sea lion
Shannon Conway, South
Fremantle, Western Australia

'The sea lions would just
dive down and beckon you
to play. This cheeky monkey
just posed for a few seconds,
looking very angelic.'
Kangaroo Island, South
Australia

Nikon D2x, Subal Housing,
12-24mm, 1/125, f8,
ISO 100, flash
2008 4-11 Exhibition

Highly Commended,
Underwater Subject
**Bellinger River snapping
turtle**
Mark Spencer, Boambee,
New South Wales

'The Bellinger River
snapping turtles were quite
approachable, which is a
blessing when photographing
underwater animals. I was
astounded by the richness of
the freshwater region.'
Bellinger River, New South
Wales

Nikon D200, 17-70mm,
1/15, f16, ISO 160, flash
2008 4-8 Exhibition

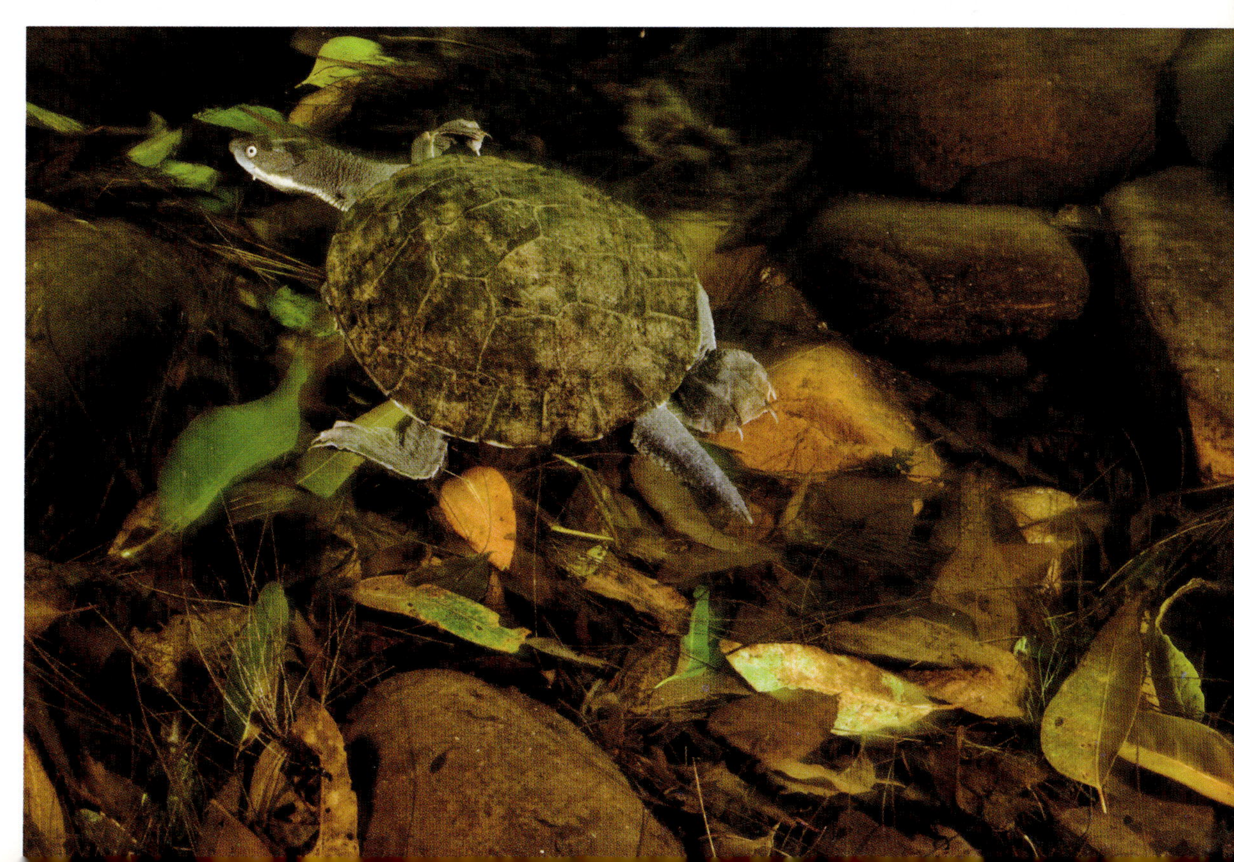

Section 5, Wilderness Landscape

The landscape or seascape must have minimal evidence of human interference.

Prize: $1,000

Winner, Wilderness Landscape
Last of the evening light
Tony Hopkins, Gooseberry Hill, Western Australia

'As the sun was setting on the horizon I noticed the lovely low light shining through the waves, bringing a warm glow to the rock. Fortunately I already had my camera set up on a tripod.' Kalbarri, Western Australia

Judges' comment: 'An evocative landscape photograph, given power because of the strong focal point.'

Canon EOS 5D, 100-400mm, 6 sec, f16, ISO 100
2008 5-1 Exhibition

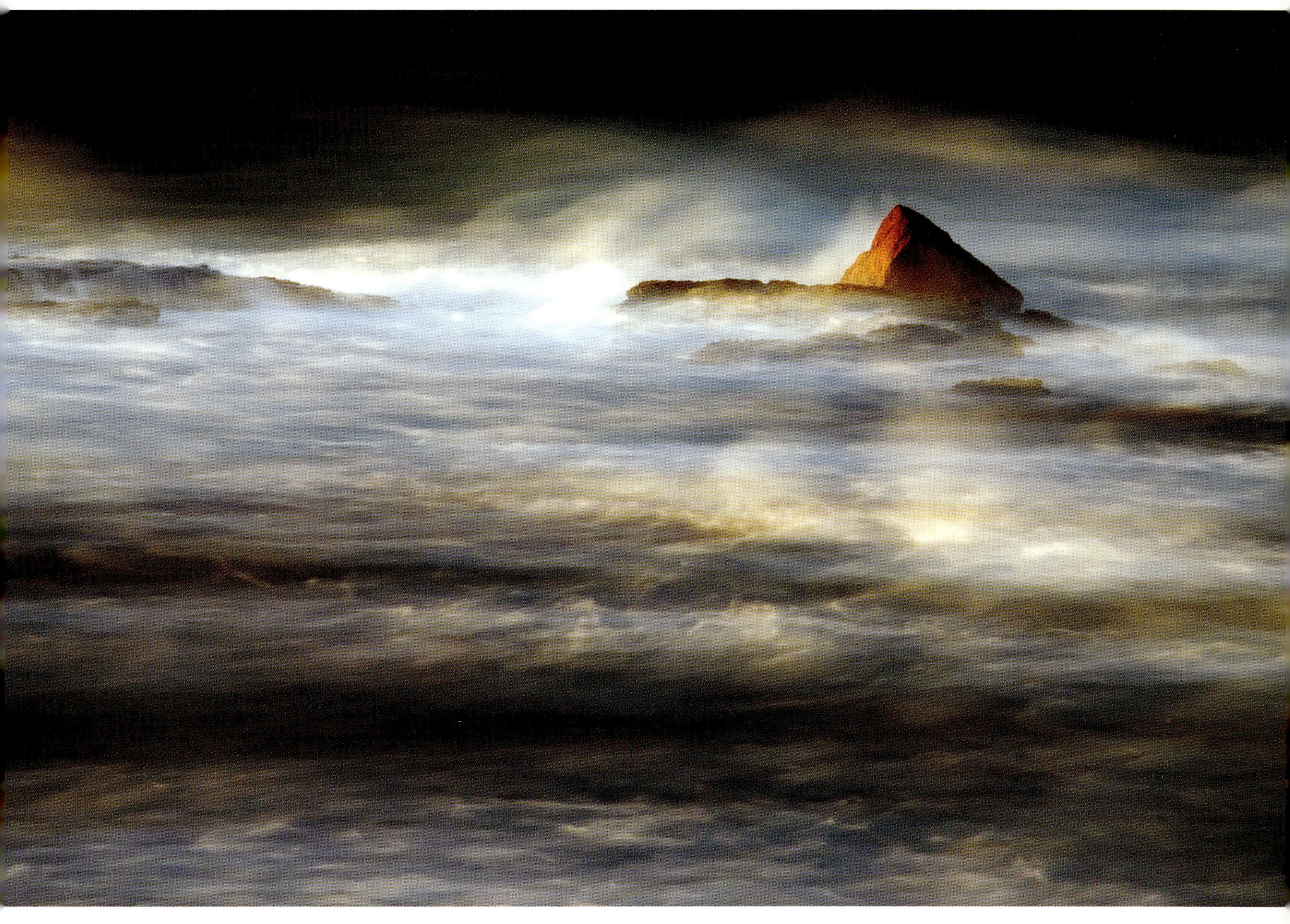

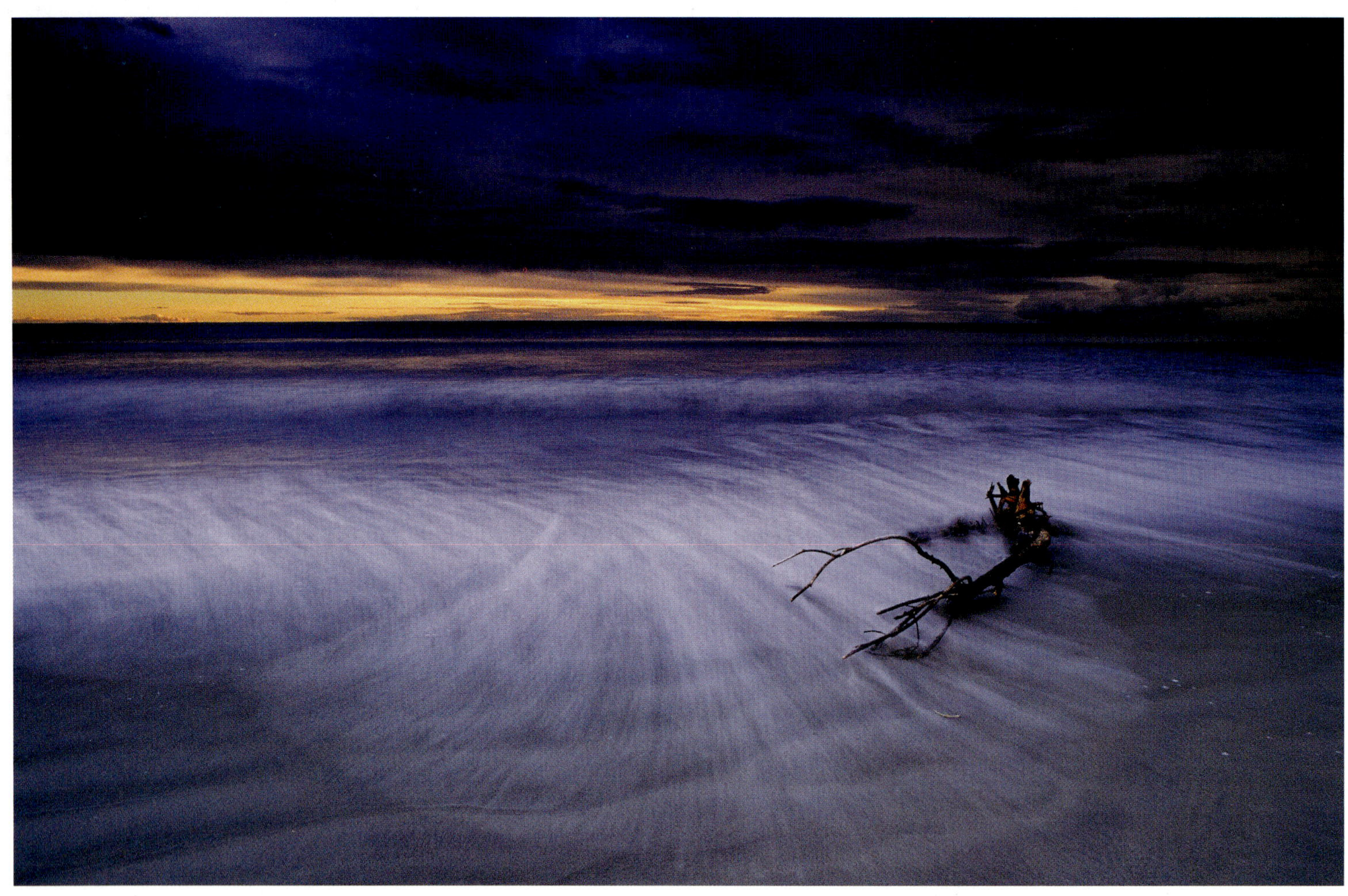

Runner-up, Wilderness Landscape
Driftwood on beach
Andrew Trowbridge, Halswell, Christchurch

'I was much more intent on keeping warm than taking photographs in the pre-dawn of this winter morning. When I came across this piece of driftwood and the warming light on the horizon I knew I had to stop.'
Southshore, Christchurch, New Zealand

Judges' comment: 'You feel the wind when looking at this image.'

Nikon F5, 17-35mm, 3 Stop ND Filter, Velvia, ISO 50
2008 5-2 Exhibition

Highly Commended, Wilderness Landscape
Silver snow daisies after sunset
Jeremy Turner, Stirling, Australian Capital Territory

'The wildflowers were in spectacular bloom. The weather was changeable and clouds formed behind the granite peak adding to the drama of the shot. The silver snow daisies in the foreground were leading up to the peak. The light was fading, adding to the moodiness of the photo.'
Kosciuszko NP, New South Wales

Pentax 645, 35mm lens, 4 sec, f22, Fujichrome Velvia 50
2008 5-3 Exhibition

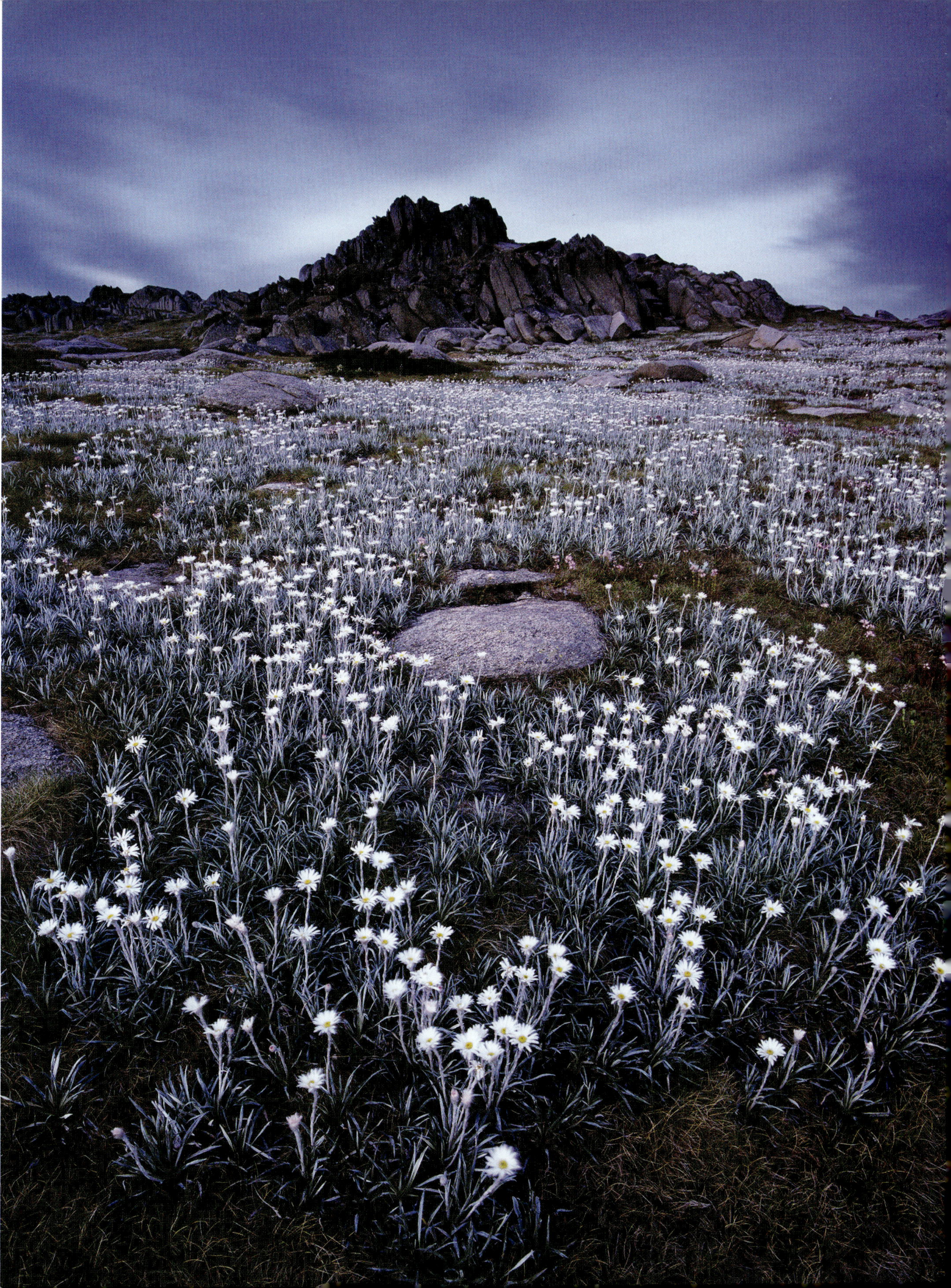

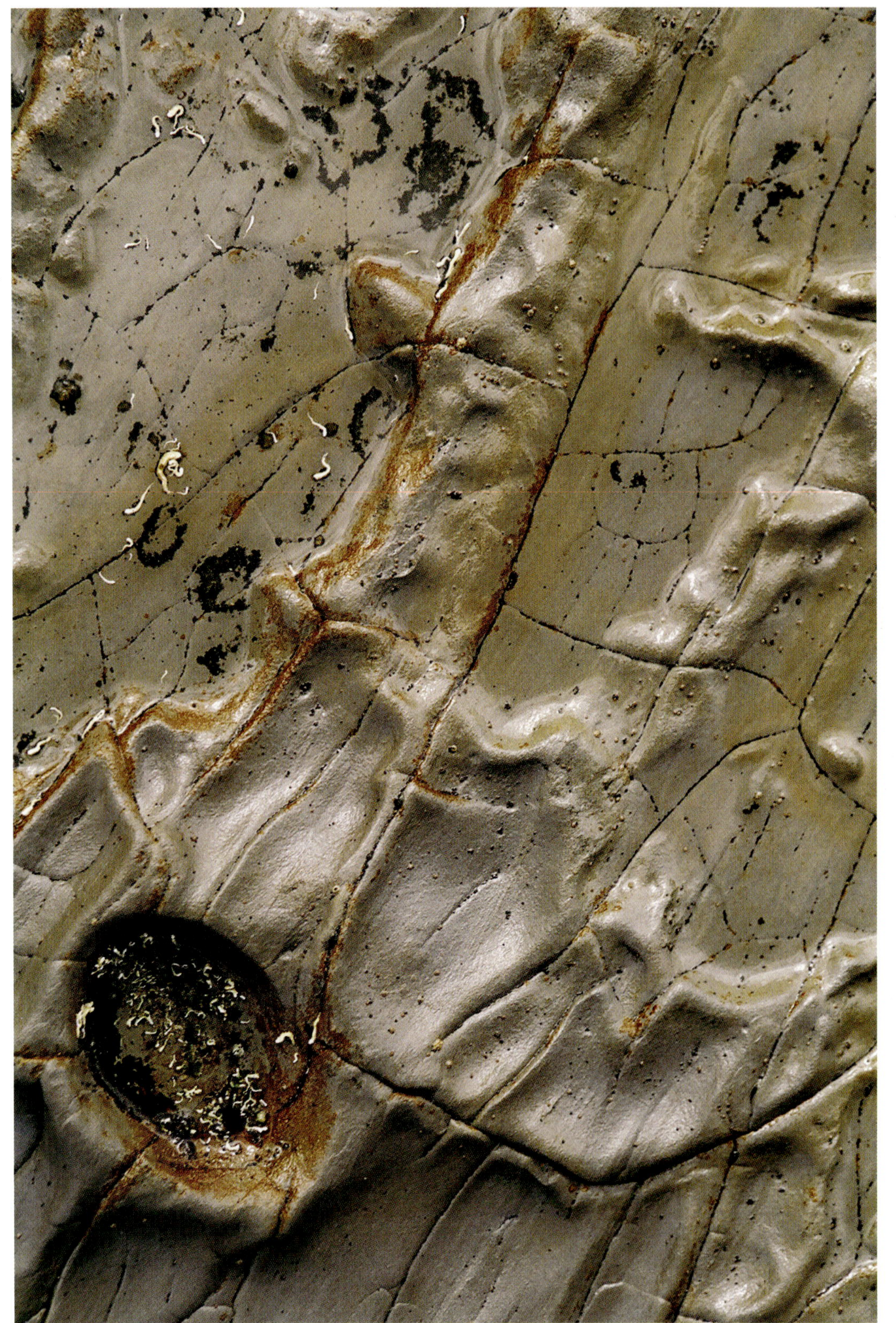

Highly Commended, Wilderness
Landscape
Rock design, Chinaman's Beach
Sandra Neill, Surat, Queensland

'The early morning sunlight
skimmed the rock shelf, enhanc-
ing the rhythmic lines and folds
of wet rock, while the shadow
rock pool was positioned beautifully to anchor my composition.'
Bundjalung NP, New South
Wales

Canon EOS 3, 24-70mm, Kodak
200, 1/250, f11
2008 5-5

Highly Commended, Wilderness
Landscape
Cement Creek
Louise Wolfers, Ringwood East,
Victoria

'This part of the creek is lower
down the mountain and it is
amazing how the green moss
covers almost everything. The
water is still pure and clean and
very drinkable. Fallen leaves
provide a nice contrast to the
almost solid green scenery.'
Mt Donna Buang, Victoria

Canon 400D, 1sec, f10, ISO 100
2008 5-4

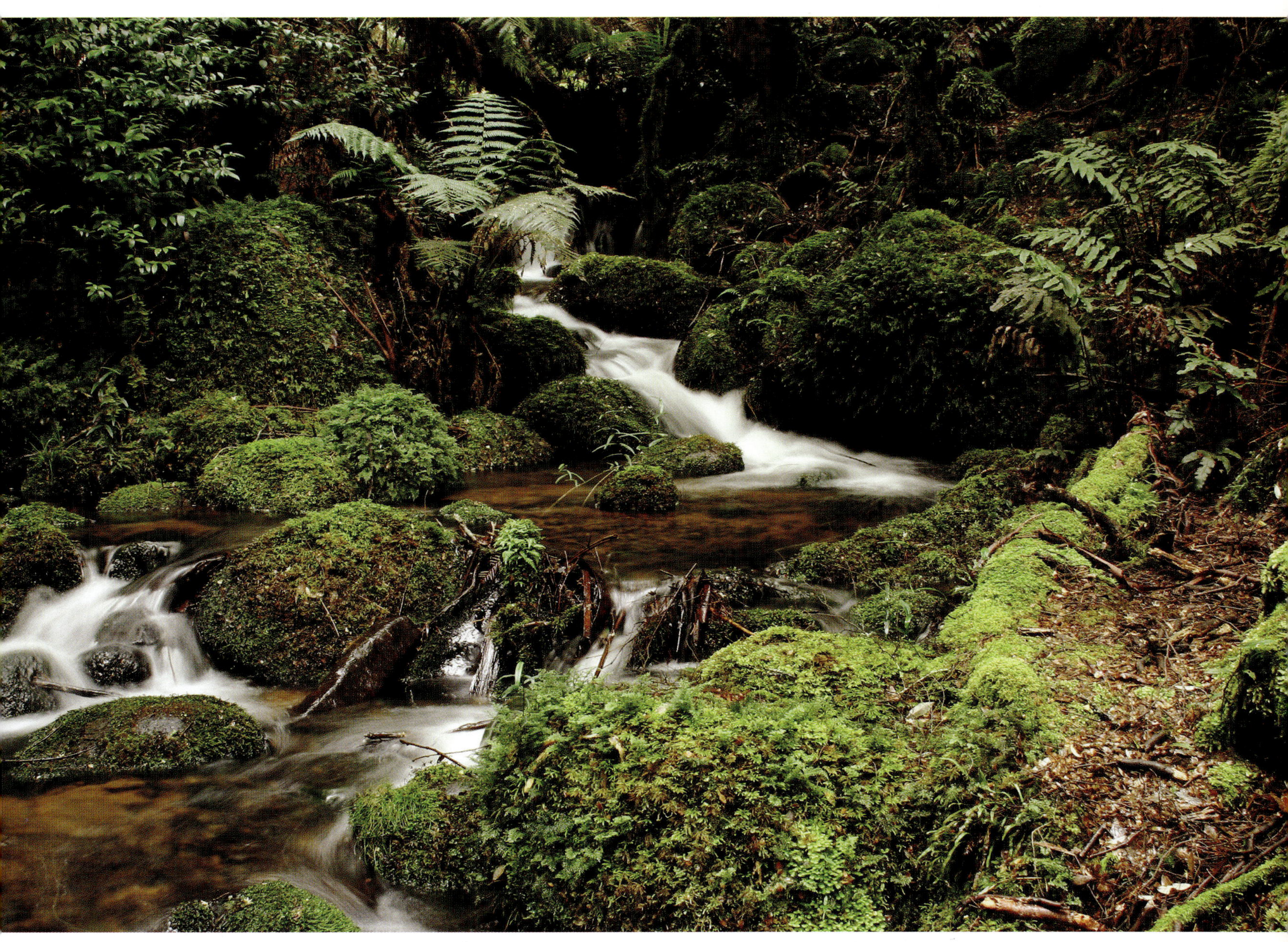

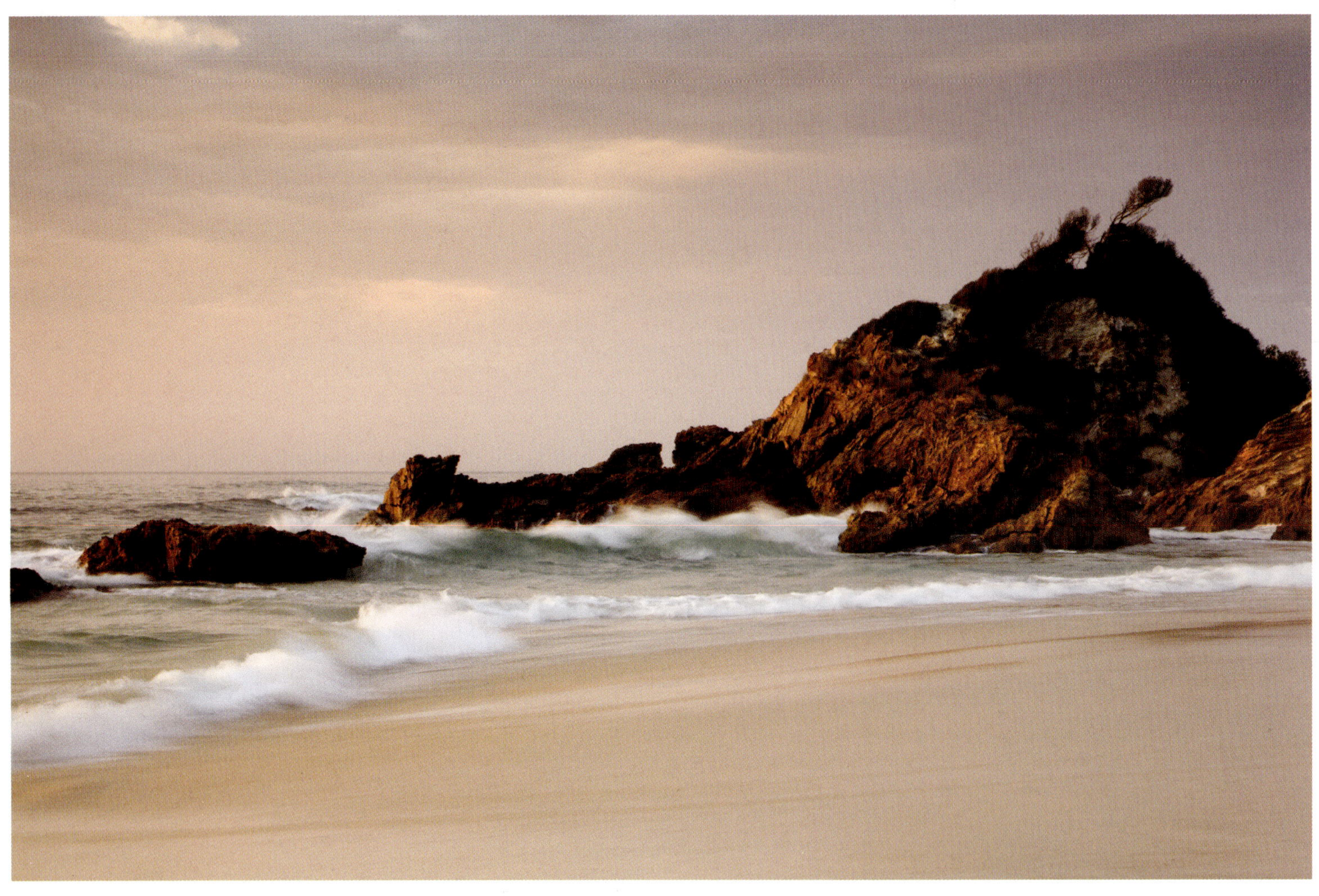

Highly Commended, Wilderness Landscape
Betka Beach sunrise
Winnie Ho, Port Melbourne, Victoria

'This image was taken moments after a blazing
sunrise. I hoped to capture the warm glow of the sea
stacks sandwiched between the smooth textures of
sand and sky.'
Croajingolong NP, Victoria

Canon 5D, 24-105mm, f22, 1/5sec, ISO 400
2008 5-6

Highly Commended, Wilderness Landscape
Taranaki
Verena & Georg Popp, Vienna, Austria

'We had waited a couple of days to have a clear
view of the mountain. When late in the afternoon
the clouds shifted, it was almost too late for us to get
to the pre-scouted location. We packed our gear and
hiked a three-hour hike in 90 minutes, proving that
you not only have to know your equipment but need
to be in good physical shape.'
Taranaki, New Zealand

Toyo Field 45 A11, 75mm, Velvia 50
2008 5-7 Exhibition

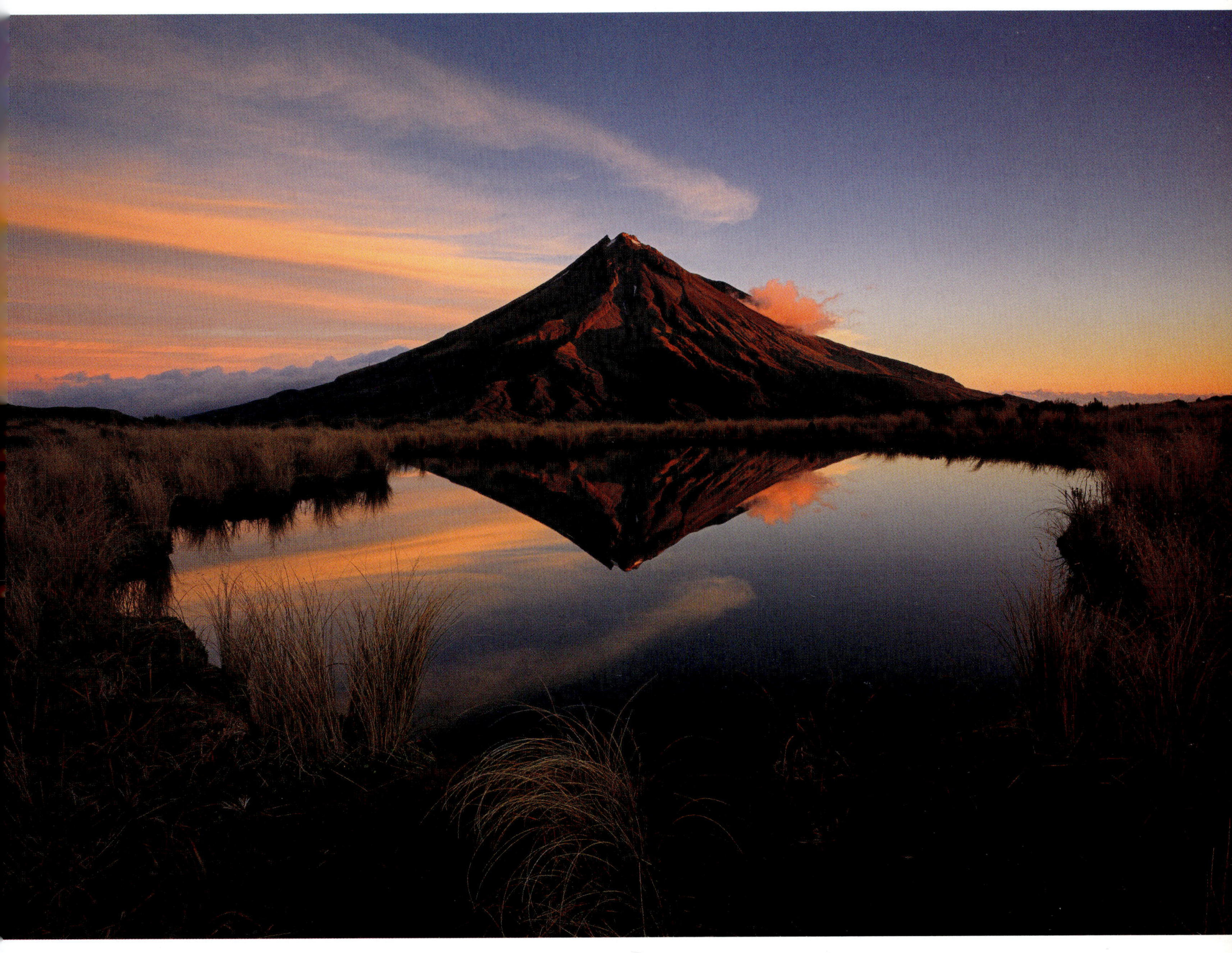

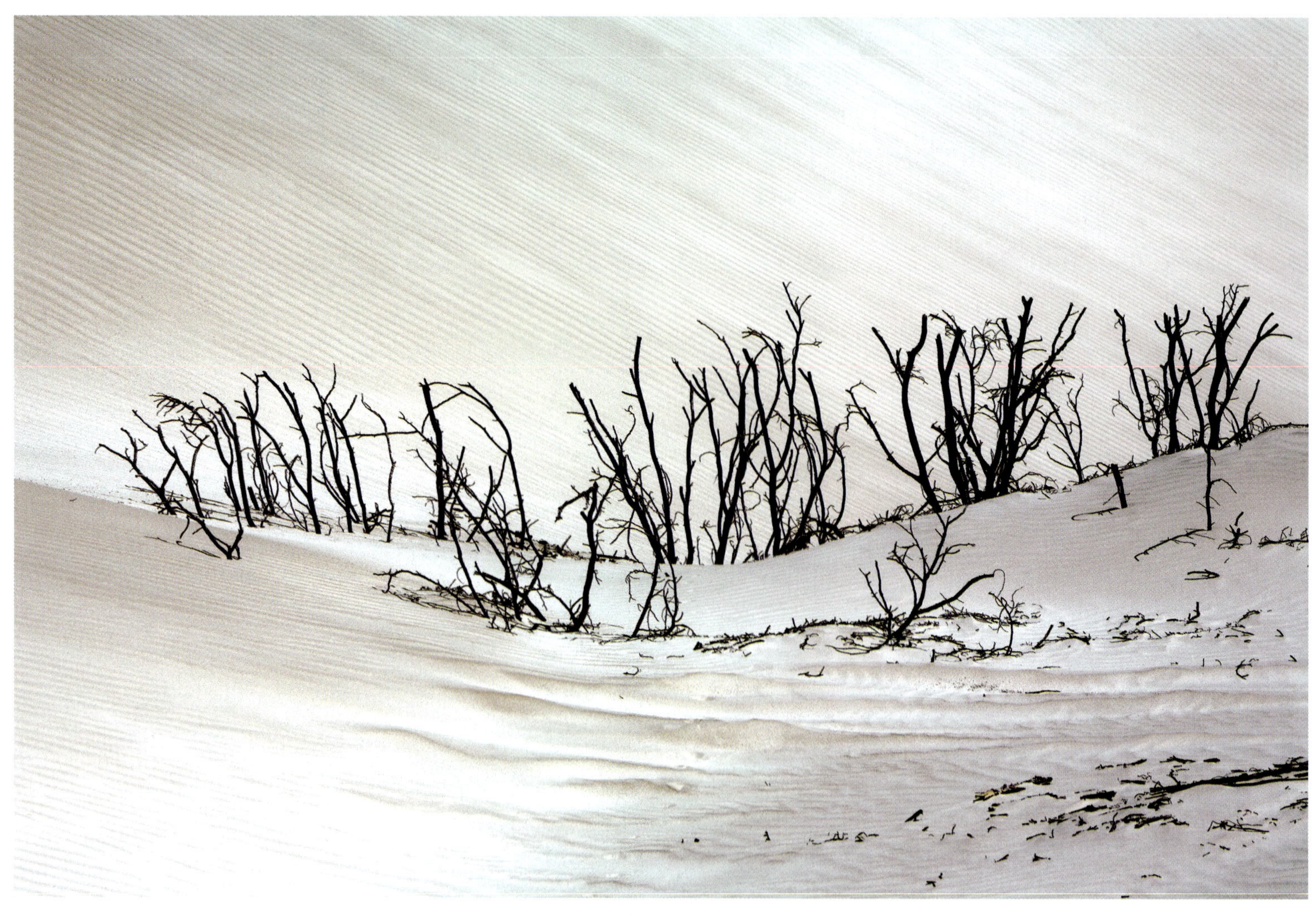

Highly Commended, Wilderness Landscape
White sand
Tony Hopkins, Gooseberry Hill, Western Australia

'I was pleasantly surprised with the outcome of this shot. It was midday and unbearably hot. Not the ideal time for photography.'
Dongara, Western Australia

Canon EOS 5D, 100-400mm, 800sec, f13, ISO 100
2008 5-8

Highly Commended, Wilderness Landscape
Misty alpine tarn
Andrew Trowbridge, Halswell, Christchurch

'I camped by this tarn for four days. The first three were nothing special, but on the last day, the sun rose and transformed "my" tarn. It reminds me of a quote from a photographer (can't remember who): "Any place in the world can be beautiful; you just have to be there at the right time."'
Arawhata River, Westland, New Zealand

Canon 5D, 24-70mm, 1/5sec, f16, ISO 100
2008 5-9 Exhibition

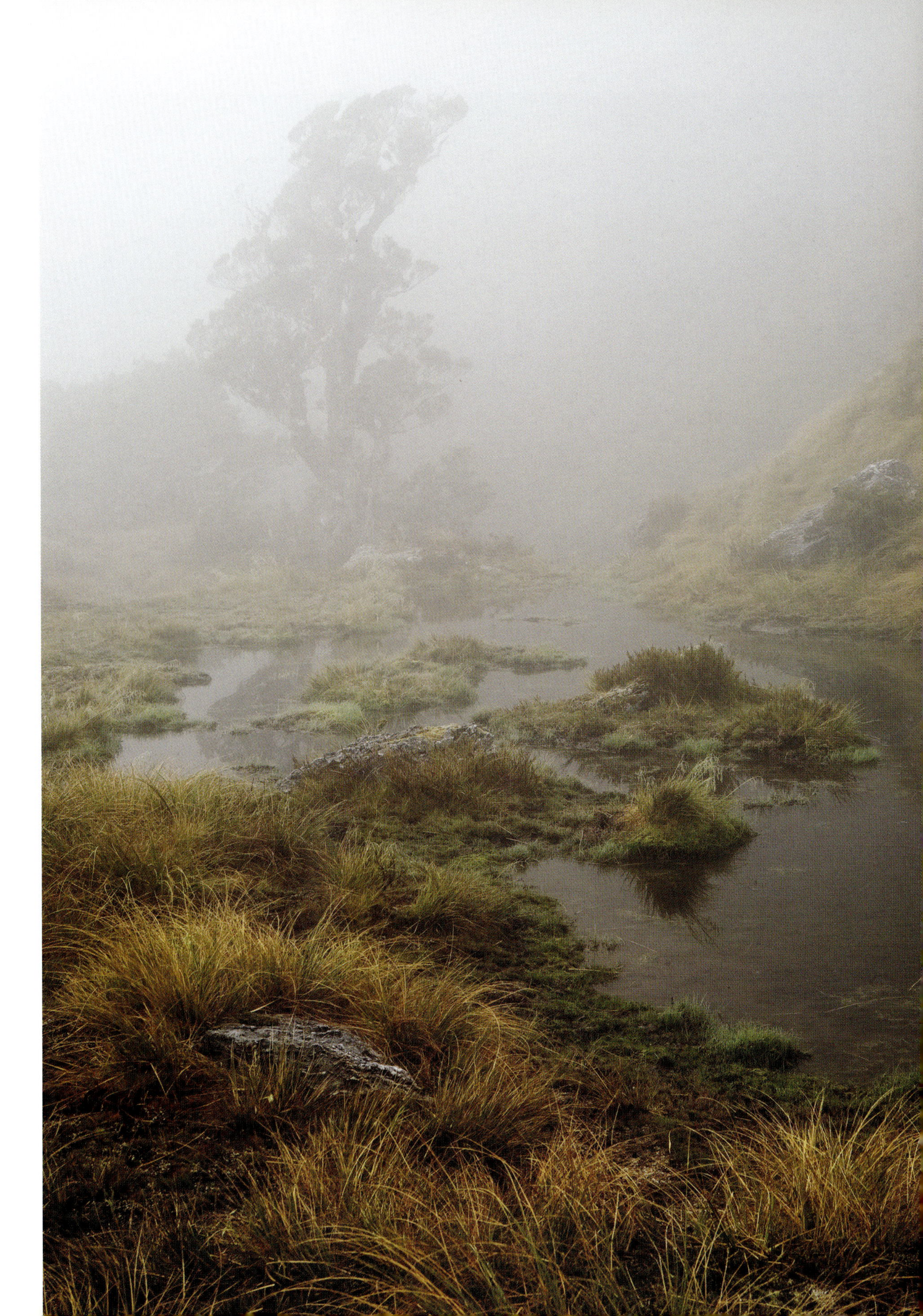

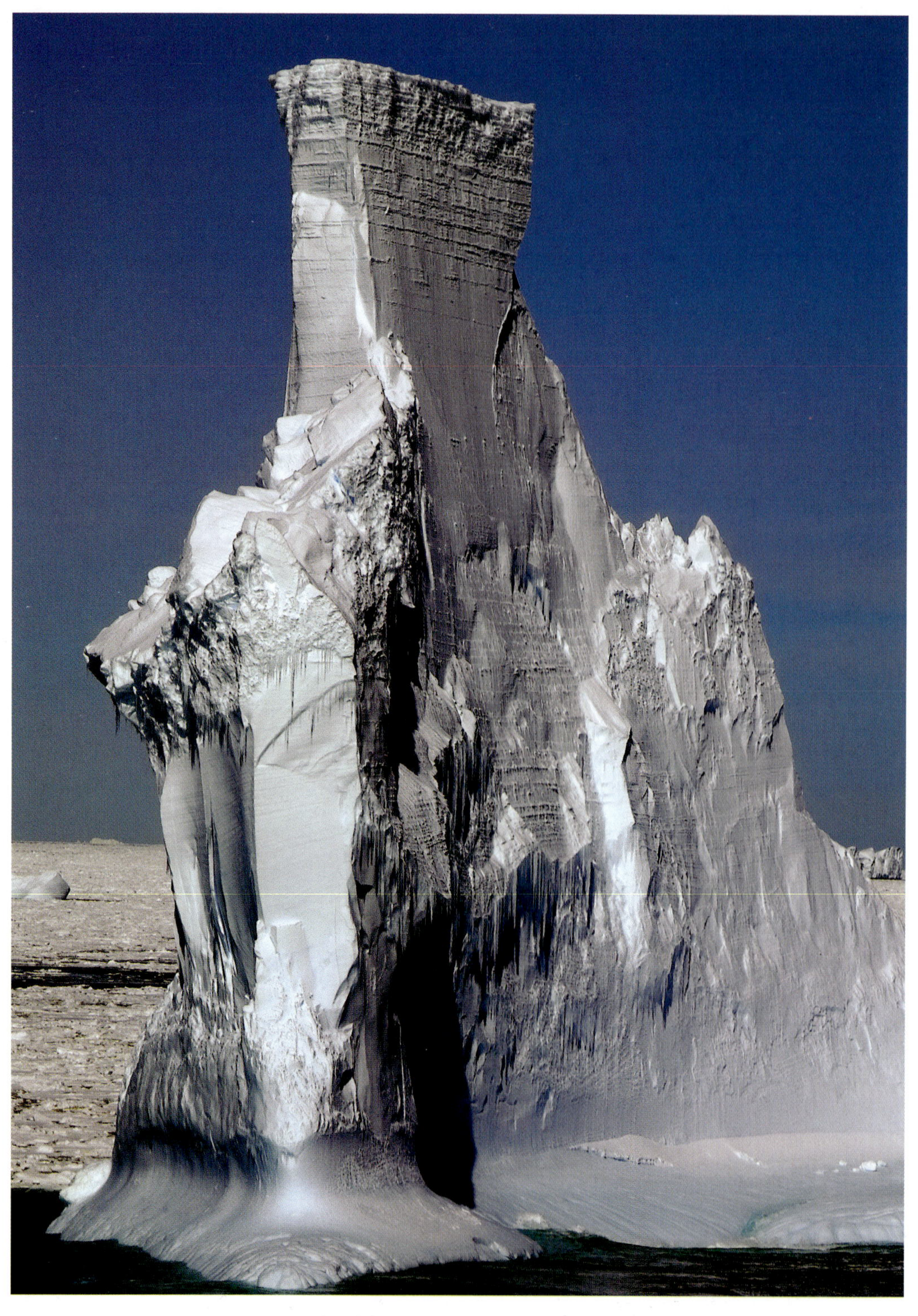

Highly Commended,
Wilderness Landscape
Skyscraper berg
Mindy Oberne, Grass Valley,
USA

'We passed through a corridor of enormous icebergs the size of multi-story office buildings. This one reminded me of a New York skyscraper.'
Phantom Coast, Antarctica

Canon EOS-1Ds, 70-200mm,
1/60sec, f22, ISO 100
2008 5-10 Exhibition

Highly Commended,
Wilderness Landscape
White berg at dusk
Ted Mead, Taroona, Tasmania

'The sun had just slipped below the horizon, which painted everything in magenta hues. It is inexplicable why a solitary iceberg in the distance retained its white defiant glow.'
Antarctica

Fuji 6x9, 65mm, f16, Fuji
Velvia
2008 5-11 Exhibition

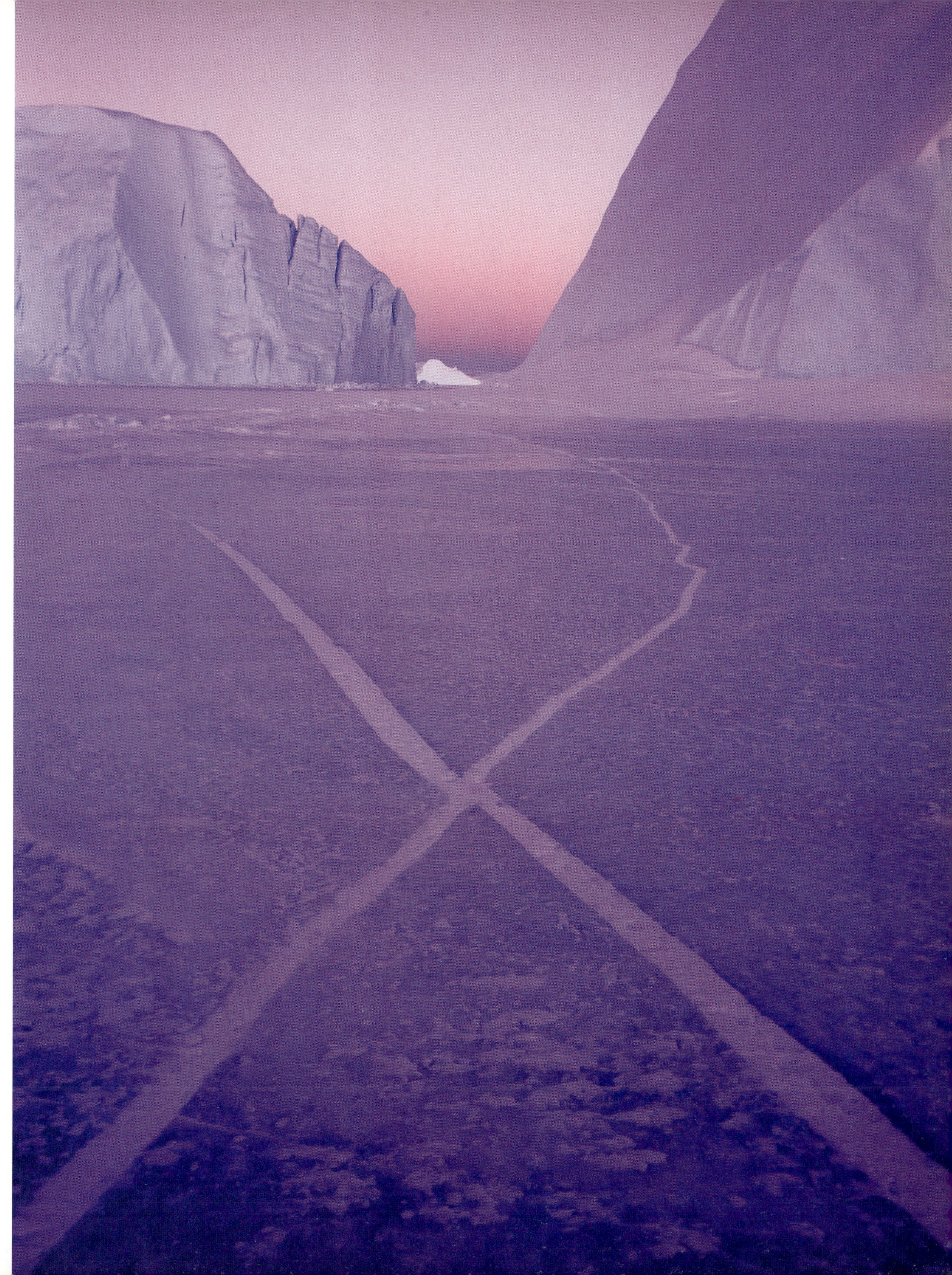

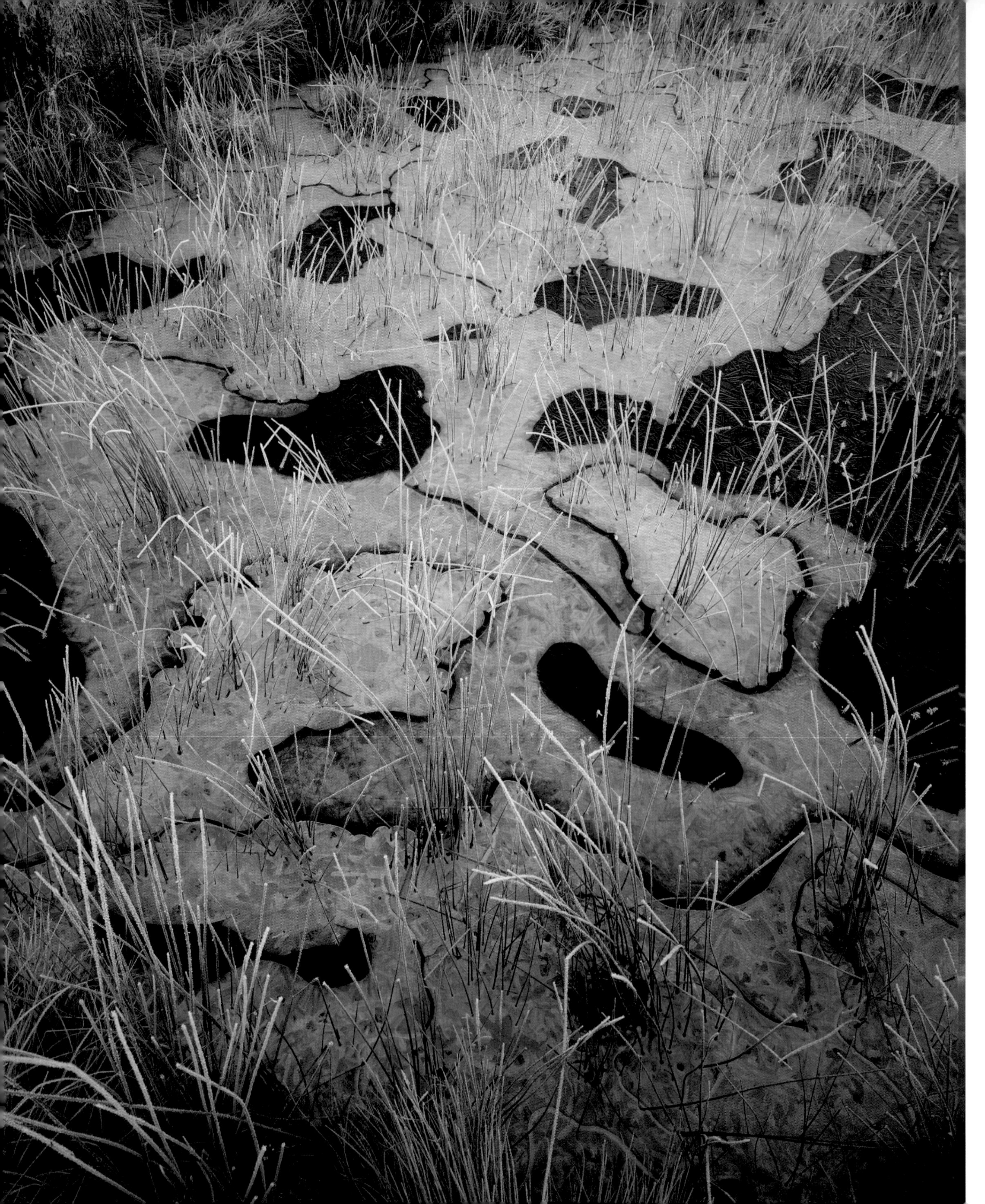

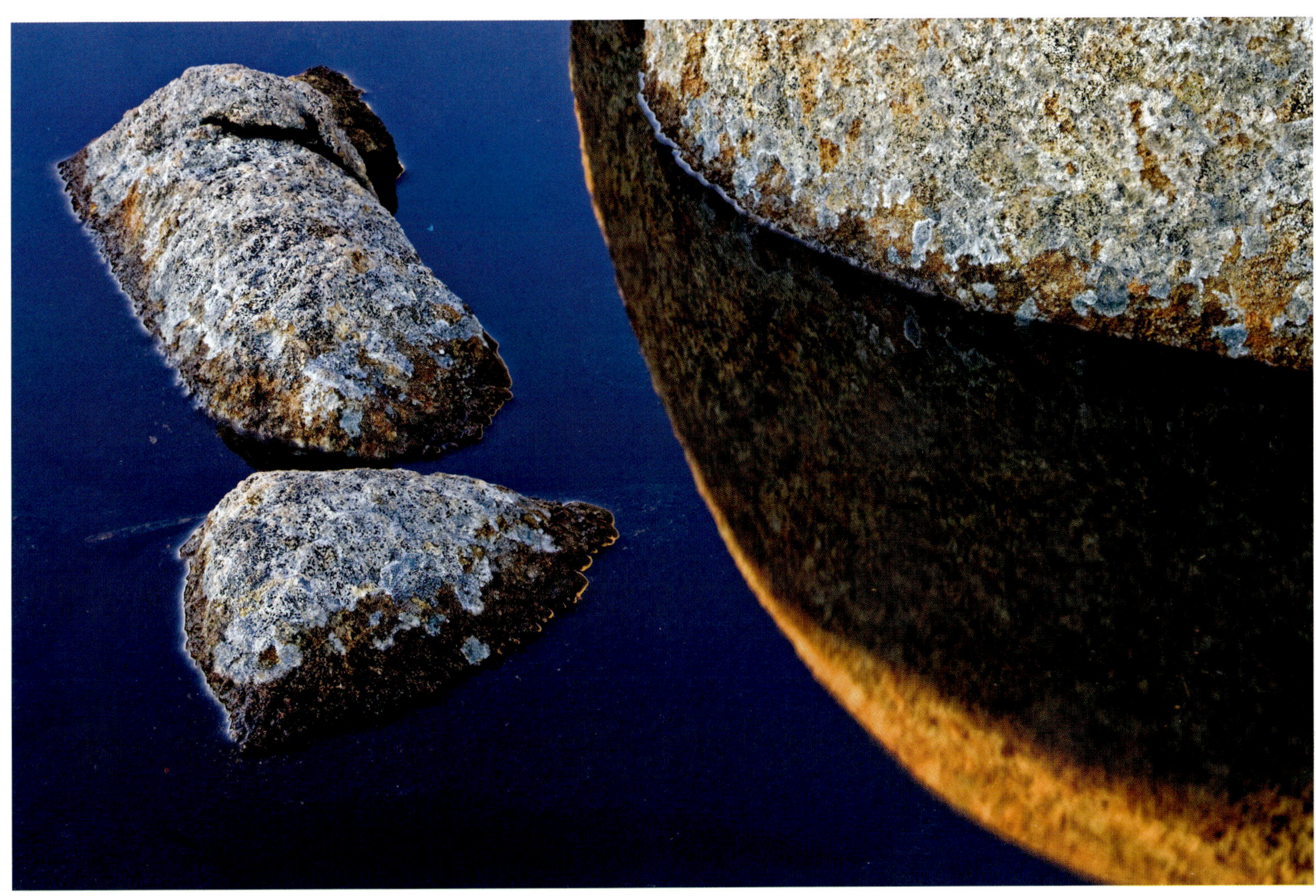

Highly Commended, Wilderness Landscape
Frozen tarn and reeds
Ted Mead, Taroona, Tasmania

A heavy overnight minus-20°C frost coated everything in a delicate cloak of winter, painting this tarn in an artistic array of shapes and chilling colour. Tasmanian Highlands, Tasmania

Mamiya 6x7, 43mm, f22, Fuji Velvia
2008 5-12

Highly Commended, Wilderness Landscape
Eclipse
Kah Kit Yoong, Port Melbourne, Victoria

'Late one afternoon I came across a series of pools reflecting the blue sky and dolerite boulders. With the sky acting as a reflector and the rocks in the shade, it was a perfect opportunity for an intimate landscape shot.'
Mt Wellington, Tasmania

Canon 40D, 24-105mm, 2.5 sec, f16, ISO 100
2008 5-15 Exhibition

Section 6, Threatened Animals or Plants

The subject or subjects may be photographed in any of the following ways:

- In portrait
- Engaged in natural activity
- In natural habitat.

All entries in this section must be accompanied by an official reference (valid for any of the previous five years prior to the date of close of entries) from the relevant country's government agency concerned with flora and fauna verifying the subject's threatened, rare, vulnerable or endangered status.

Prize: $1,000

Winner, Threatened Animals or Plants
Female New Zealand falcon and chick in nest
Andrew Trowbridge, Halswell, Christchurch

'A friend and I spent three weeks getting a hide within eight metres from this nest. We wanted to have this done before the eggs were laid. We spent many days in the hide observing the pair incubate and then feed the two chicks until they fledged.'
Oreti River, Southland, New Zealand

Judges' comment: 'A classic bird at nest shot.'
Canon 5D, 500mm, 1/125sec, f8, ISO 400, fill flash
2008 6-1 Exhibition

Distribution and status: The New Zealand falcon is New Zealand's only endemic falcon and the only remaining bird of prey endemic to New Zealand. The New Zealand falcon is mainly found in heavy bush and the steep high country in the South Island and is rarely seen north of a line through the central area of the North Island. A small population also breeds on the Auckland Islands. Although protected since 1970, it is considered to be a vulnerable species.

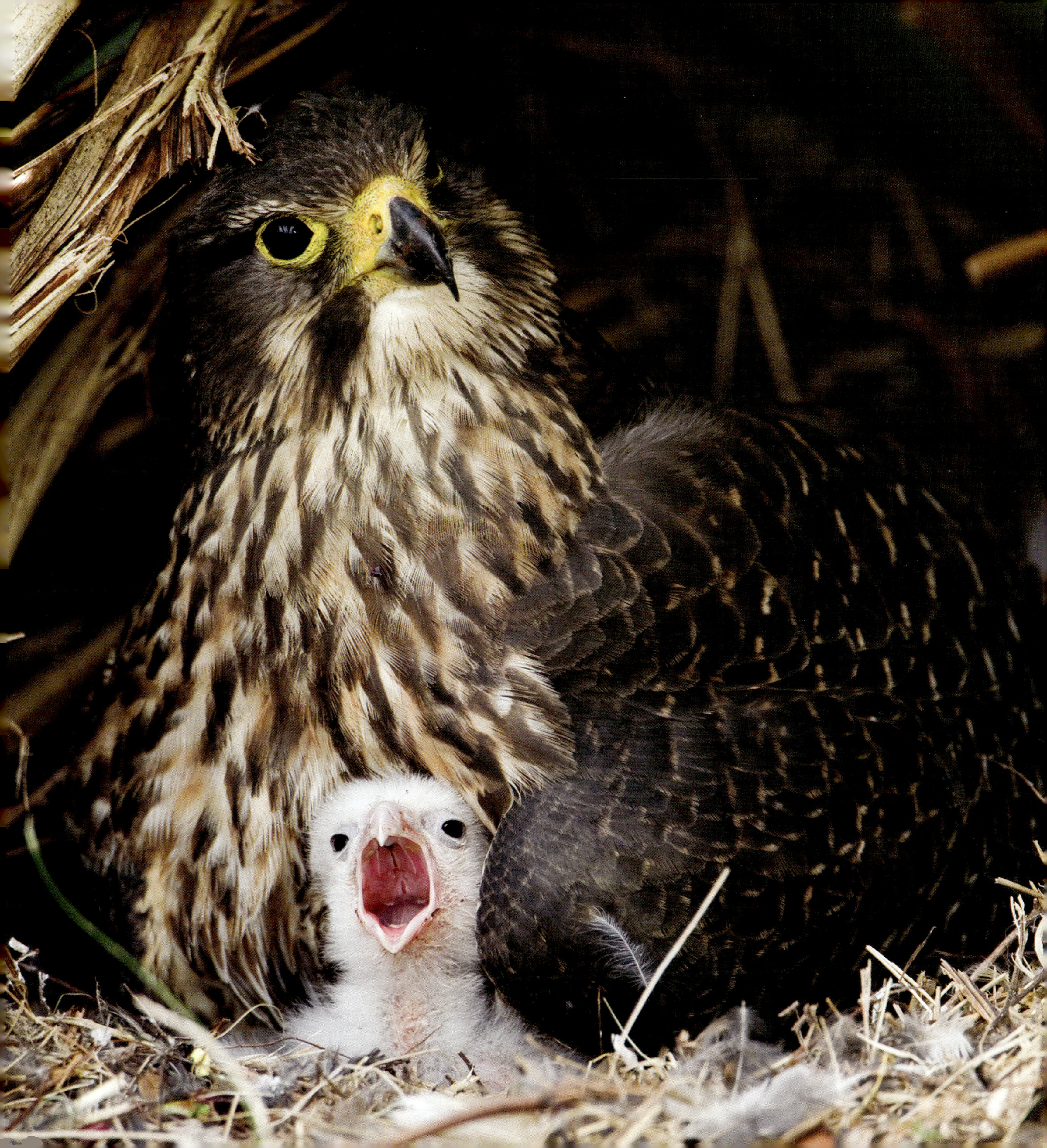

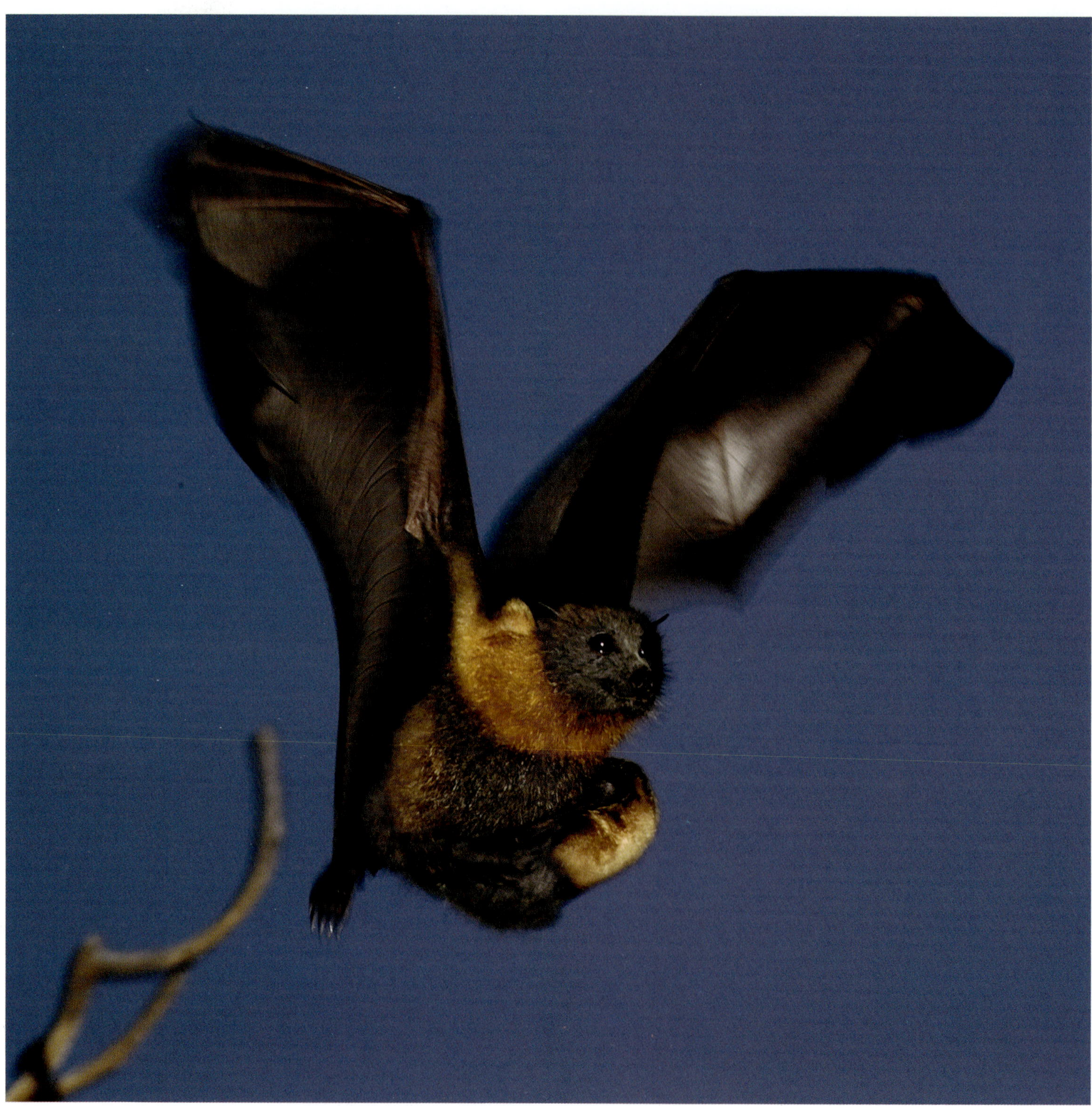

Runner-up, Threatened Animals or Plants
Flight to an uncertain future
Nick Edards, Crows Nest, New South Wales

'For the first few weeks after birth the young of
the grey-headed flying fox stay with their mothers,
travelling up to 50 kilometres to feed every night.
If separated from their mothers it is certain death.
The exposed position of the young shows just how
vulnerable they are.'
Royal Botanic Gardens, Sydney, New South Wales

Judges' comment: 'A difficult shot well executed.'
Nikon D200, 70-200mm, 1/160sec, f4.5, ISO 200,
flash
2008 6-2 Exhibition

Distribution and status: The grey-headed flying fox
is endemic to the south-eastern forested areas of
Australia, principally east of the Great Dividing
Range. Grey-headed flying foxes are exposed to
several threatening processes, including loss of
foraging and roosting habitat, competition with
the black flying fox, and mass die-offs caused by
extreme temperature events.

Highly Commended, Threatened Animals or Plants
Barbara – 50-year-old southern cassowary
Susan Kelly, Mission Beach, Queensland

'The southern cassowary is threatened by
development and killed regularly on the roads. It
is remarkable that Barbara has survived for almost
50 years. She was named by Freda Jorisson who
bequeathed her land as National Park to maintain a
safe refuge for the cassowary that live in the area.'
Mission Beach, Queensland

160mm, f5.6, ISO 200
2008 6-3

Distribution and status: The southern cassowary is
found in New Guinea, and north-eastern Australia.
The population is estimated at 2,000 birds and is
declining. In Australia, it is threatened by habitat
loss and fragmentation. In New Guinea, the species
is heavily hunted, captured and traded close to
populated areas, being of high cultural importance,
and constituting a major food source for subsistence
communities.

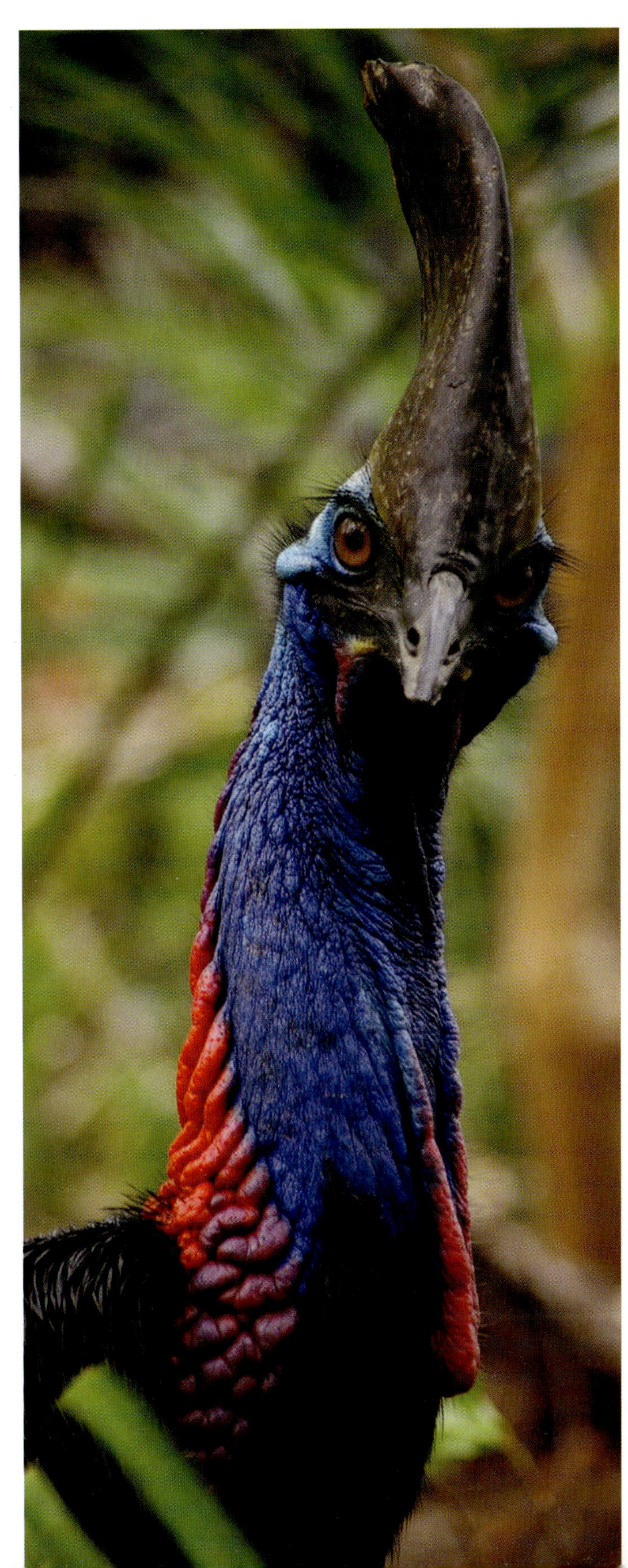

Highly Commended, Threatened Animals or Plants
Cave dwellers
Justin Gilligan, Anna Bay, New South Wales

'I sat at the back of the cave in the dark looking towards the opening, holding my breath so as not to scare the shark or the thousand bulls-eye fish. When the shark was a metre away, with the light of the cave opening in the right place, I took the picture.' Off South West Rocks, New South Wales

Nikon D80, 10.5mm, f4, ISO 100, flash
2008 6-4 Exhibition

Distribution and status: The grey nurse shark lives near the coast in sub-tropical to cool-temperate waters near most continental land masses (not in the eastern Pacific Ocean off North and South America). There are few grey nurse sharks found in northern Australia though they are relatively abundant in the southern part of the eastern and western Australian waters. The population declined dramatically in recent decades, especially in the 1960s and 1970s. After 20 years of protection the population is still declining and there are approximately 400 to 500 grey nurses left in eastern Australia. This has led to increased public awareness, and conservation of these sharks is now greatly supported.

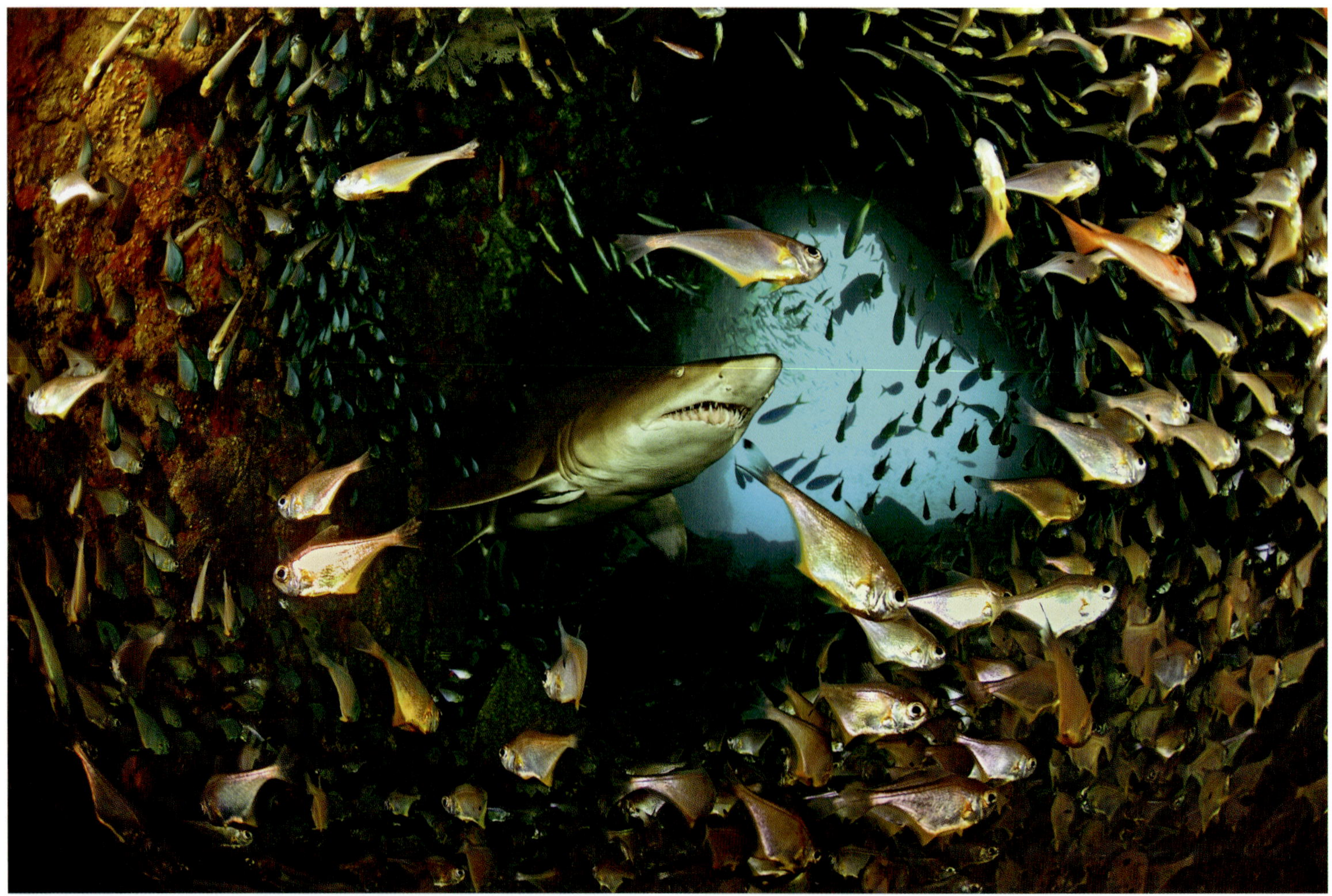

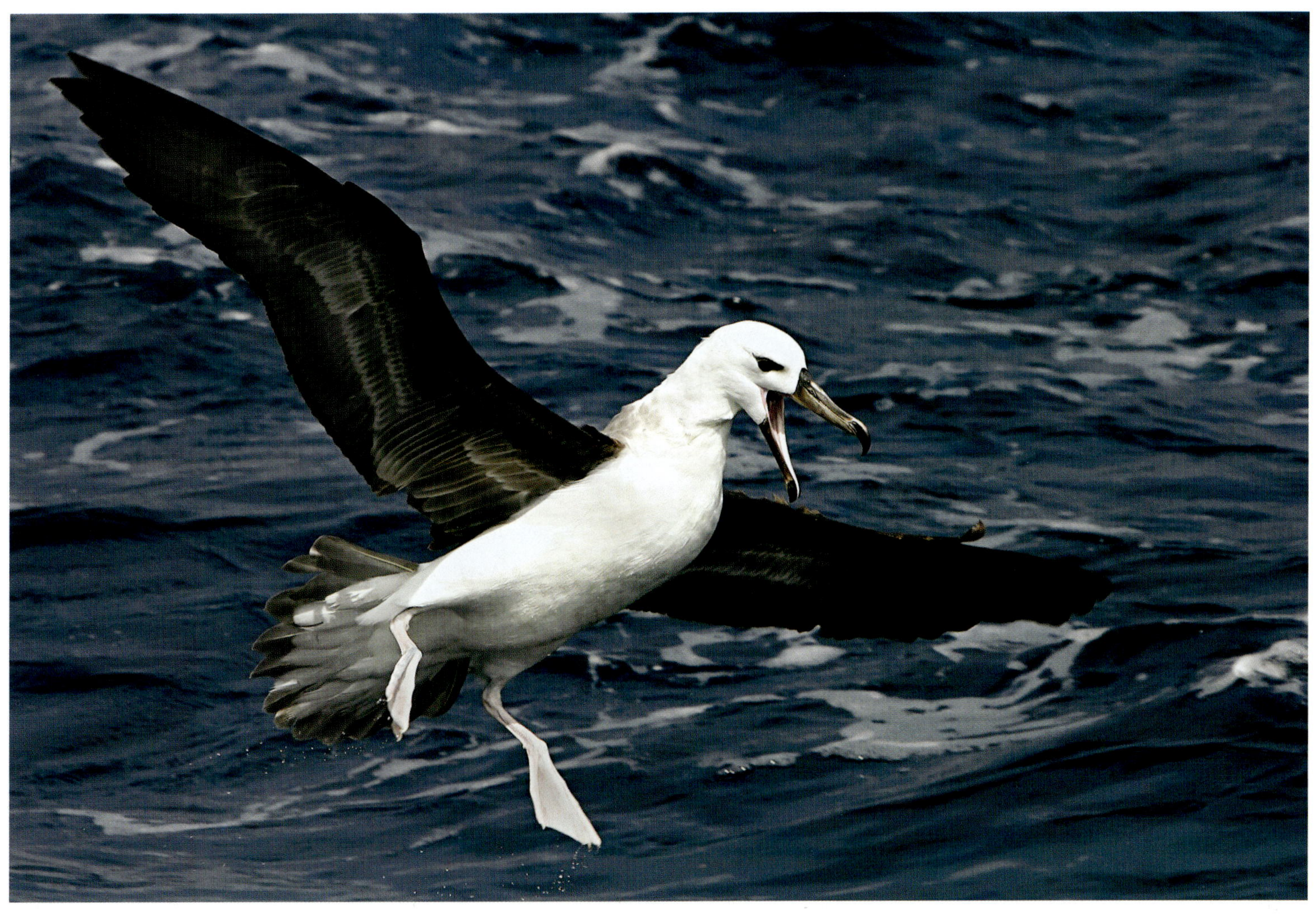

Highly Commended, Threatened Animals or Plants
Black-browed albatross landing
Jessica Drake, Berowra Heights, New South Wales

'I travelled on an ex-fishing trawler for about 60 nautical miles. Such trips are at best uncomfortable, at worst dangerous. All thoughts of discomfort vanish when you see one of these graceful birds. So many are lost to long-line fishing.'
Off Wollongong, New South Wales

Canon 400D, 50-500mm, f10, 1/1000, ISO 400
2008 6-5

Distribution and status: The black-browed albatross has a circumpolar range over the Southern Ocean, and is seen off the southern Australian coast mainly during winter. This species migrates to waters off the continental shelf from approximately May to November. Due to their feeding habits, the most significant threat to these and many other albatross is long-line fishing. Distribution of black-browed albatross populations coincides with long-line fishing grounds and it is estimated that tuna fishing boats kill up to 1,000 of these graceful birds each day in waters south of Australia.

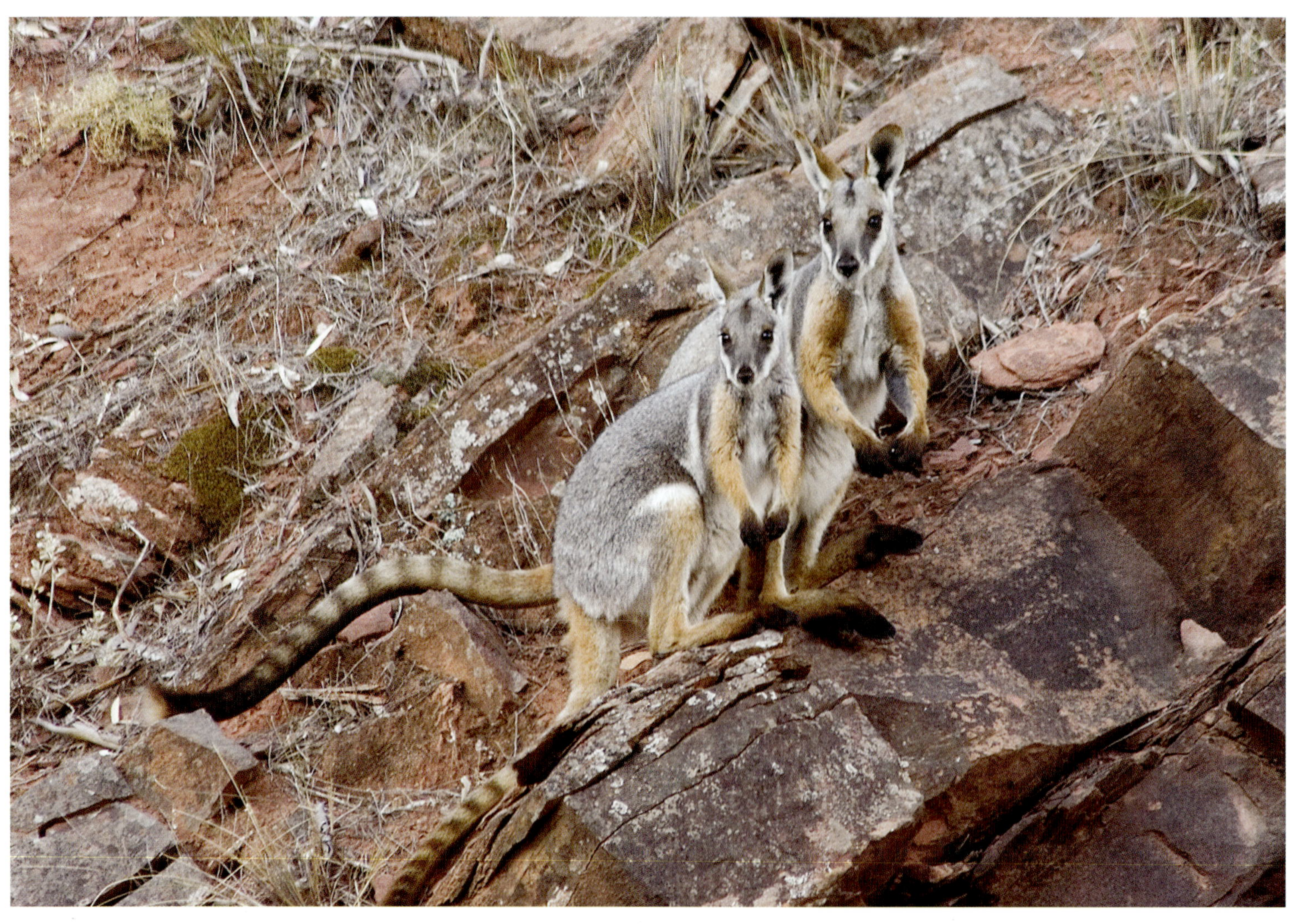

Highly Commended, Threatened Animals or Plants
Yellow-footed rock wallaby
Terry Morley, Salisbury South, South Australia

'While watching yellow-footed rock wallaby these two jumped casually up a few rocks and turned back to watch us, in doing so giving me an opportunity to take this photograph.'
Flinders Ranges, South Australia

Canon 20D, 75-300mm, f5.6, 1/4
2008 6-6

Distribution and status: This rock wallaby is found in western New South Wales, north-western Victoria, the east of South Australia and parts of southern Queensland. It does not usually live in places near humans, for it prefers a rocky environment. It is threatened by fox predation, competition with domestic and wild introduced animals (particularly goats, rabbits and sheep) and wildfires.

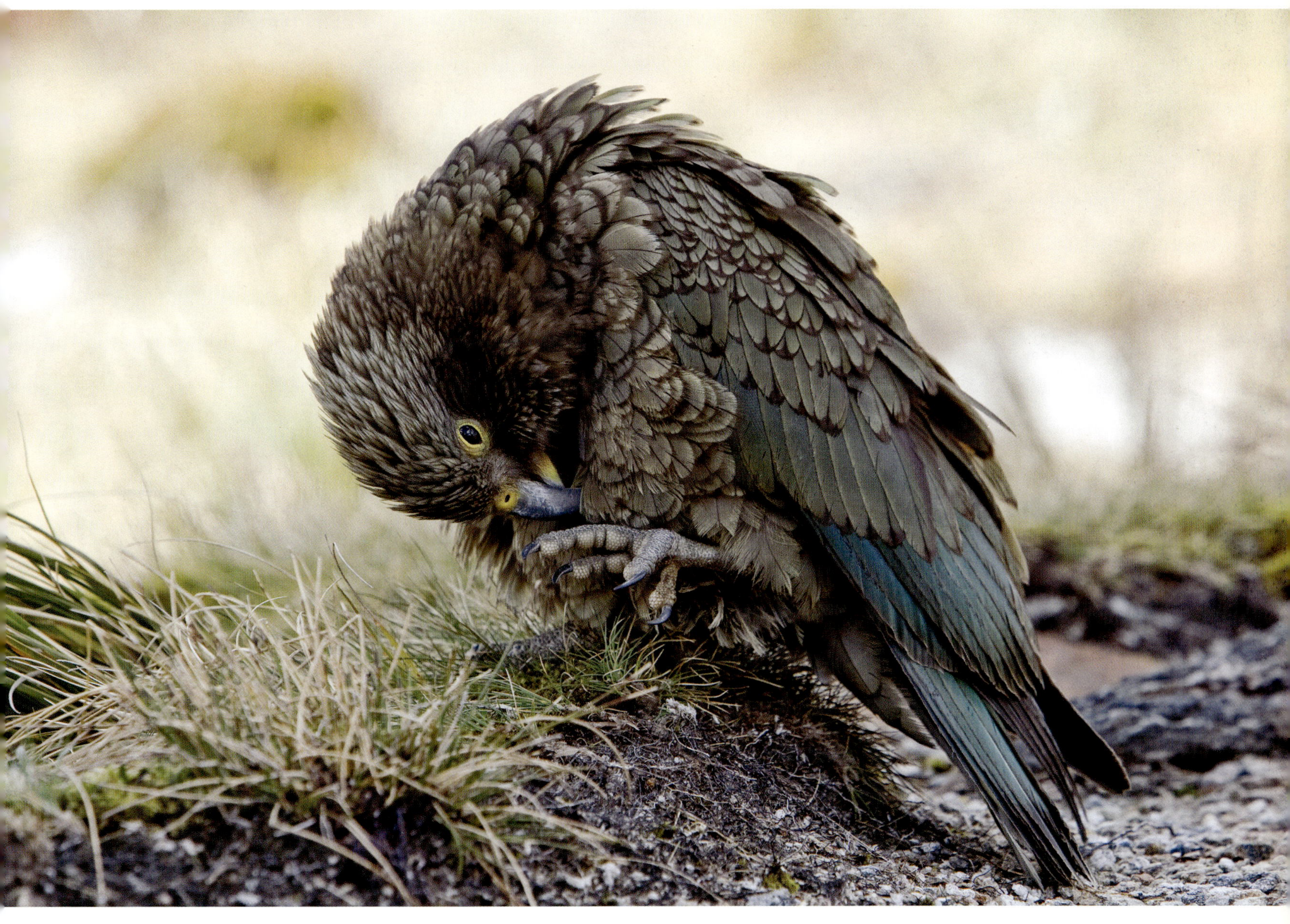

Highly Commended, Threatened Animals or Plants
Kea preening
Andrew Trowbridge, Halswell, Christchurch

'It was a glorious day, made even better by the fact that about seven or so keas wanted to share it with us. This particular bird was hell bent on getting into my pack but after about 20 minutes it gave up and started to preen its feathers.'
Milford Track, Fiordland NP, New Zealand

Canon 5D, 70-200mm, 1/320 sec, f8, ISO 400, flash   2008 6-8 Exhibition
Distribution and status: The kea ranges from lowland river valleys up to the alpine regions of the South Island closely associated throughout its range with the southern beech (*Nothofagus*) forests in the alpine ridge. Its notorious urge to explore and manipulate, combined with strong curiosity, makes this bird a pest for residents but an attraction for tourists. Population estimates range from 1,000 to 5,000 individuals, but the kea's wide distribution at low density prevents accurate estimates.

73

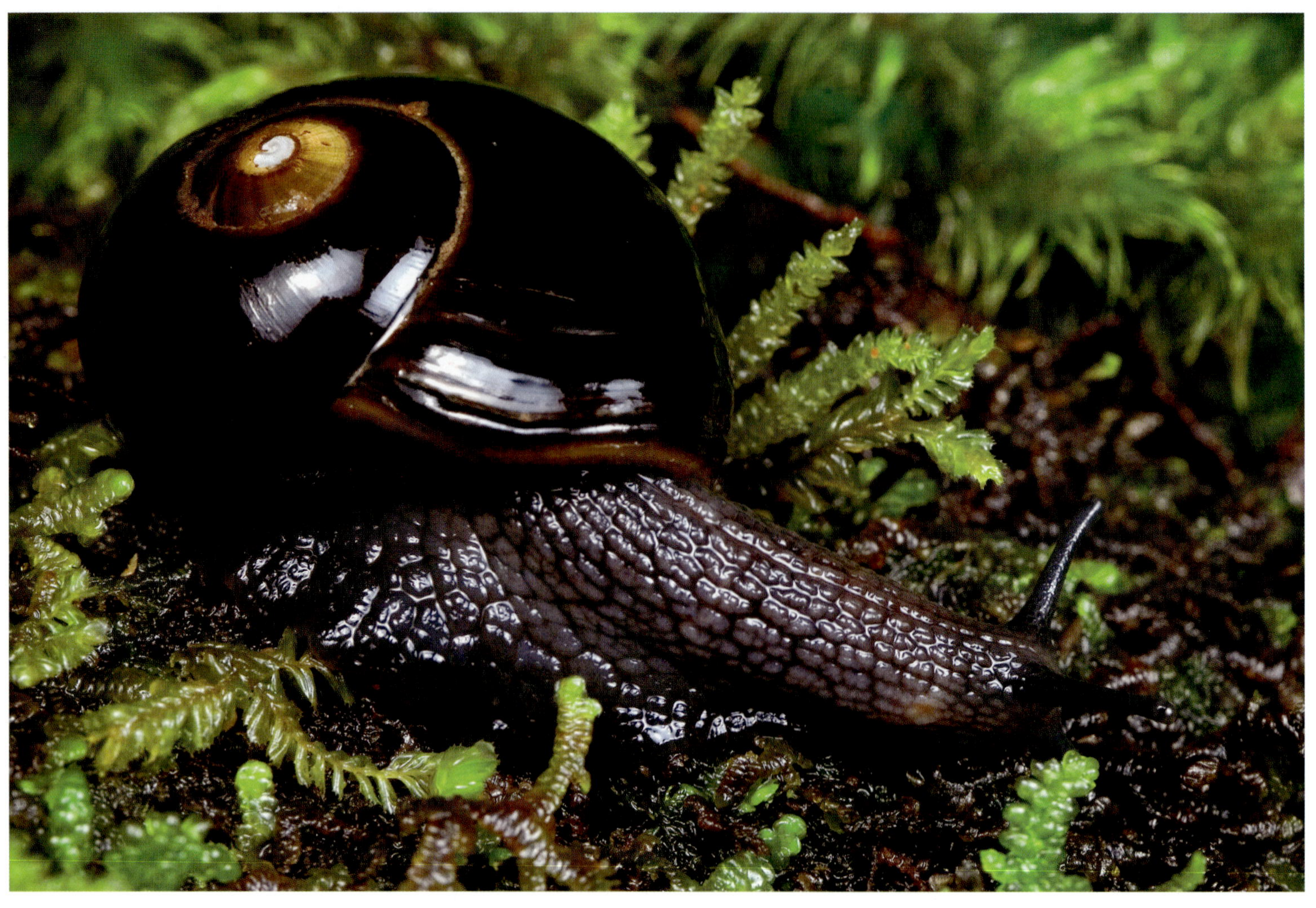

Highly Commended, Threatened Animals or Plants
Otway black snail
Michael Williams, Newport, Victoria

'The snail was difficult to photograph, even though slow moving.'
Otway Ranges, Victoria

Canon 20D, 105mm Macro, 1/250, f14, 1/250, ISO 100, flash
2008 6-9 Exhibition

Distribution and status: When surveyed in 2004 the Otway black snail was found at three locations in the Otway Ranges –
temperate rainforest (gullies), wet forests (ridges) and the ecotone between these two (slope). It was found predominantly around
the base of trees and in leaf litter, and fewer were found associated with logs and/or the tree trunks.

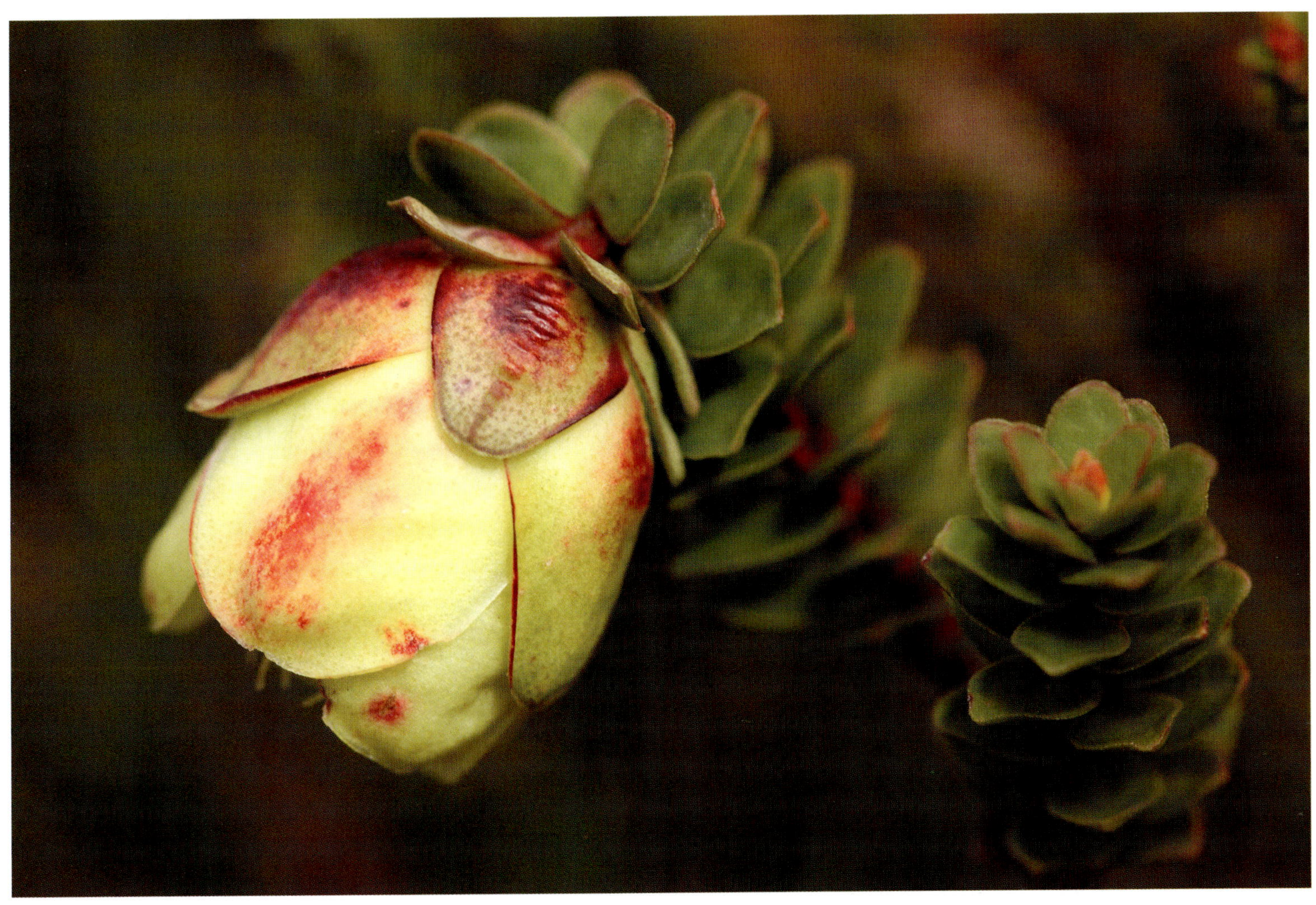

Highly Commended, Threatened Animals or Plants
Darwinia collina
Alice Gillam, Crawley, Western Australia

'It was just after sunrise, cloudy, raining and very windy. The clouds lifted a few seconds at a time, and I waited for the gusts of wind to subside at the same time so that I could get a photograph before freezing.'
Bluff Knoll, Stirling Range, Western Australia

Canon EOS 400D, 100mm Macro, 1/125, f5, ISO 100
2008 6-10

Distribution and status: This is a very rare species that occurs only near the summit of several of the highest peaks in the Stirling Range in the south-west of Western Australia.

Section 7, Black and White

A subject or subjects must be chosen that would qualify for any of the first six sections. This section includes all monochrome photography e.g. sepia-toned and infra-red photographs.

Prize: $1,000

Winner, Black and White
Elephant seals breeding
Graham Morgan, Sussex Inlet, New South Wales

'This image was shot in wet and windy conditions, and the surf was crashing over the mating pair. I had to scamper down the beach between waves to capture the shot. The location was an explosion of wildlife activity with the beta males trying to sneak mating opportunities while the beach master was otherwise engaged.'
South Georgia, Southern Ocean

Judges' comment: 'The choice of black and white concentrates the viewer on the massive form of the subject.'
Canon EOS 1D Mk III, Canon 70-200F4mm, 1/800, f11, ISO 200
2008 7-1 Exhibition

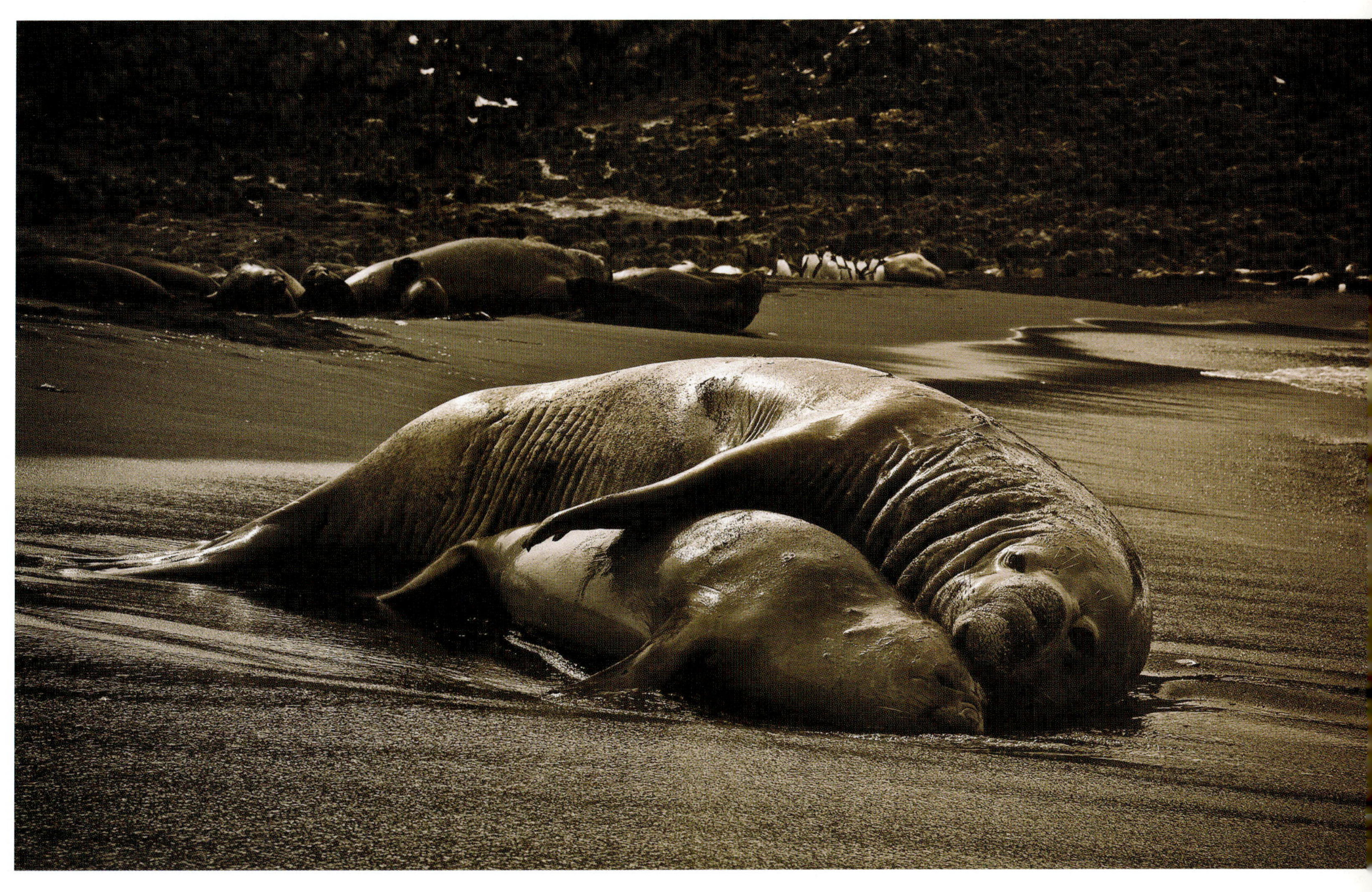

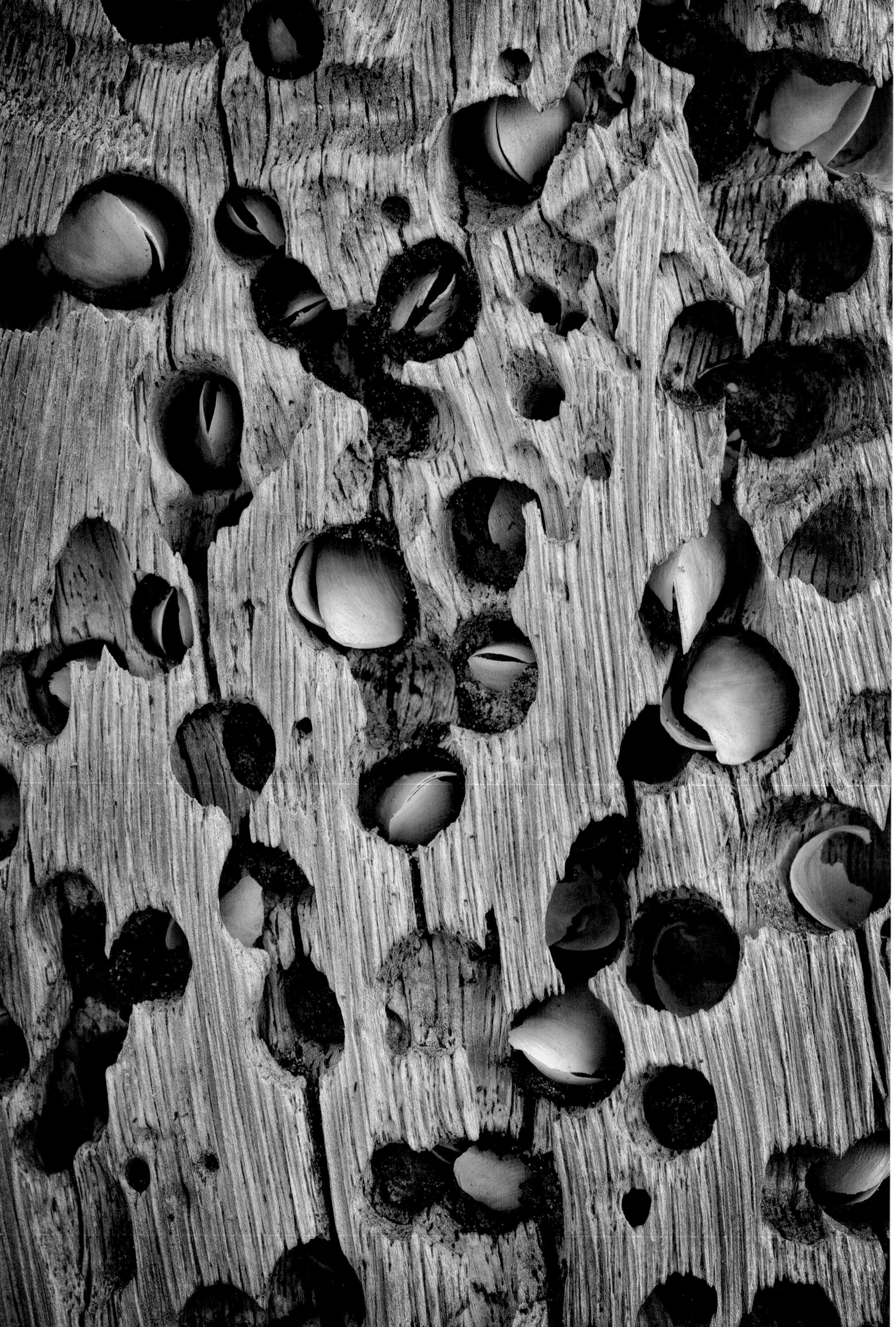

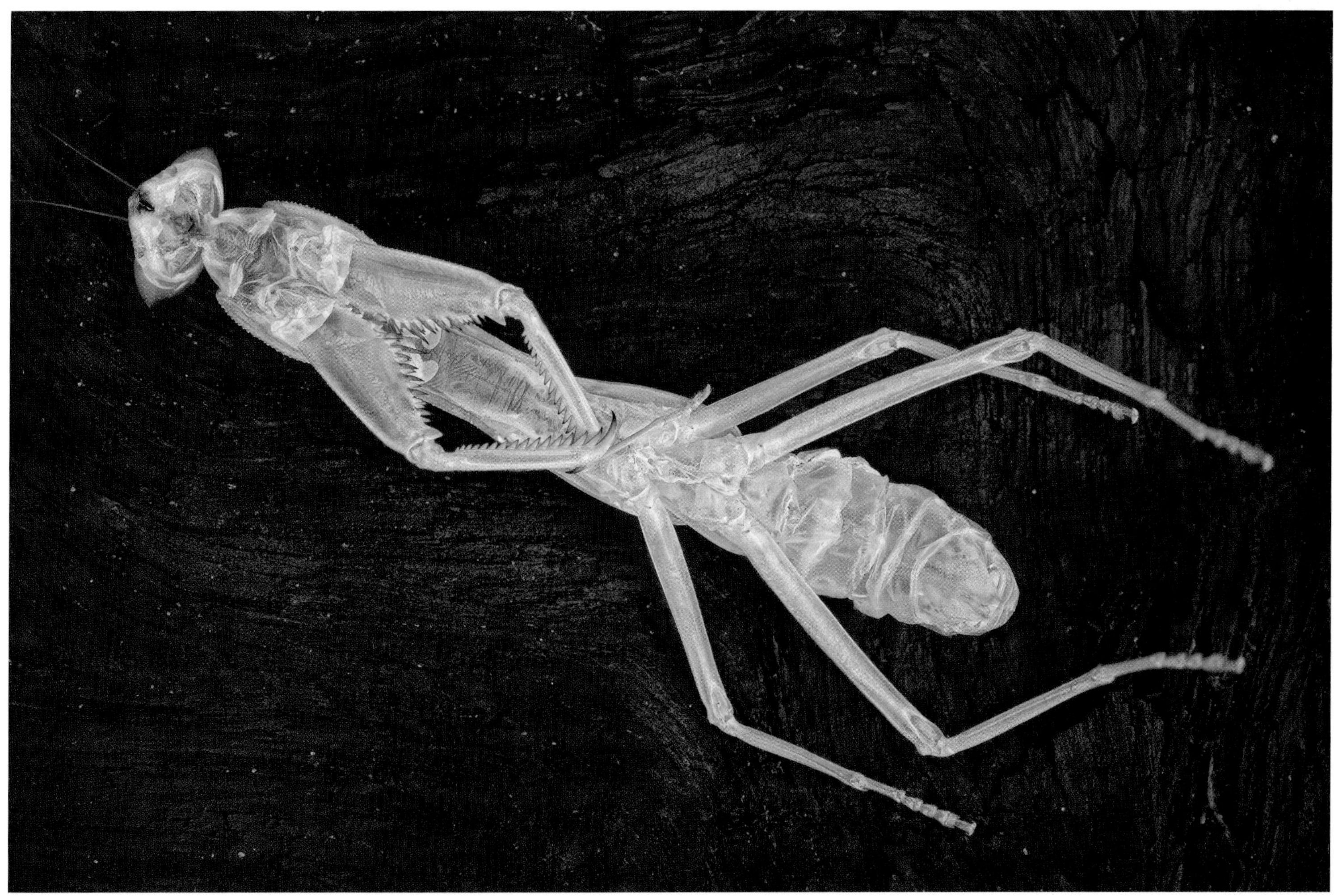

Runner-up, Black and White
Community – marine borers in driftwood
Stanley and Kaisa Breeden, Malanda, Queensland

'A long-dead piece of driftwood washed up on the beach was packed with life. It was stuffed with communities of little marine borers peeking out from their tunnels.'
Cape Tribulation, Queensland

Judges' comment: 'A beautiful study in monochrome full of texture.'

Canon 1Ds Mk II, 100mm macro, f16,
2008 7-2 Exhibition

Highly Commended, Black and White
Cast skin of a praying mantis
Stanley and Kaisa Breeden, Malanda, Queensland

'The cast skin drifted from high in the canopy down to the rainforest floor, landing on a dark, dead branch. It contrasted beautifully with textures of the dark wood. The contrast was enhanced by de-saturating what little colour there was, converting to black and white.'
Cape Tribulation, Queensland

Canon 1Ds Mk II, 100mm macro, f16
2008 7-3 Exhibition

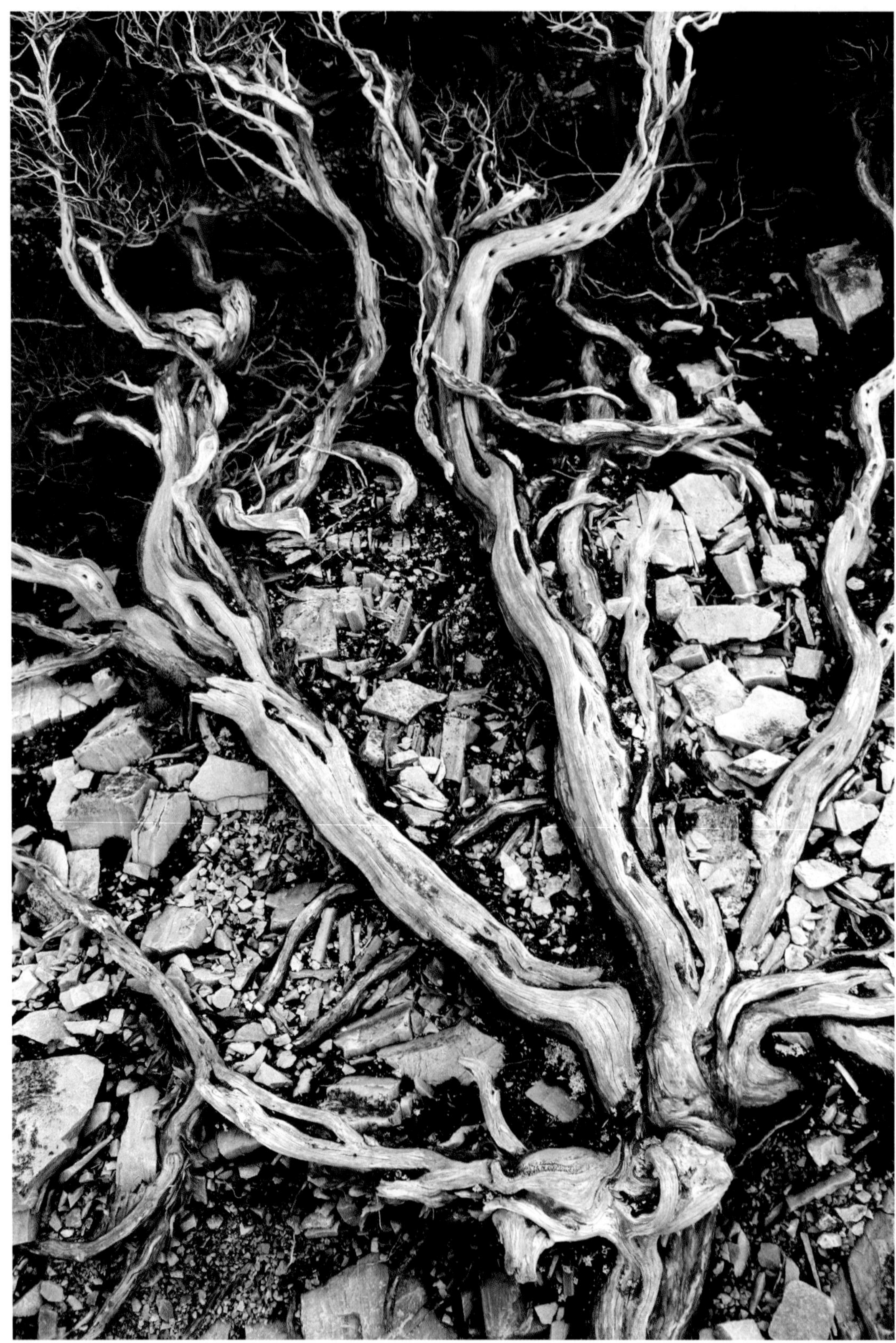

Highly Commended, Black and White
Beech bonzai
Louise Wolfers, Ringwood East, Victoria

'When I found this myrtle beech tree I was amazed
by its "bonsai" like shape. It had been worn by
decades of cold, wind and weather in such an
exposed situation, yet still survived.'
Cradle Mountain, Tasmania

Canon 400D, 1/80, f7.1, ISO 400
2008 7-4 Exhibition

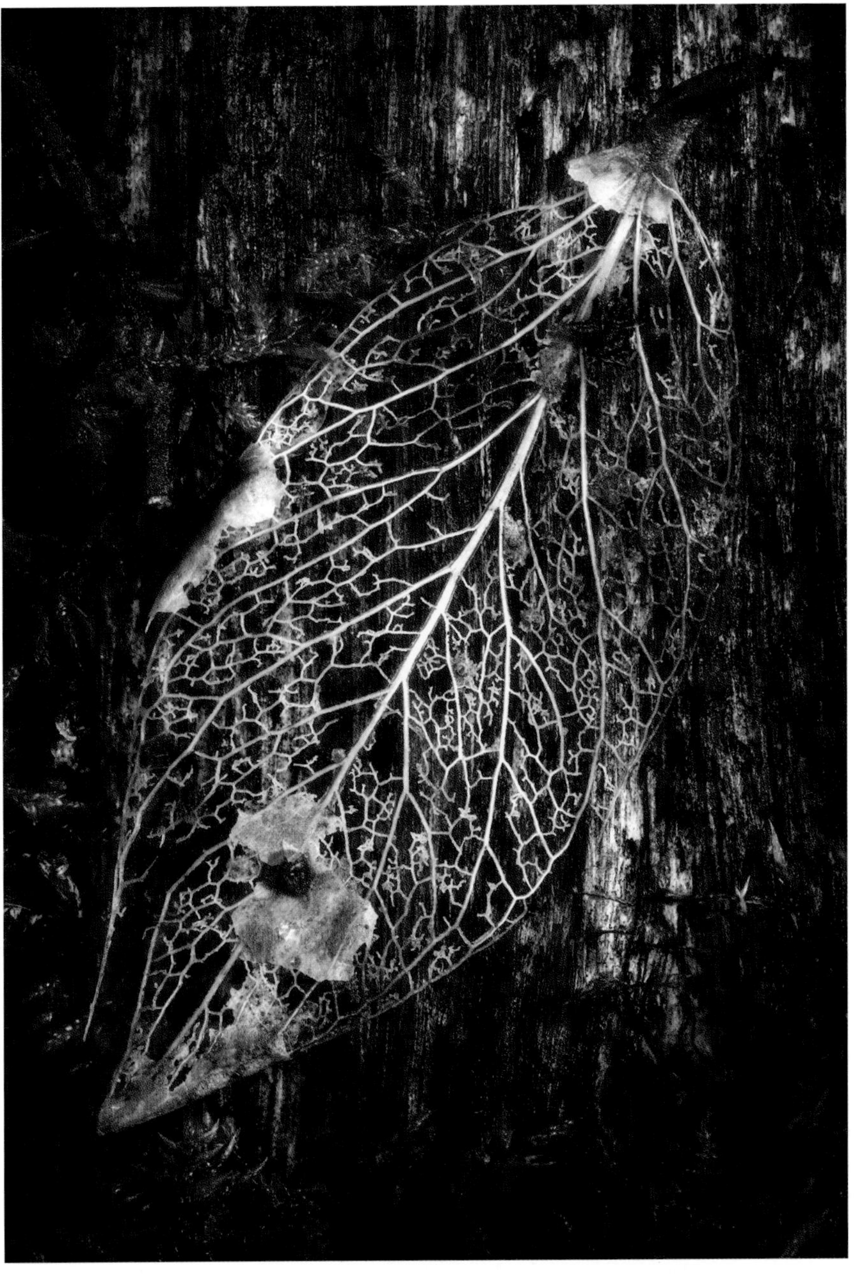

Highly Commended, Black and White
Decaying leaf
Wolfgang Glowacki, Sandy Bay, Tasmania

'The decaying leaf was found in the forest of the
unique Styx Valley of giant old-growth eucalyptus,
some of the tallest in the southern hemisphere.
I hope to raise awareness of an ecosystem that
is under threat from big business interests and
commercial-scale logging.'
Styx Valley, Tasmania

Canon D5, 1/4, f16
2008 7-6

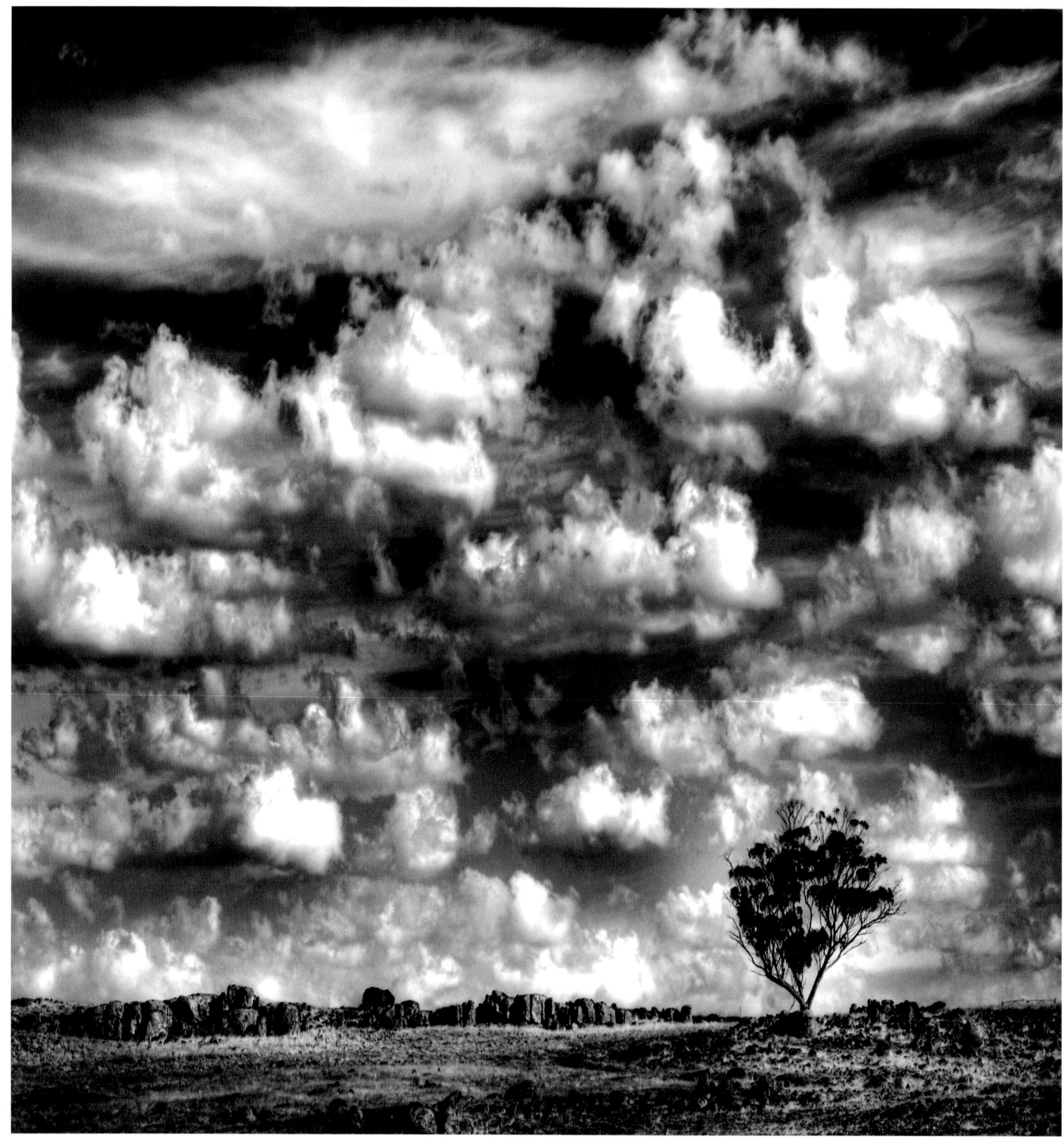

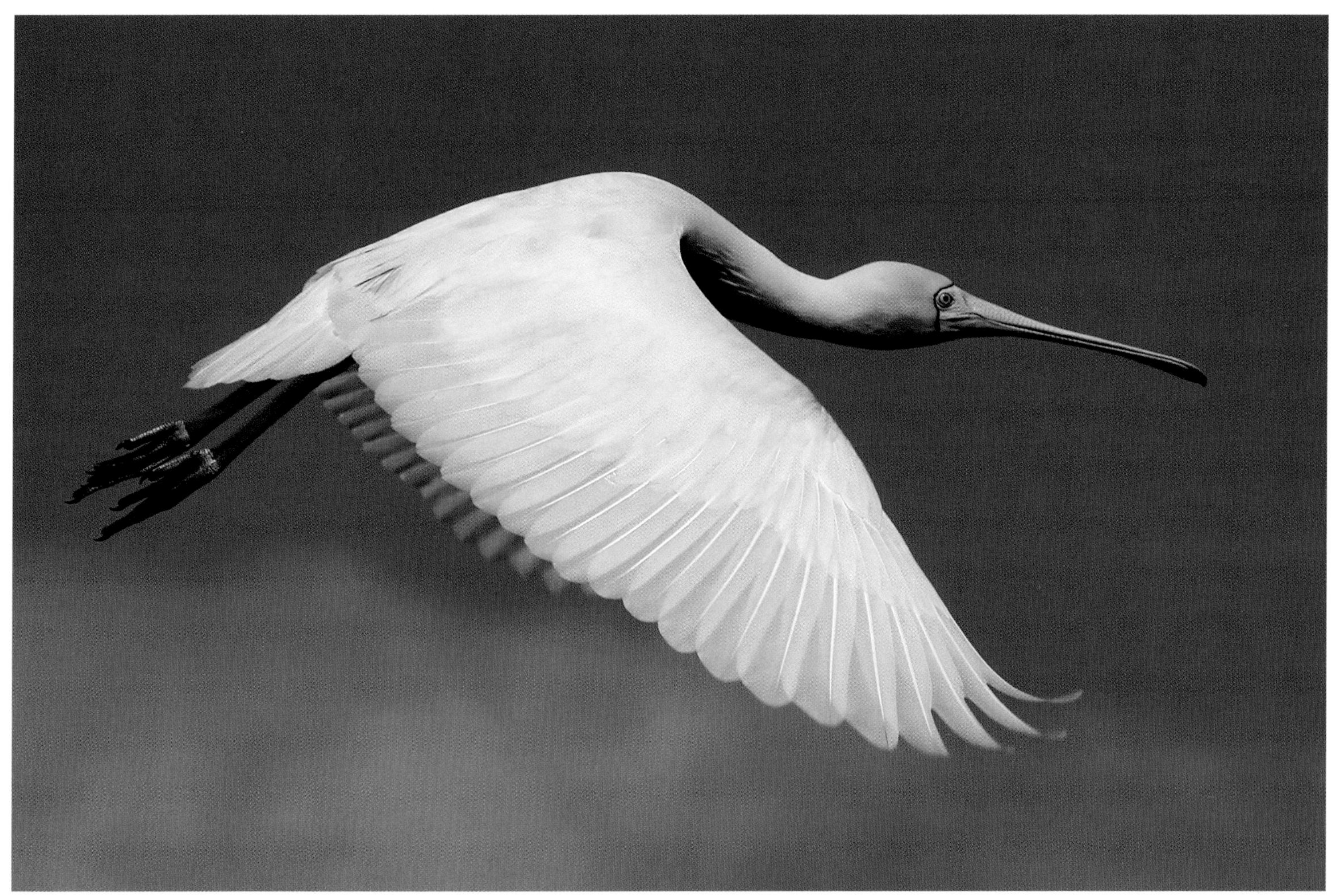

Highly Commended, Black and White
York back roads
Andrew Davoll, Dianella, Western Australia

'It was a very hot day and the clouds were forming rapidly, being blown by strong wind. I noticed a eucalypt on the horizon and realised it would look good as a silhouette against the sky. It would also serve as a contrast, showing the size and grandeur of the sky.'
York, Western Australia

Nikon D200, 1/25, f22
2008 7-7

Highly Commended, Black and White
Above the clouds
David Rennie, Ravenswood, Western Australia

'At 6.30am I went out to a swamp nearby to try out my new 100–400mm lens. After several hours of wading around in the water, I found two nesting spoonbills. I am now hooked on the spoonbills and their antics.'
Lake Barragup, Mandurah, Western Australia

Canon 40D, 100-400mm, 1/1000, f6.3, ISO 200
2008 7-8

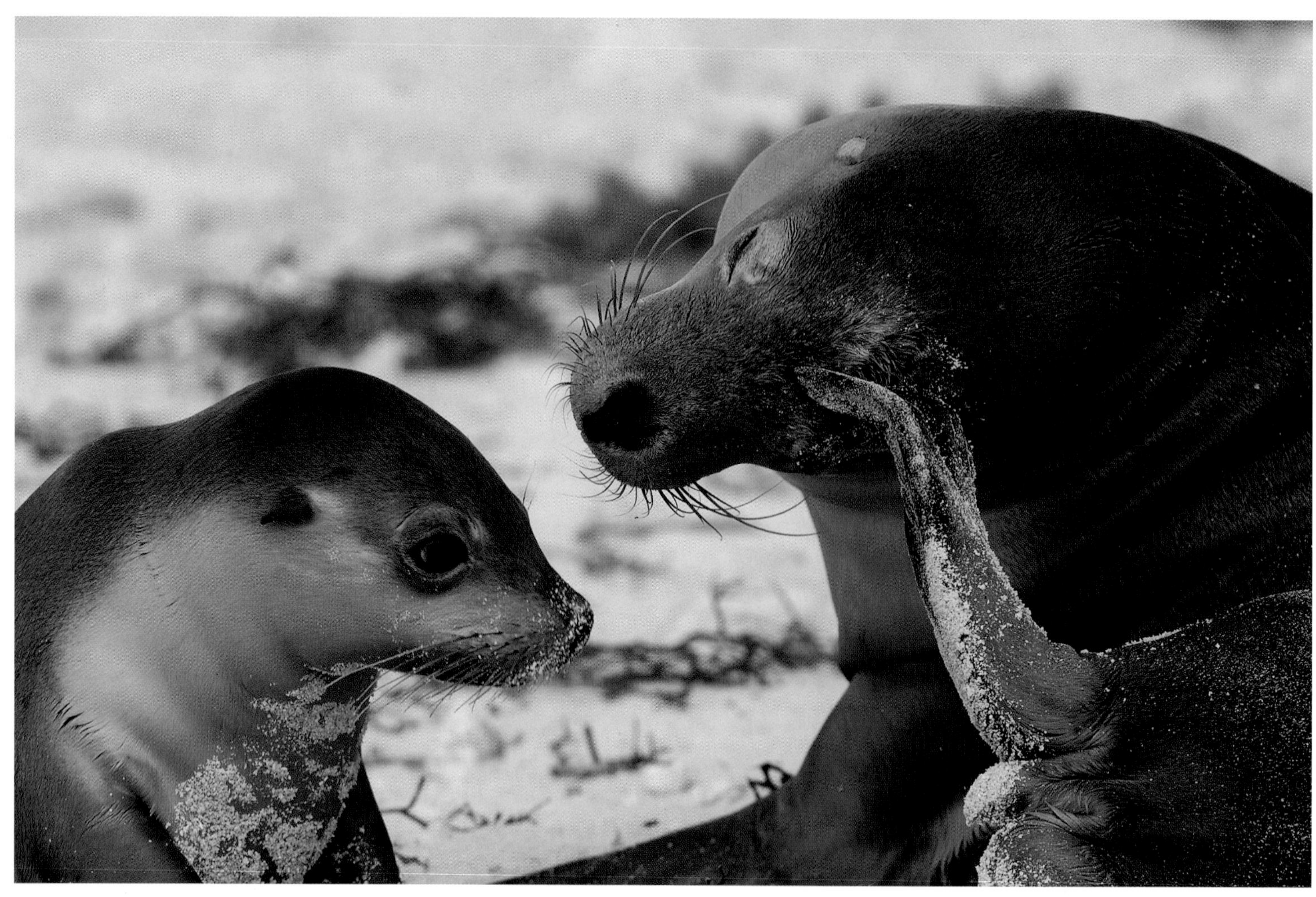

Highly Commended, Black and White
Australian sea lion pup
Pam Osborn, Applecross, Western Australia

'This pup was the youngest in the colony and
anxious to access some of mum's milk. When the
mother went fishing the pup's cries could be heard
until she returned.'
Abrolhos Islands, Western Australia

Nikon D200, 300mm, 1/1000, f4.5, ISO 320
2008 7-11

Highly Commended, Black and White
Button grass plains
Louise Wolfers, Ringwood East, Victoria

'This photograph was taken from one of the many
boardwalks. The dense growth of these grasses
makes them almost impenetrable. They survive
extreme weather conditions. I thought that the range
of tones in the grasses would really suite black and
white.'
Cradle Mountain, Tasmania

Canon 400D, 1/60, f16, ISO 200
2008 7-13 Exhibition

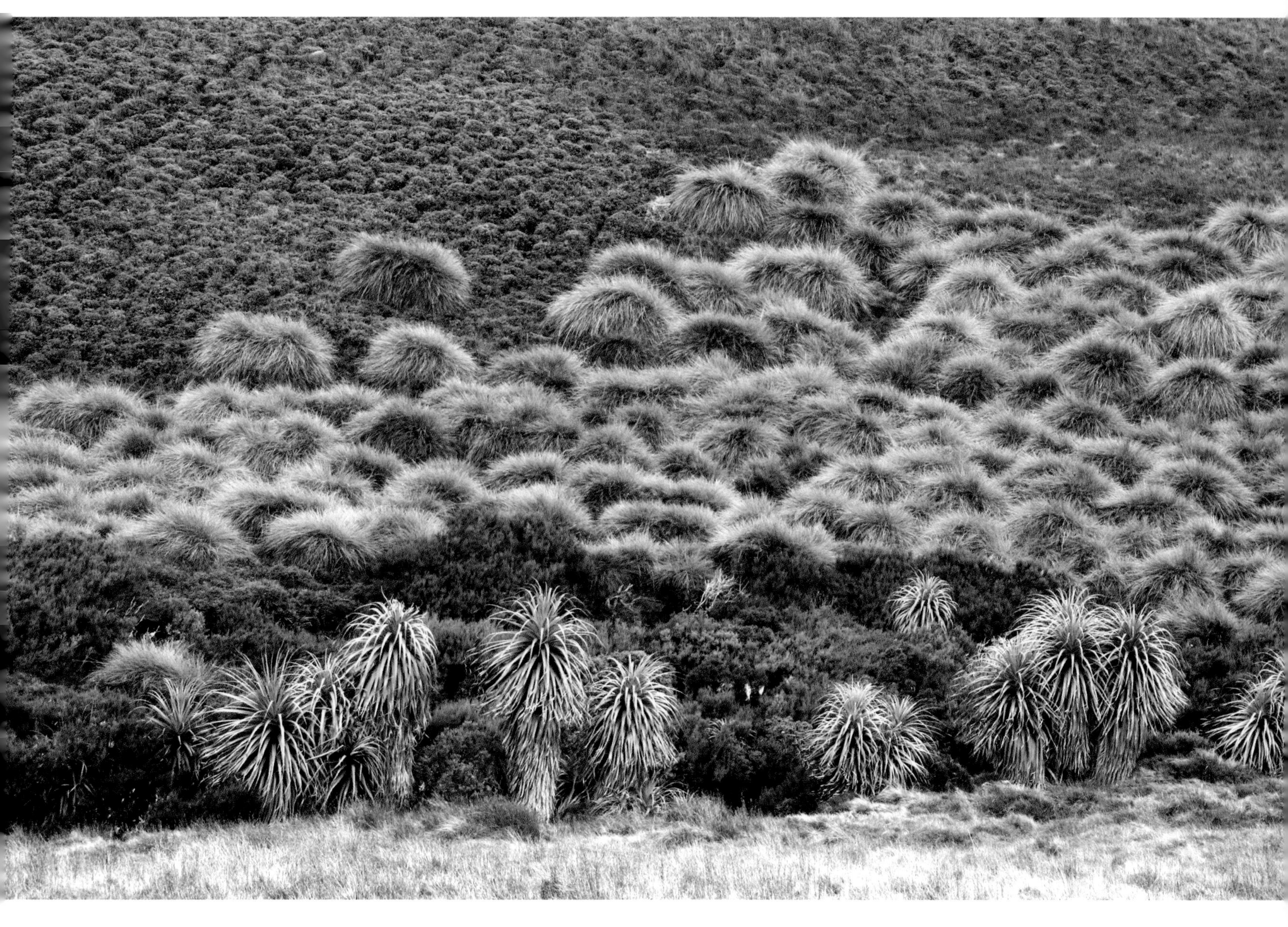

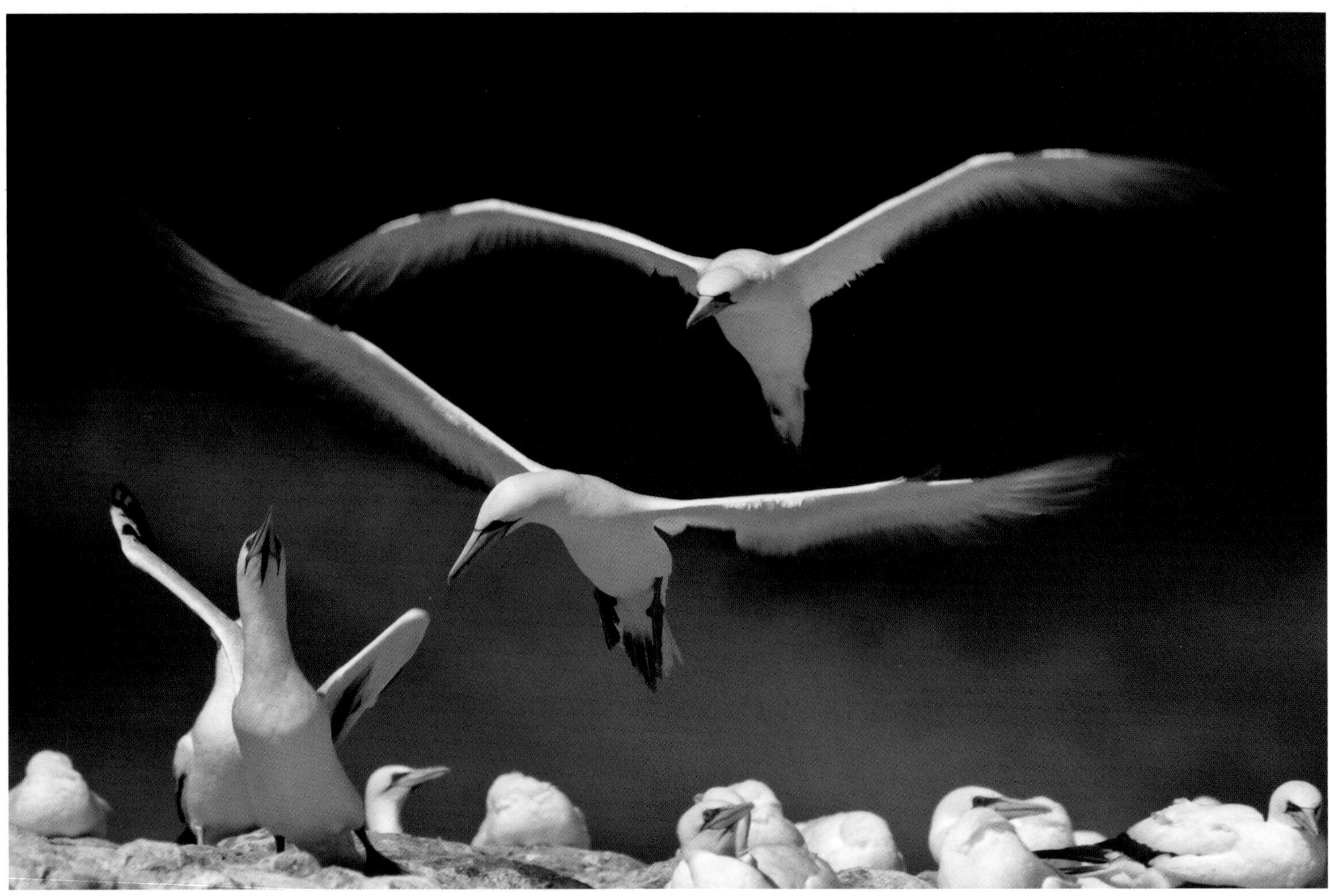

Highly Commended, Black and White
Gannets
David Burren, Middle Camberwell, Victoria

'I spent several days watching and photographing birds flying in and out of their nesting areas. Here the bird on the left is being disturbed by the centre bird about to land nearby, while a third bird in the background is still searching out its own landing spot.'
Victoria

Canon EOS 350D/IR, 100-400mm, 1/320, f8, ISO 400
2008 7-10

Highly Commended, Black and White
Tubastrea
Wayne Osborn, Applecross, Western Australia

'Tubastrea live in colonies in caves and underhangs. They have well defined mouths and muscular tentacles resplendent with stinging cells.'
Off Rottnest Island, Western Australia

Nikon D2X, 105mm, 1/160, f22, ISO 100, flash
2008 7-12

Runner-up, Interpretive Photography
Secret life of gum trees
Jessica Drake, Bankstown, New South Wales

'This image is meant to convey the life of a snow
gum over time. I sense that there is a long history
of endurance – the life of a well adapted botanic
wonder – as it thrives despite the extremes of
seasons, fire and snow.'

Judges' comment: 'A complex and absorbing
collage.'

2008 8-2 Exhibition

Highly Commended, Interpretive Photography
Bark of eucalyptus with leaf from same tree
Len Stewart, Joondalup, Western Australia

'The pastel colours and texture of these trees when
they shed bark provide an opportunity to create an
abstract image. A separate photograph of a leaf from
the same tree was combined to create a focal point,
combining nature's colours found in the tree.'

Nikon D200, 55mm, 1/50, f5.6, ISO 100
2008 8-4

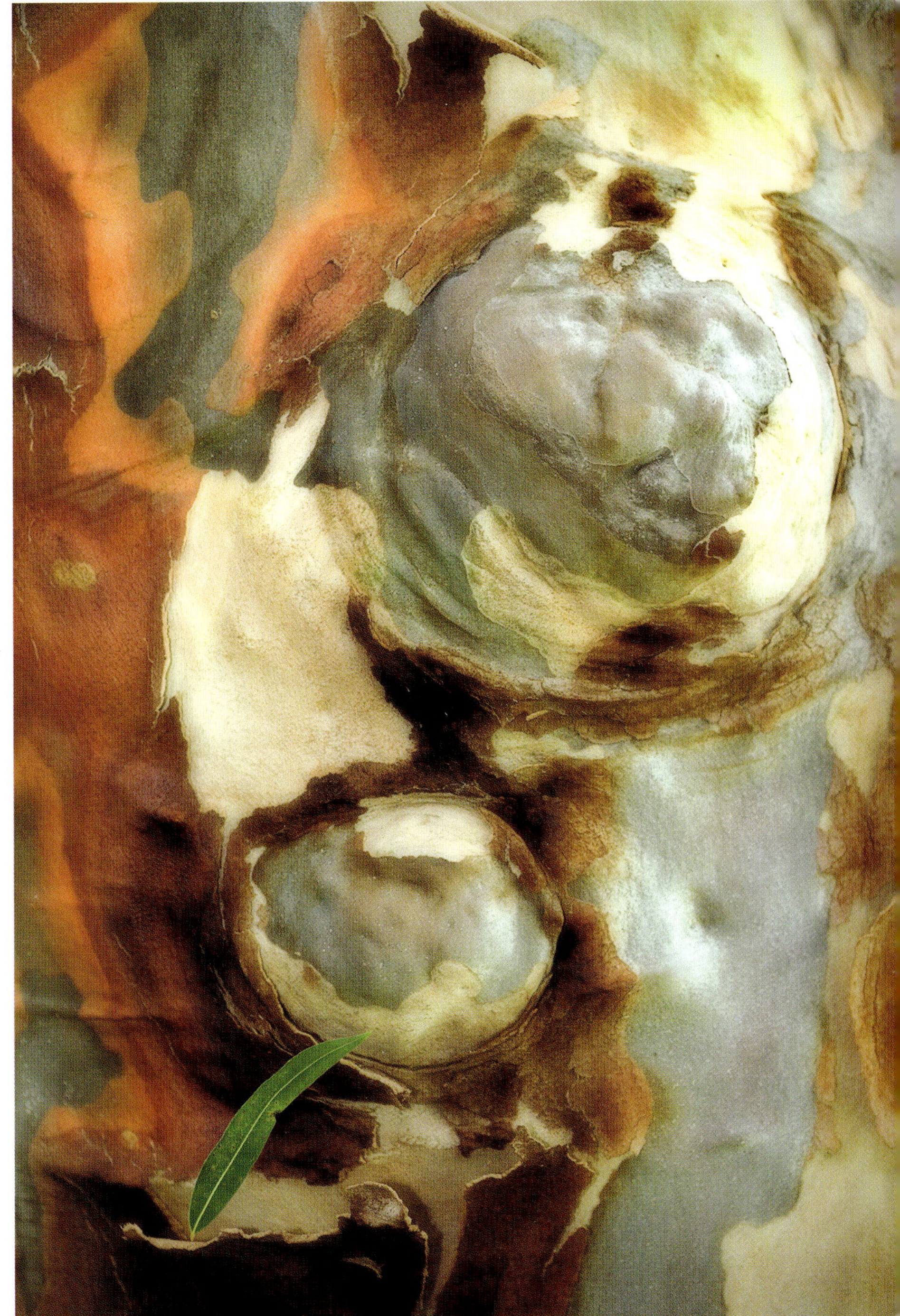

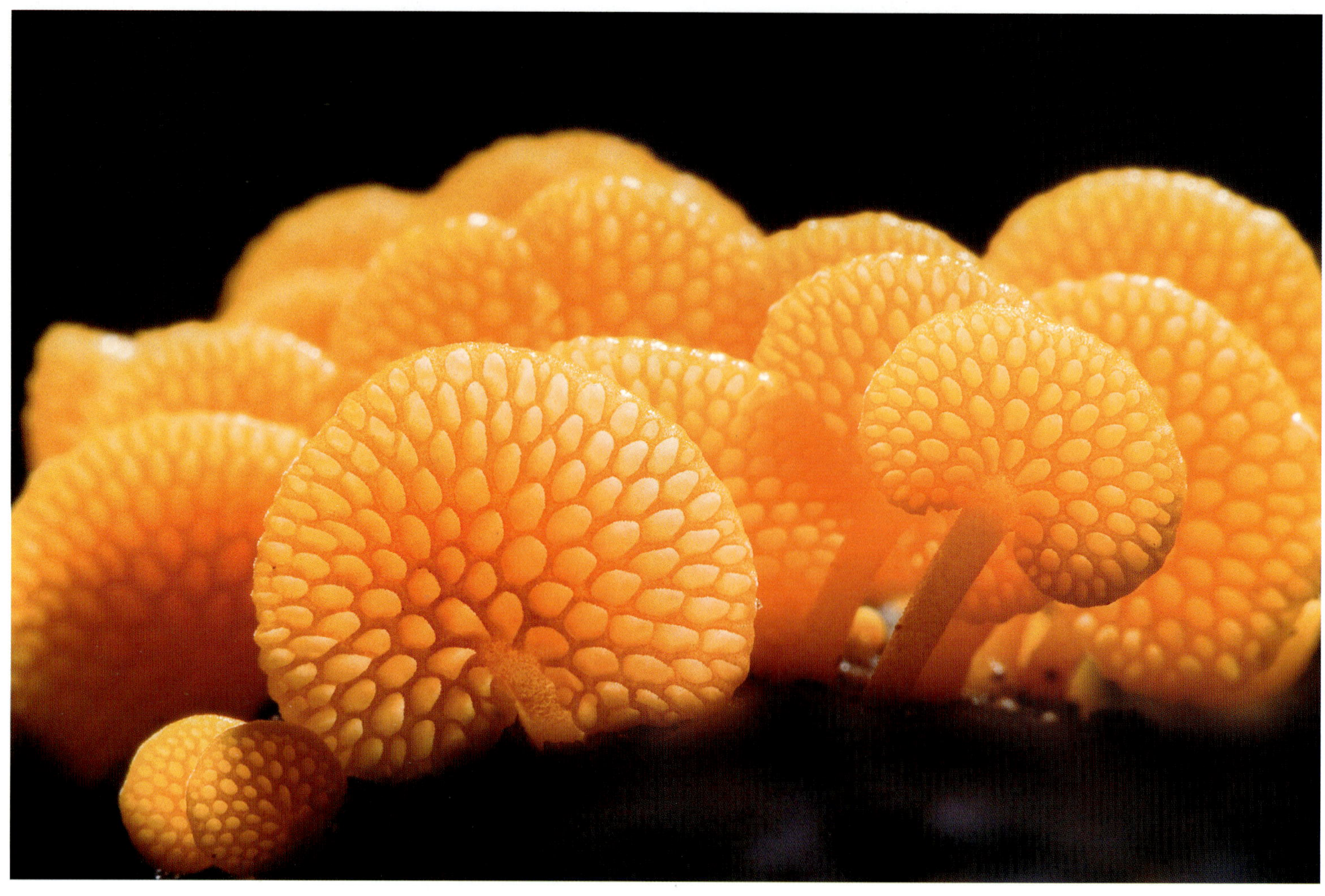

Highly Commended, Interpretive Photography
Netted patterns
Darran Leal, Coolum Beach, Queensland

'After lots of rain I found these beautiful mushrooms, the largest about the size of a thumbnail. I can remember lying in the mud being "explored" by leeches, trying to get the best angle.'
Lamington NP, Queensland

Canon EOS5, 100mm macro, 1/125, f22, ISO 100, flash
2008 8-5

Highly Commended, Interpretive Photography
Three friends
Darran Leal, Coolum Beach, Queensland

'Leaf-tailed geckos are skilled hunters and very adept climbers. I shot these two at a photo workshop. It was not until I looked at the image on the computer screen that I discovered the spider.'
Lamington NP, Queensland

Canon EOS5, 100mm macro, 1/125, f22, ISO 100, flash
2008 8-6 Exhibition

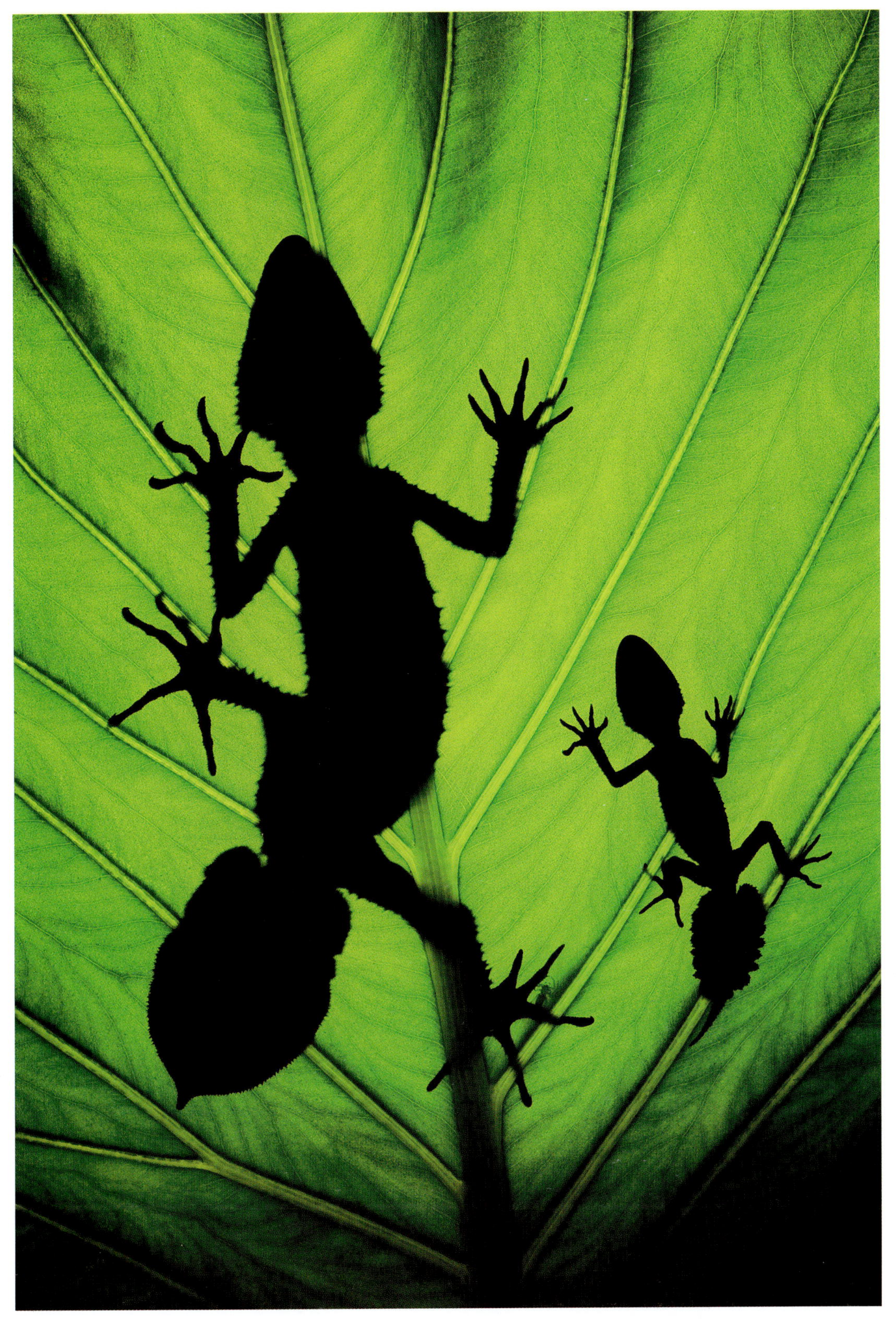

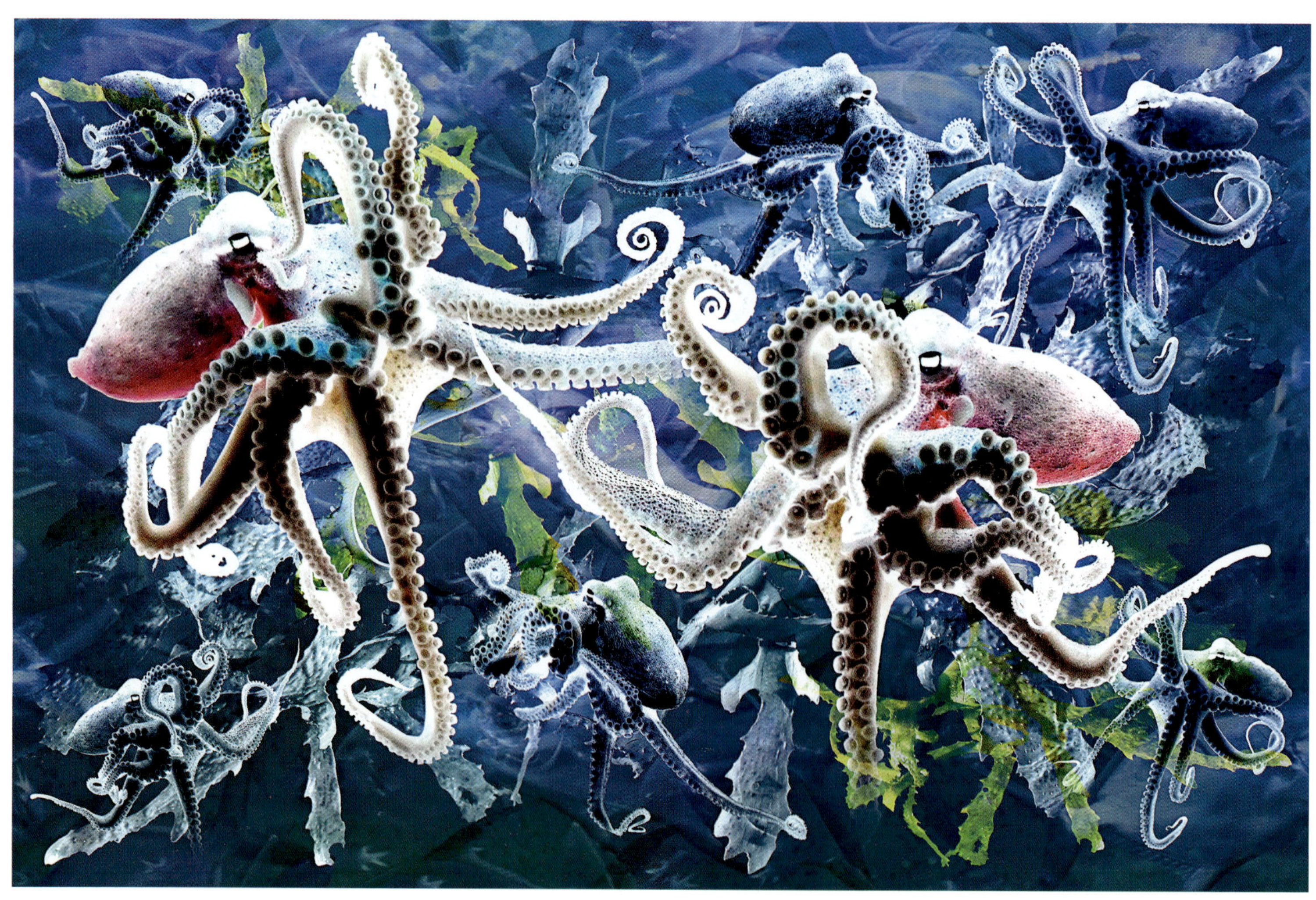

Highly Commended, Interpretive Photography
Octopus battle
Jessica Drake, Bankstown, New South Wales

'This image represents the daily squabbles for
territory and food that occur all the time, when
no-one is looking, in the life of one of our small,
common octopus species.'

2008 8-7

Highly Commended, Interpretive Photography
Fish to the power of four
Wayne Osborn, Applecross, Western Australia

'The original subject was a silver drummer. The
strong geometric lines and texture of the fish
appealed to me. Mirror imaging the original and
duplicating this again gave me the effect I was
looking for.'
Off Rottnest Island, Western Australia

Nikon D2X, 105mm, 1/160, f14, ISO 100
2008 8-8

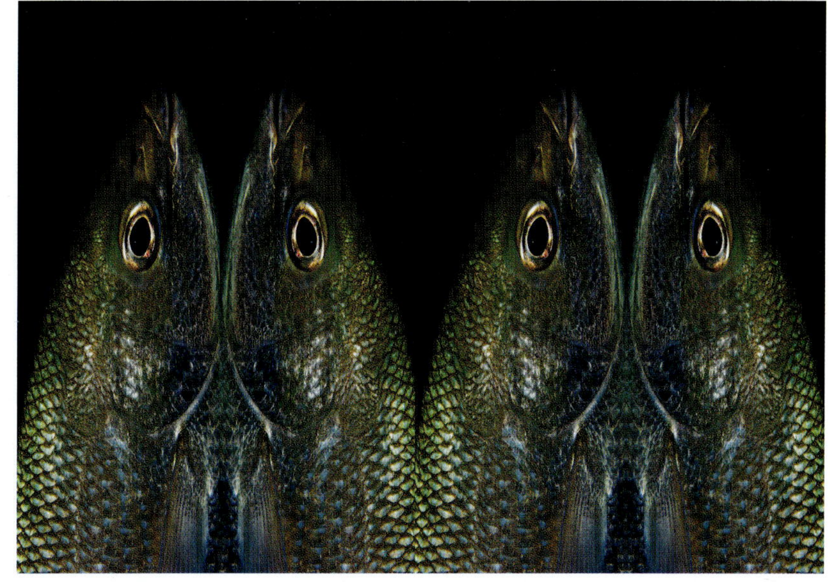

Highly Commended, Interpretive Photography
Feather duster worm
Wayne Osborn, Applecross, Western Australia

'This aptly named marine animal anchors to the
substrate with a calcium tube and extends its gills
to feed on passing nutrients. It presents a challenge
to photograph, as any disturbance of the water will
make the worm retract the gills.'
Off Rottnest Island, Western Australia

Nikon D2X, 105mm, 1/160, f13, ISO 100
2008 8-9 Exhibition

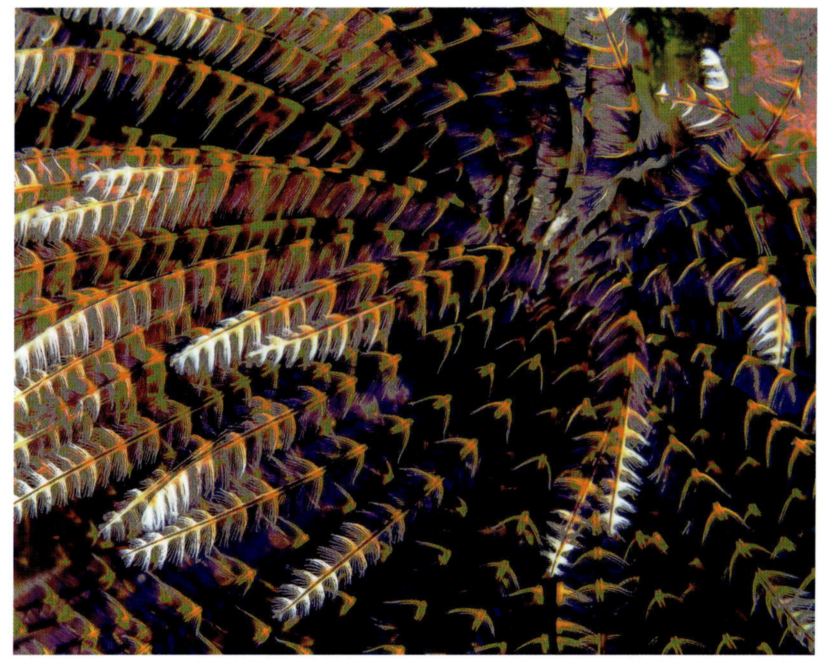

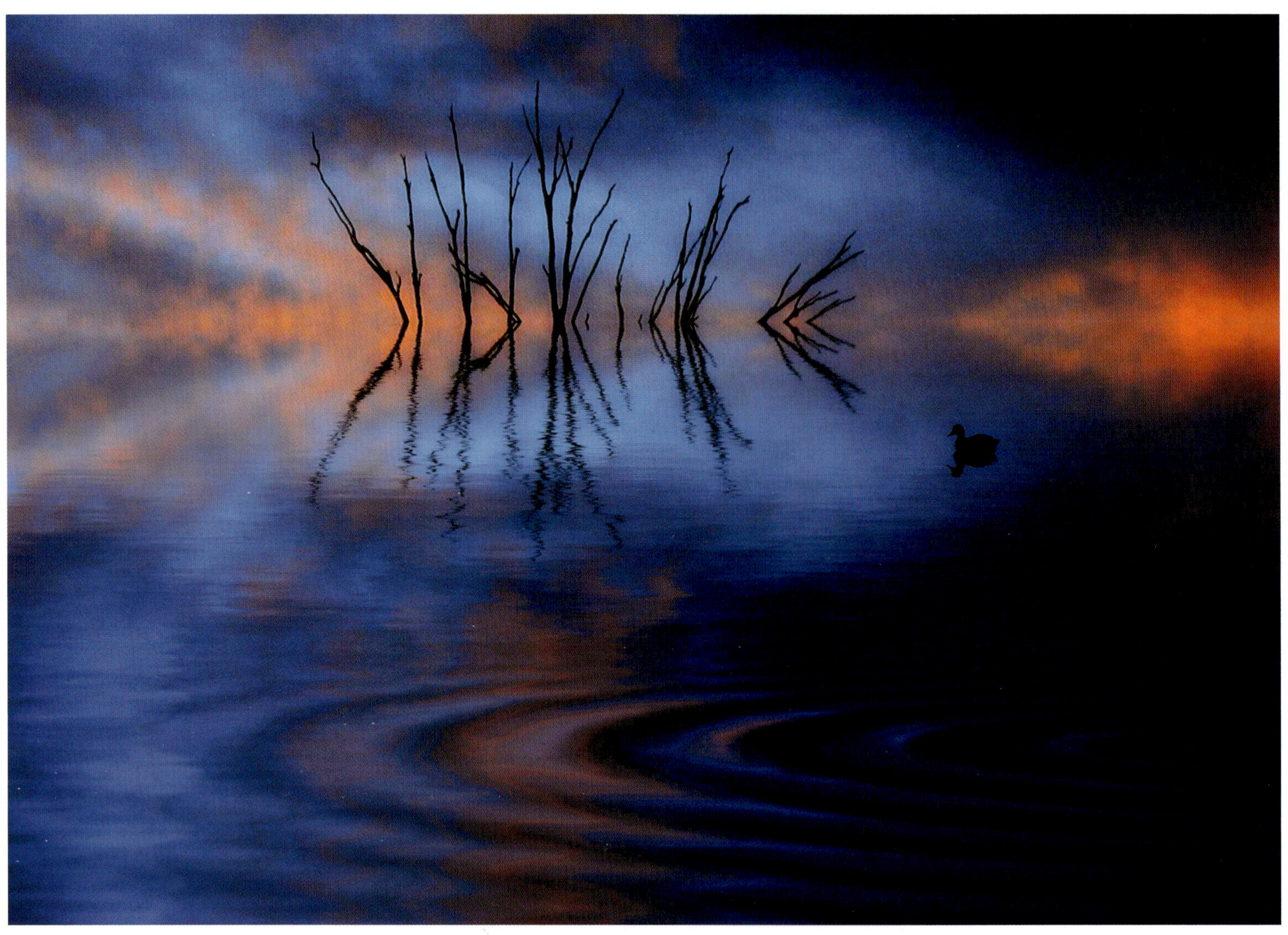

Highly Commended, Interpretive Photography
Trees, lake and duck
Annette Blattman, St Marys, New South Wales

'This is a combination of two different pictures – the dead trees in the lake and their reflection at sunset, plus the duck to show that something so small has its special place in nature.'

Canon 300D, 18-200mm
2008 8-3

Highly Commended, Interpretive Photography
Rainforest flora
Sandra Heuston, Rosebank, New South Wales

'This region is a fragile environment known for its rich diversity. I take individual photographs of each item and then collate them in a harmonious coexistence as nature might intend. In this collage images are of decaying strangler fig leaf, bleeding heart leaf and tulipwood leaf. There is no end to the inspiration that can be found on the rainforest floor.'
Northern River region, New South Wales

Nikon Coolpix 8800   2008 8-11 Exhibition

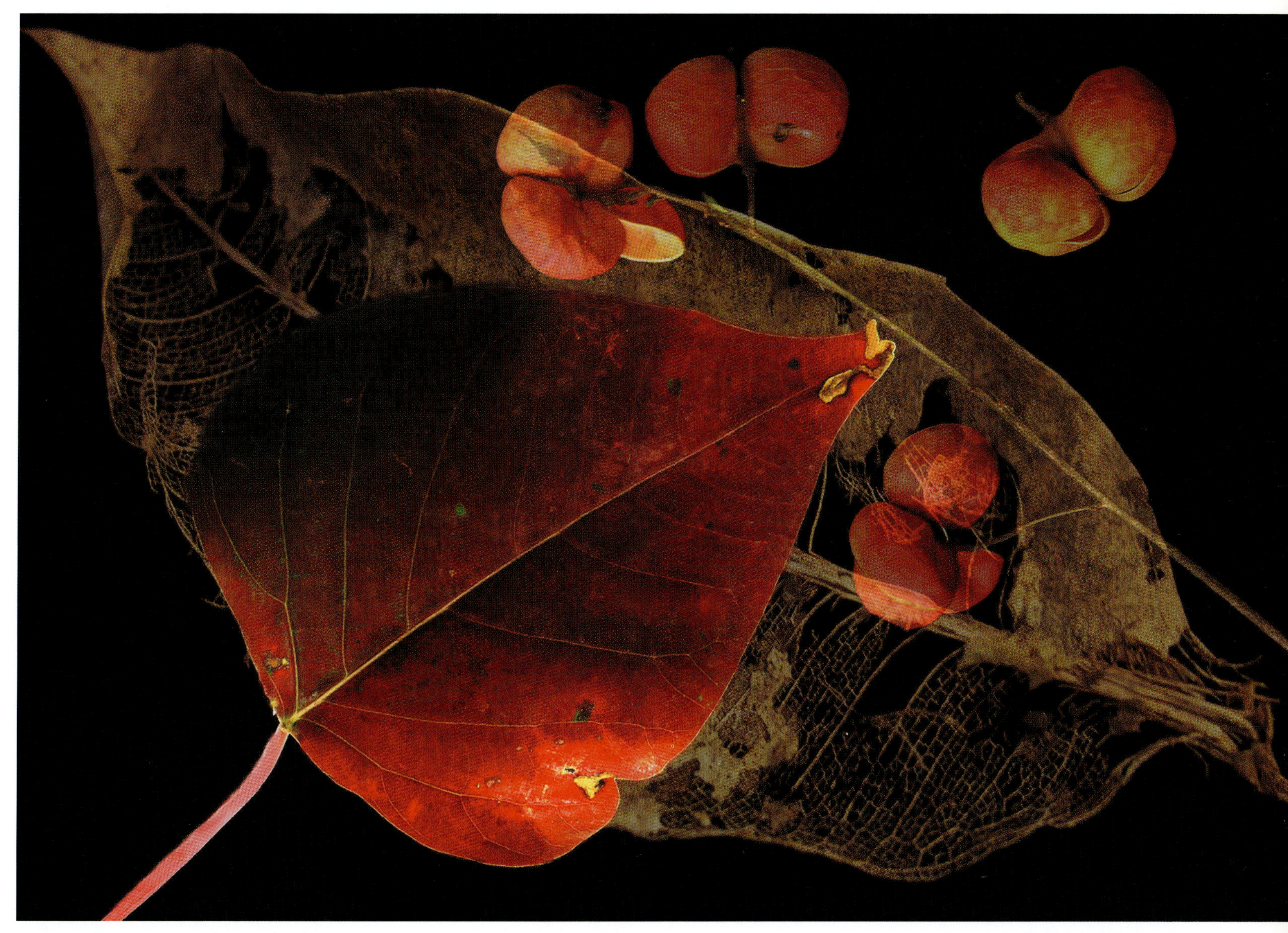

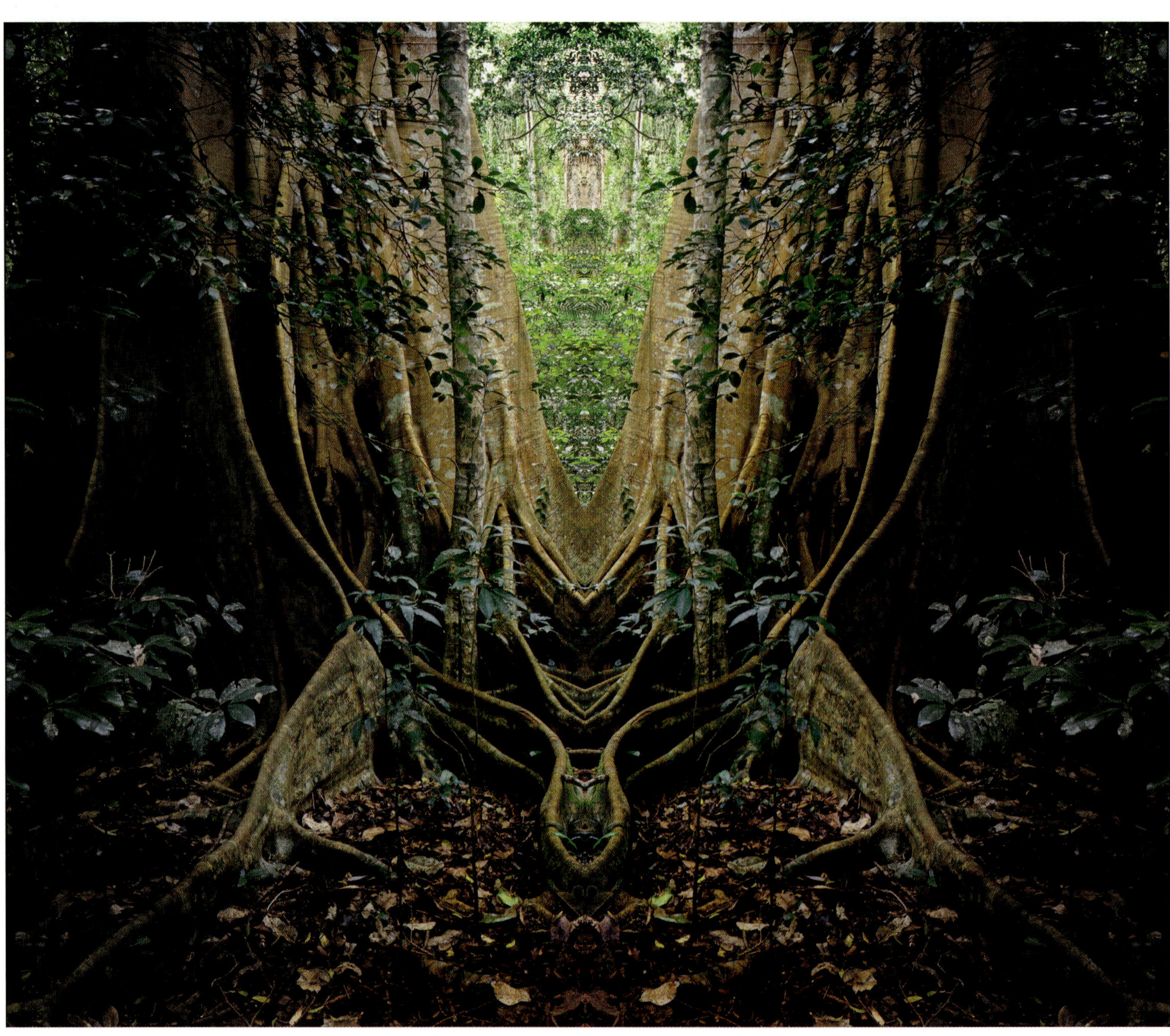

Highly Commended, Interpretive Photography
Birds of the rainforest
Sandra Heuston, Rosebank, New South Wales

'This image is a small representation of the avifauna
that visit my sacred place. My challenge is to
capture the individual uniqueness and beauty of the
subject matter. I hope this makes the viewer aware
of the fragile environment.'
Northern River, New South Wales

Nikon Coolpix 8800
2008 8-13

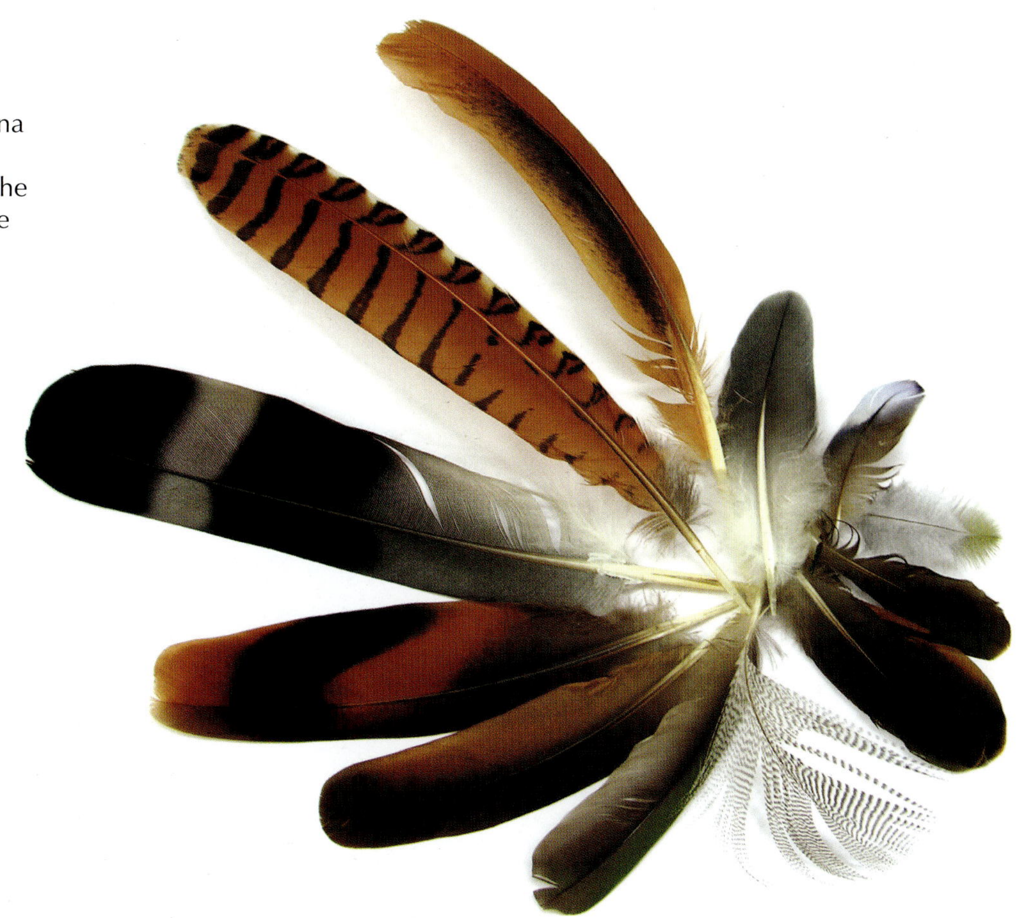

Highly Commended, Interpretive Photography
The green man – small-leaved fig
Stanley and Kaisa Breeden, Malanda, Queensland

'There are a number of places in this picture where
it seems you can see the spirit of the rainforest.'

Mamiya 7, 600mm, 6x7 Fuji Provia
2008 8-12

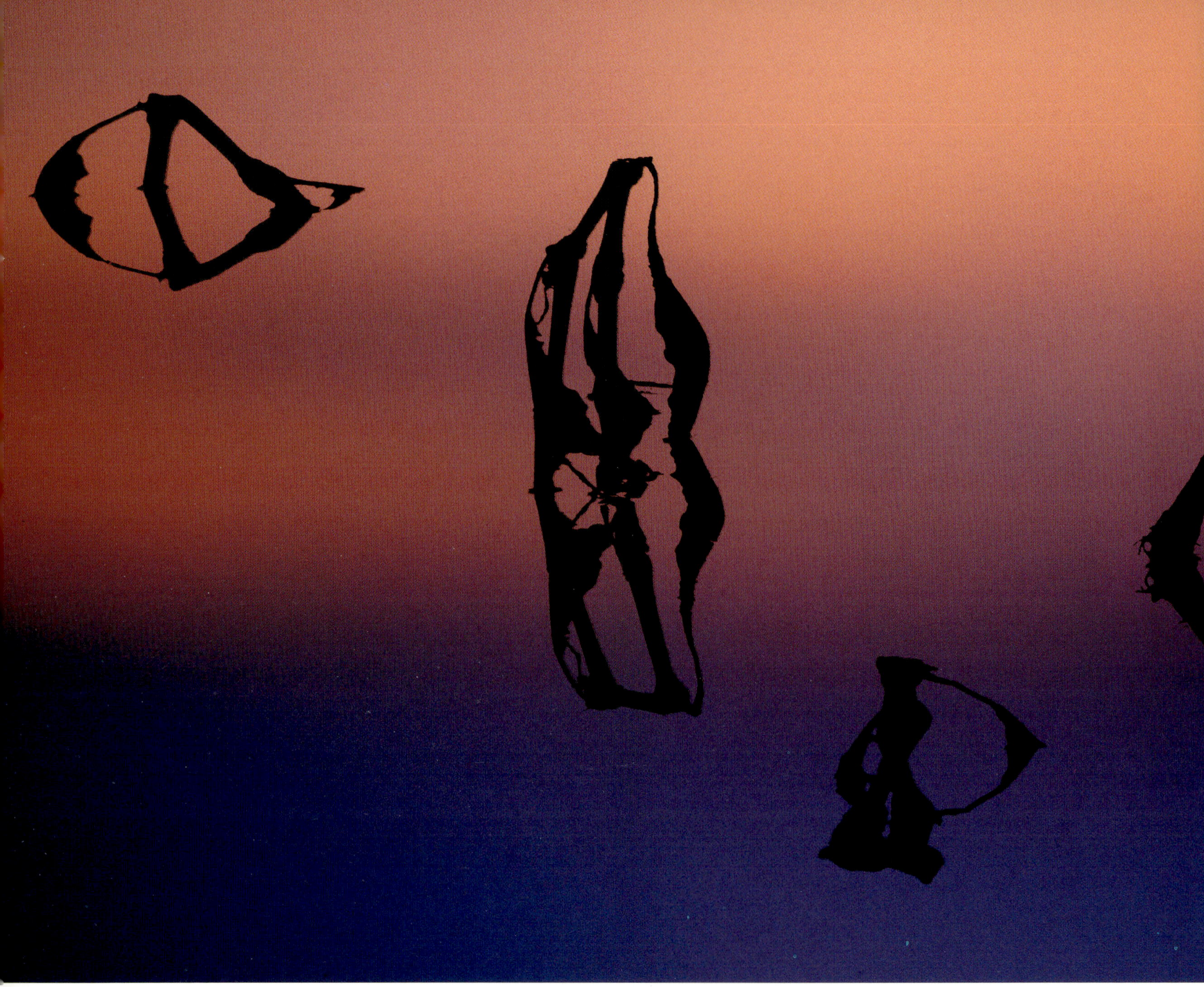

Highly Commended, Interpretive Photography
Dying reed shapes
Andrew Davoll, Dianella, Western Australia

'In the early morning I came across these reeds in colourless, motionless water, yet 10 metres away the water was beautifully coloured by the pre-dawn sky. So I combined both photos in Photoshop.'
Carine Swamp, Western Australia
Nikon F100, Velvia 50

2008 8-10

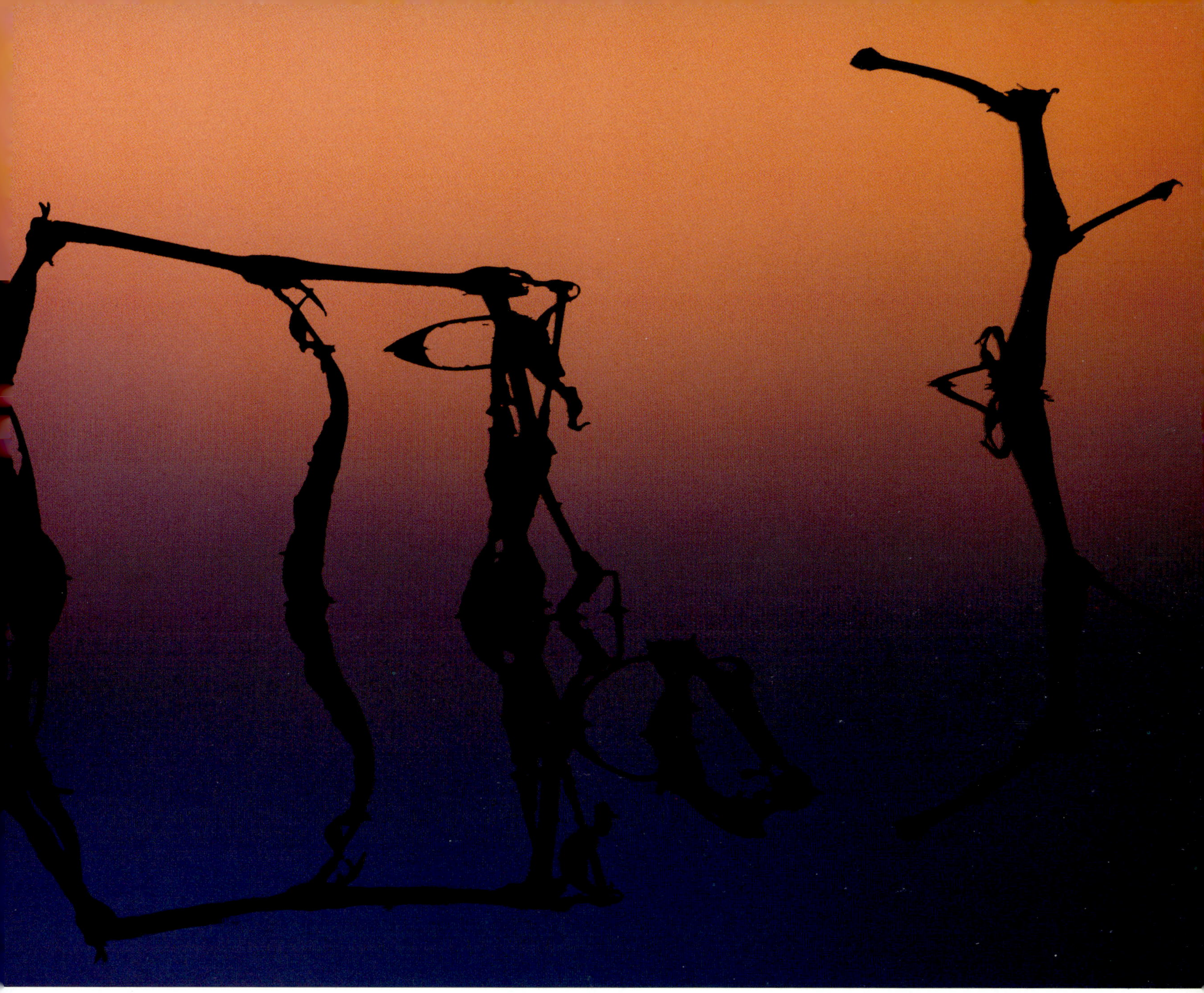

Section 9, Our Impact

The image must depict human impact on the natural environment,
be it terrestrial, marine or atmospheric. This impact may be negative
or positive. The choice of subjects is broad, including any that would
qualify for the first six sections, or may extend beyond these to subjects
relating to pollution and climate change.

Prize: $1,000

Winner, Our Impact
Thong print
Olga Barrington, Mollymook, New South Wales

'It was a drizzly grey day. The rain and previous tide had (nearly)
obliterated all evidence of man. This long-ago discarded thong
could almost fool you into thinking it was a light footprint, until
you realise it is dirty plastic that belongs in the bin – where it is
now!'
Mollymook Beach, New South Wales

Judges' comment: 'A great photograph which so simply but
adroitly epitomises man's footprint on the planet.'
Leica D2
2008 9-1 Exhibition

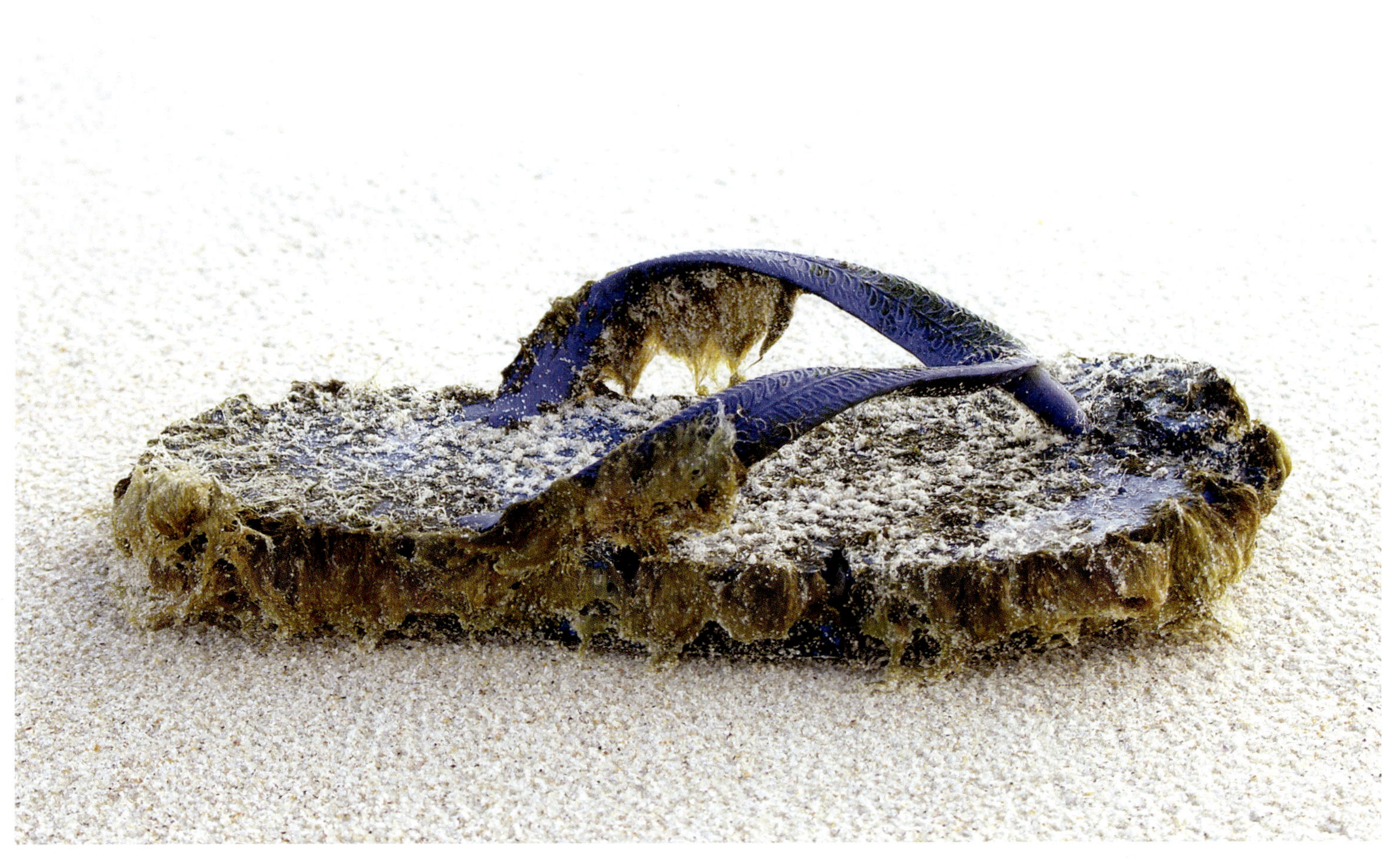

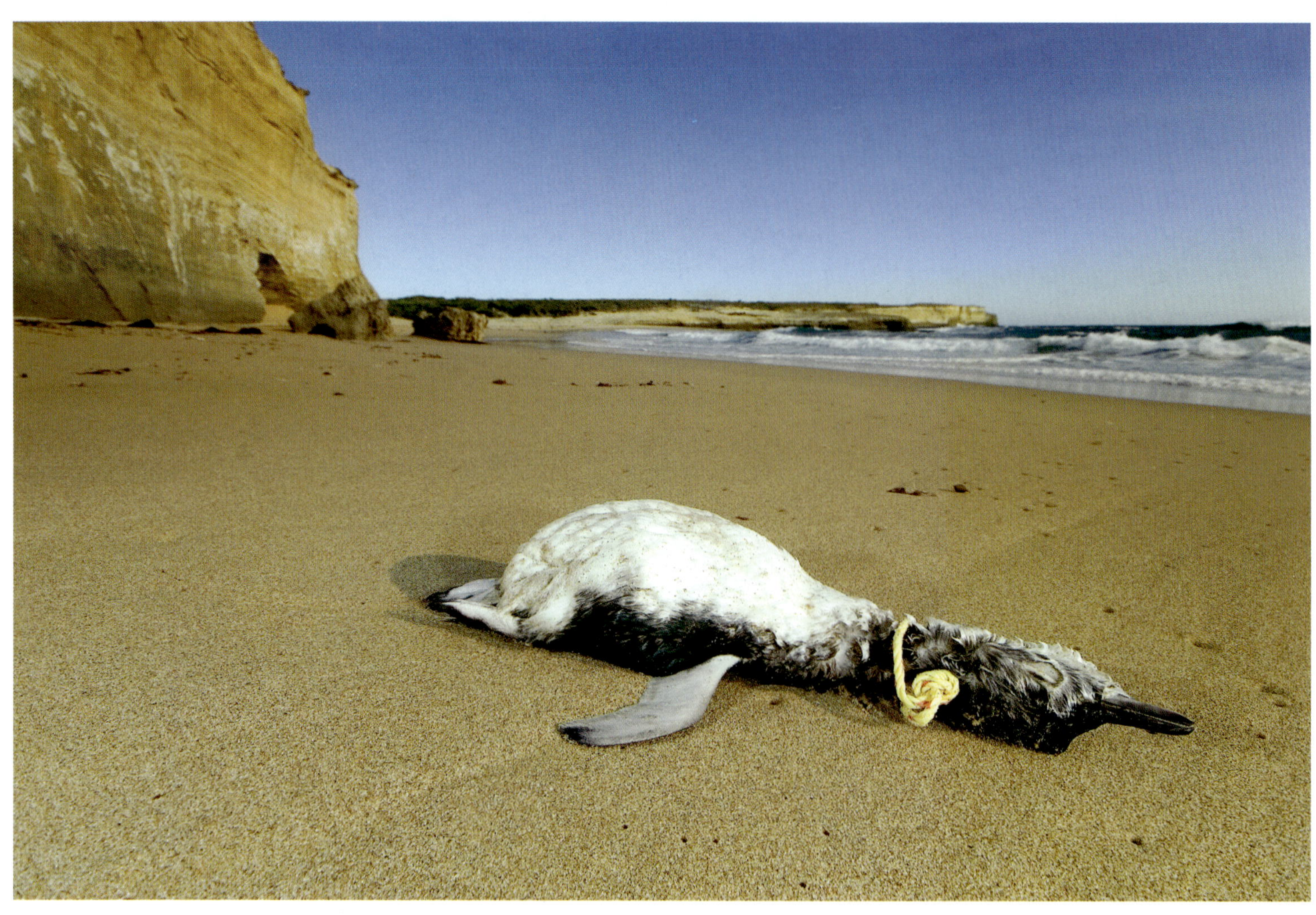

Runner-up, Our Impact
Little penguin
Michael Williams, Newport, Victoria

'Finding this little penguin in amongst washed up, discarded nets and rubbish, I set up to photograph the scene. As a huge wave pushed it further up the beach and out of the debris, the single knotted cause of its fate was exposed.'
Pt Campbell, Victoria

Judges' comment: 'Pathos captured.'

Canon 20D, Sigma 10-22mm, 1/250, f10, ISO 100, flash
2008 9-2 Exhibition

Highly Commended, Our Impact
Australasian darter – hooked
Jessica Drake, Bankstown, New South Wales

'I was dismayed to find this darter, at one of my coastal haunts, with a hook caught in his mouth and the sinker knotted around his neck. I was unable to help as he was still able to fly off.'
Killcave, New South Wales

Canon 400D Sigma 50-500mm, 1/500, f8, ISO 400
2008 9-3

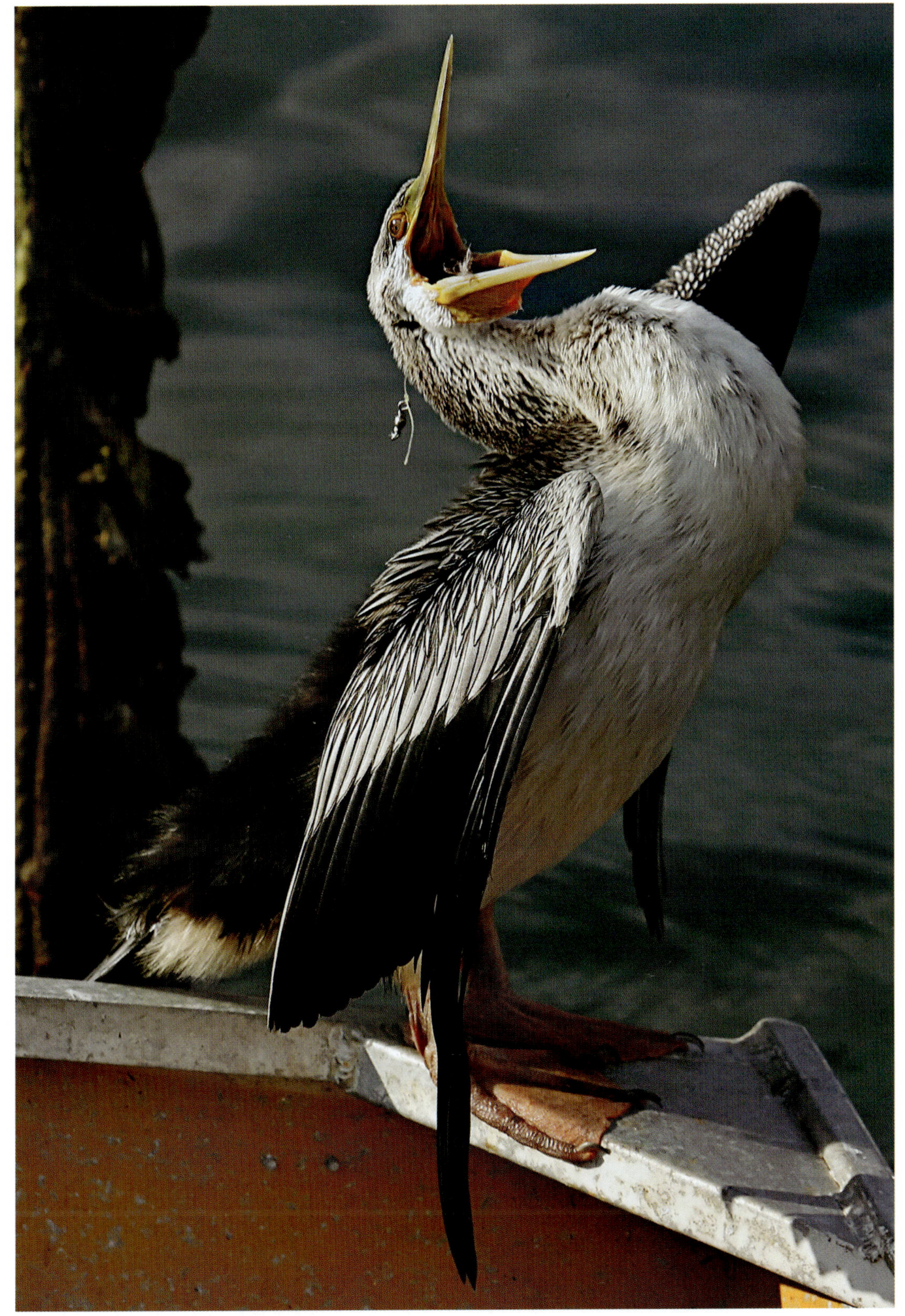

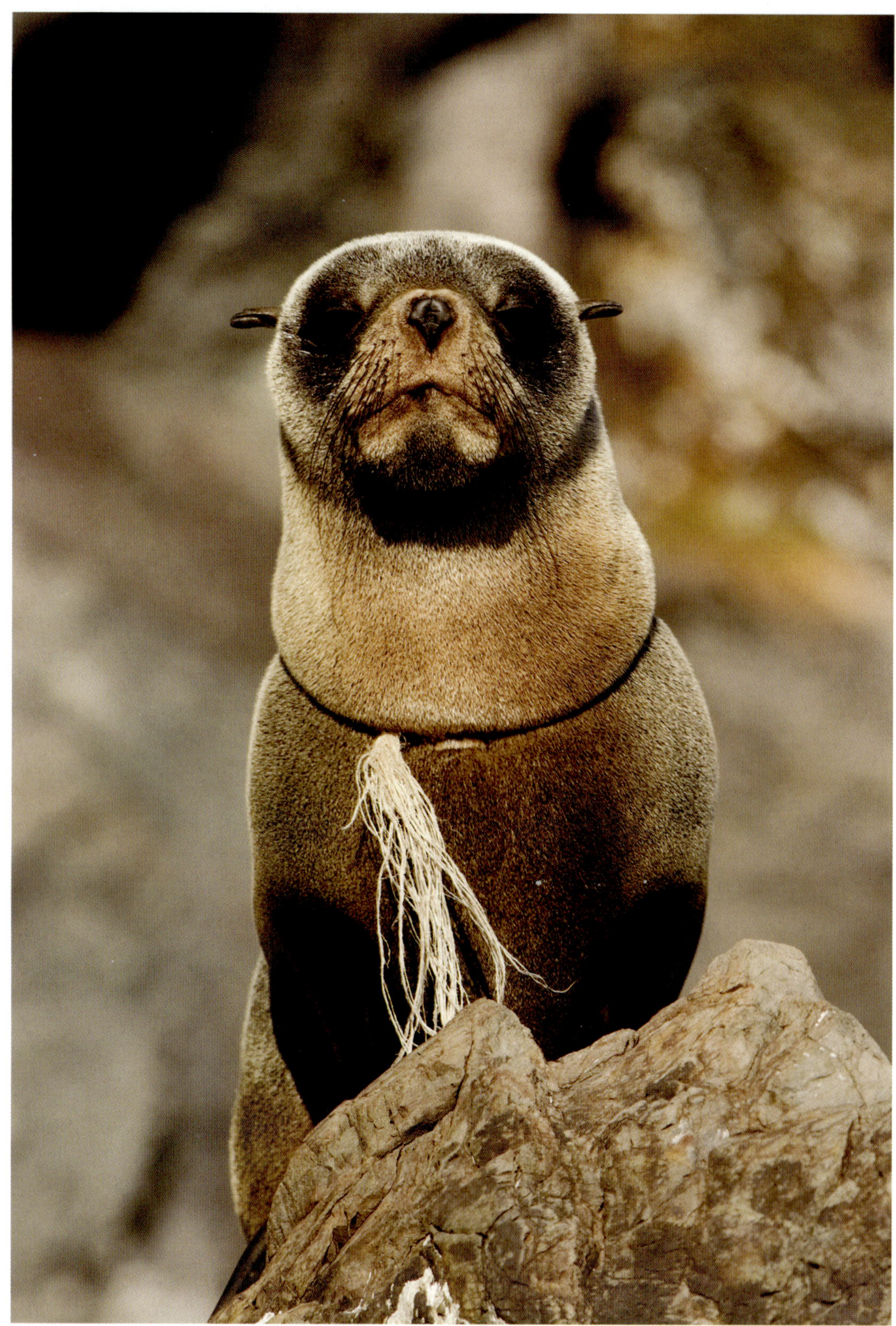

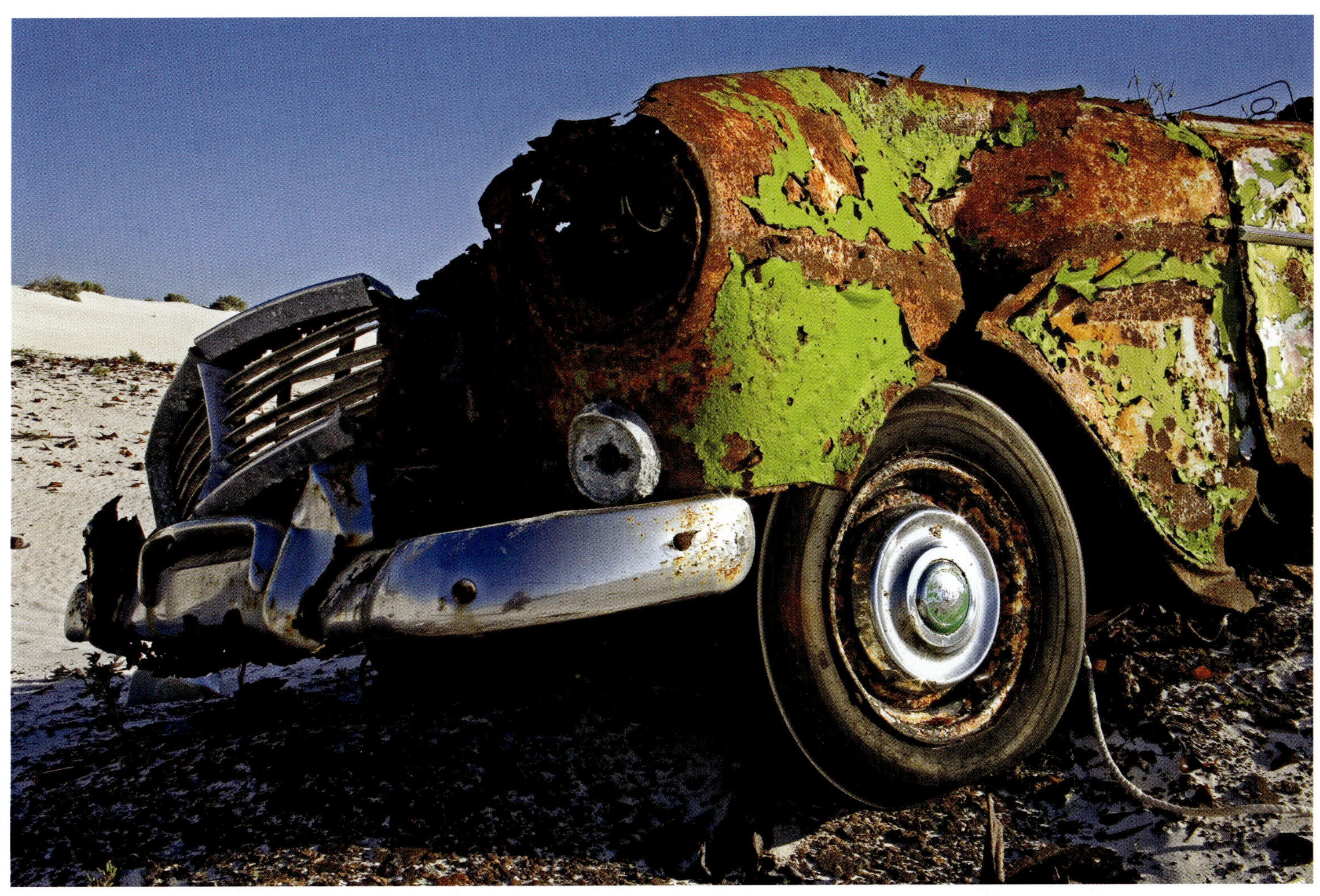

Highly Commended, Our Impact
Necklace of death
Andy Trowbridge, Christchurch, New Zealand

'After photographing this young seal, I could tell it was really struggling with the rope around its neck. I went to seek help but when we returned it had gone. Frequent visits over the next few days were unsuccessful as well.'
Murphys Beach, South Westland, New Zealand

Canon 10D, 400mm, 1/400 f8, ISO 200
2008 9-5 Exhibition

Highly Commended, Our Impact
Abandoned car
Tony Hopkins, Gooseberry Hill, Western Australia

'After climbing a beautiful white sand dune, I found I was looking down into a large crater, in it the abandoned car with the surrounding area littered with broken glass and bottles.'
Cervantes, Western Australia

Canon EOS 5D, 28-135, 1/30, f29, ISO 100
2008 9-6 Exhibition

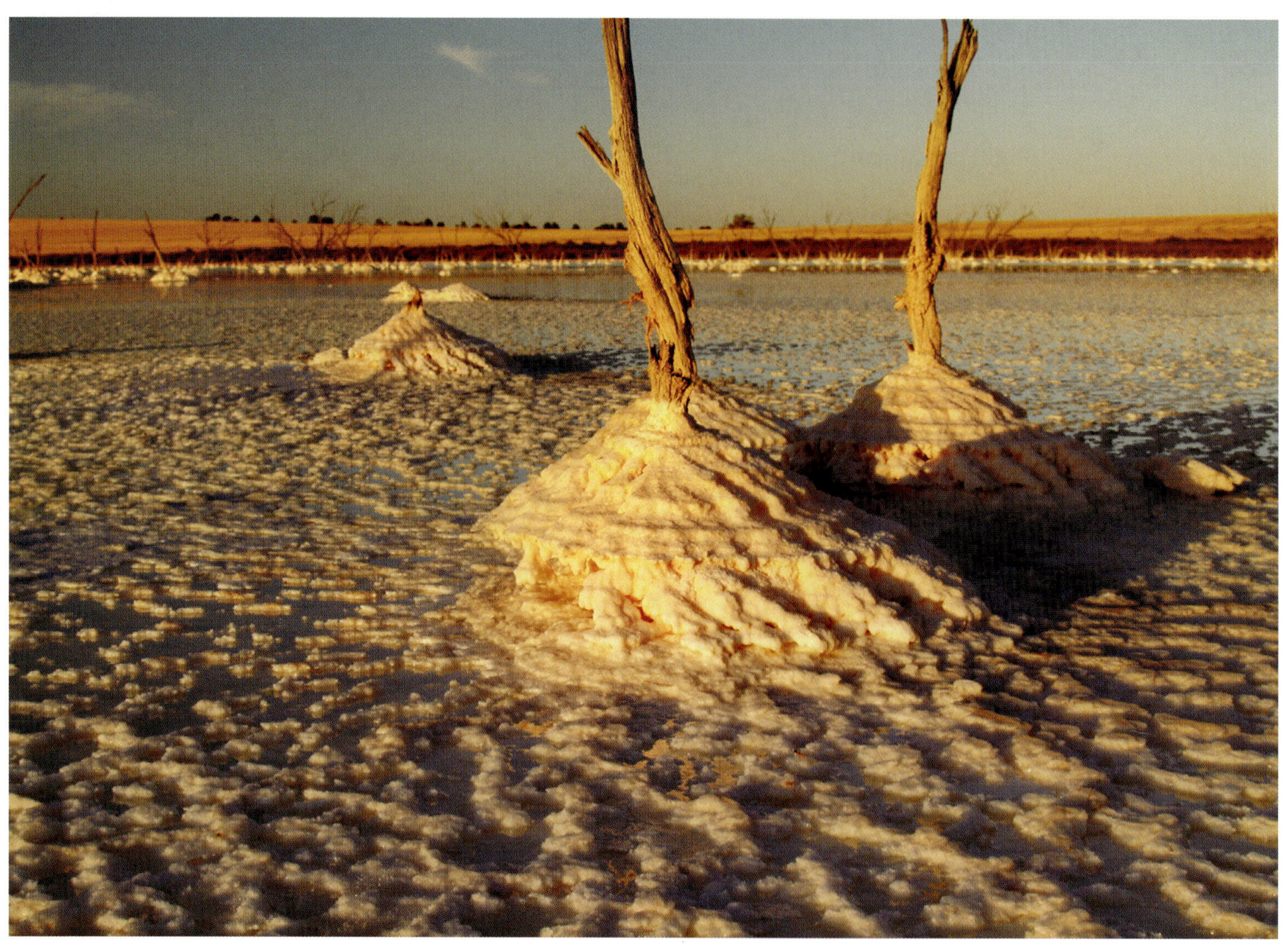

Highly Commended, Our Impact
While grain paddocks thrive, encroaching salt sterilises
Dean Zec, Greenwood, Western Australia

'The incredible amount of salt build-up in the lake made a spectacular sight in the late afternoon light, providing a stark and disturbing contrast to the healthy paddocks in the background.'
Quairading, Western Australia

Olympus E 300, 14-45, polarizing filter
2008 9-7 Exhibition

Highly Commended, Our Impact
Port Augusta profile
Keri Heart, Kingston Beach, Tasmania

'The scene from close range was stark and looming
grey, the clouds making it appear even more eerie.
The forgotten machinery had its own rustic beauty,
yet the debris that surrounded it and the thick foam
at the water's edge, plus the smoke pollution from
the refinery, made me wonder what the effect would
be on the future.'
Port Augusta, South Australia

Canon 400D, 18mm, 1/400, f7, ISO 400
2008 9-8

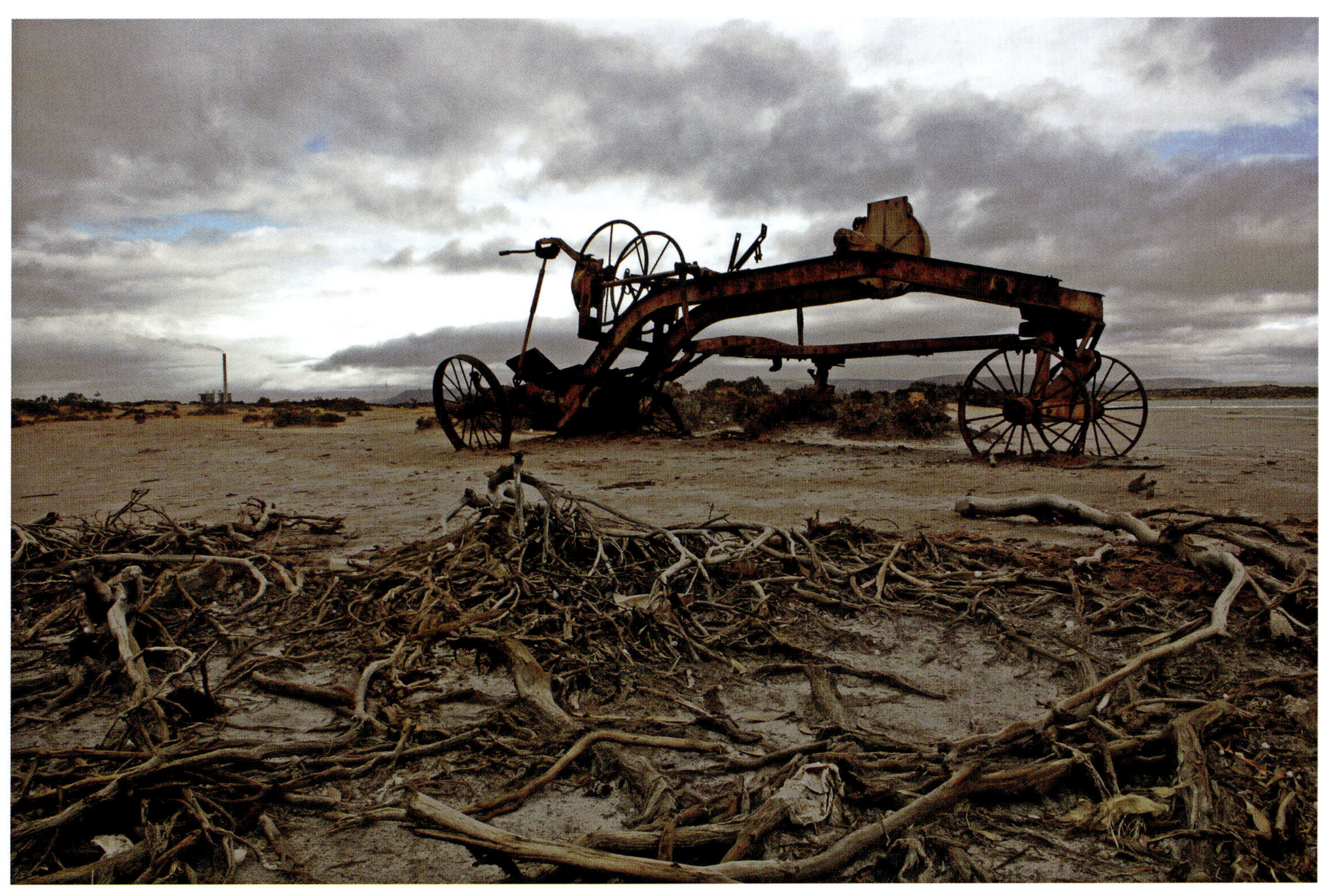

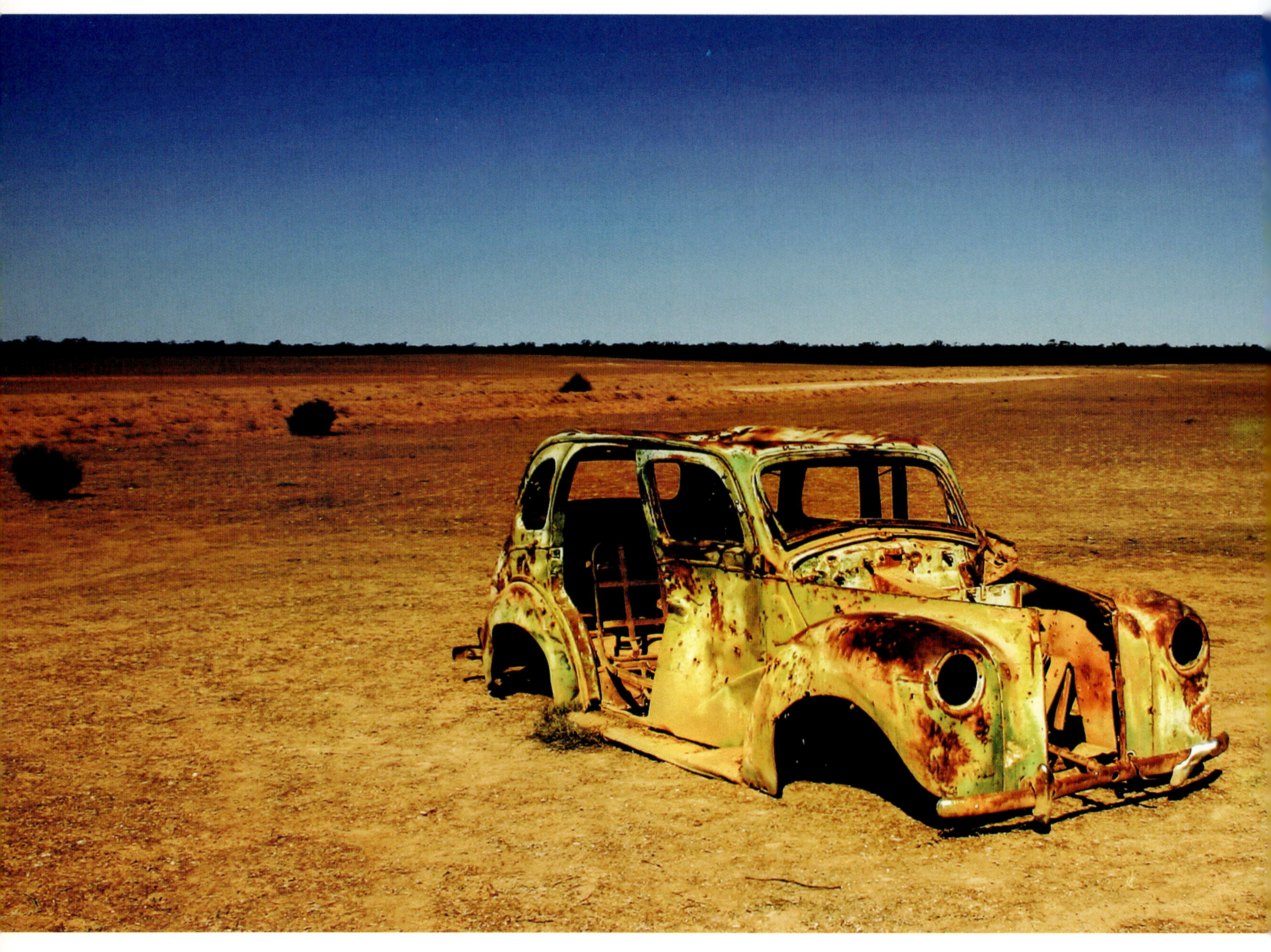

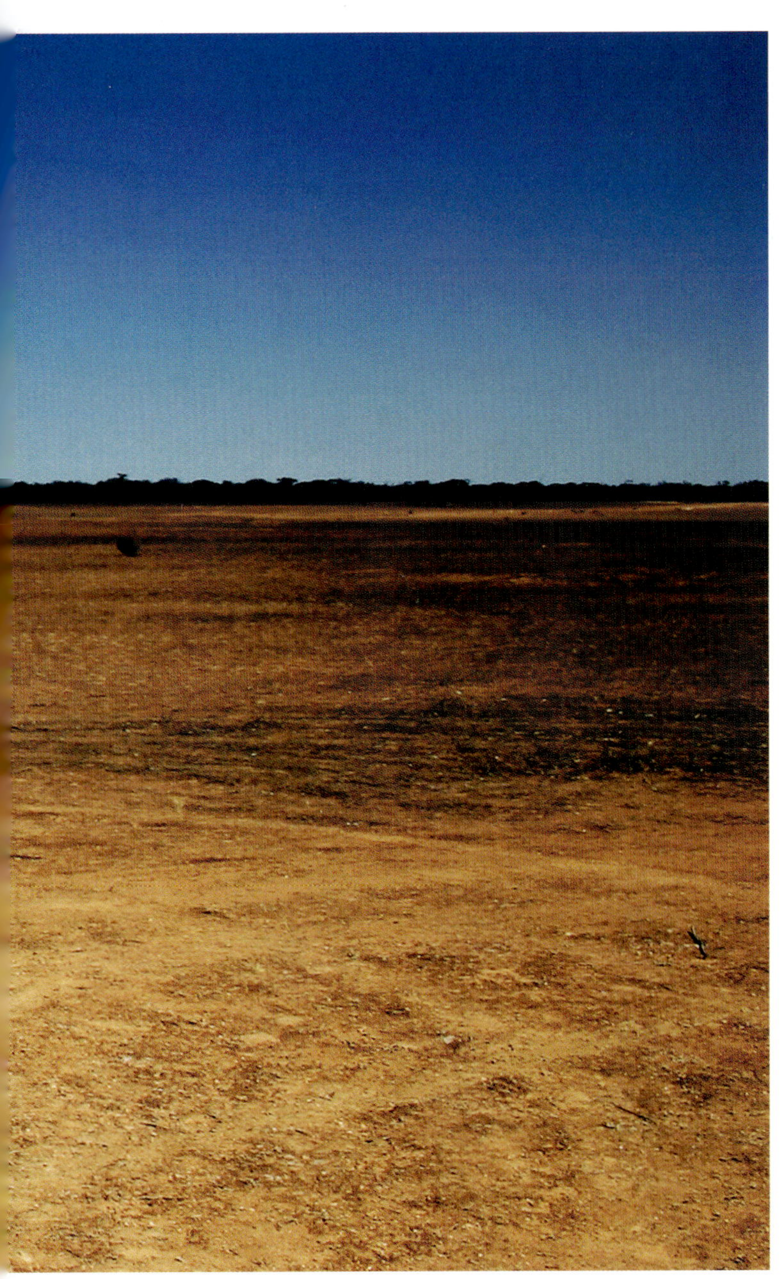

Highly Commended, Our Impact
Old car outback
Annette Blattman, St Marys, New South Wales

'I was struck by how even in the remote areas of our country man's presence is still felt.'
Outback, New South Wales

Canon 300D, 18-200mm, 1/100, f16, ISO 100
2008 9-9

Section 10, Junior Photography

The entrant must be under 18 years of age at the date of the close of entries. Entries must otherwise qualify for any of the first eight sections.

Prize: $300

Winner, Junior Photography
Bug eat bug world
Kireina Johnston, Cocos (Keeling) Islands, Western Australia

'I was looking for something small and interesting to photograph, when I saw this robberfly land. It was not until I downloaded the photo that I realised it had caught its dinner – a common house-fly.'
Cocos (Keeling) Islands, Western Australia

Judges' comment: 'Well executed!'

Olympus C760, super macro mode
2008 10-1 Exhibition

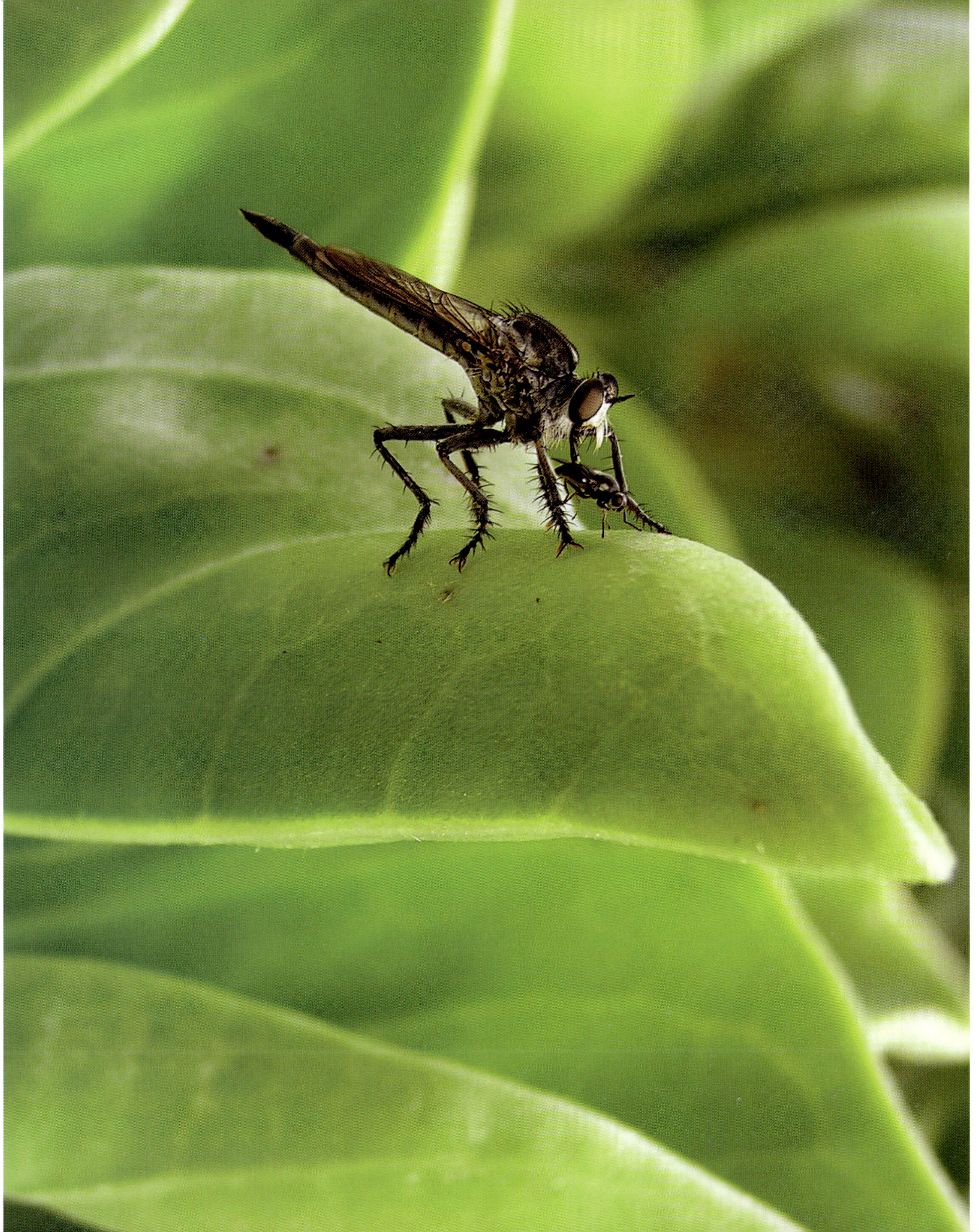

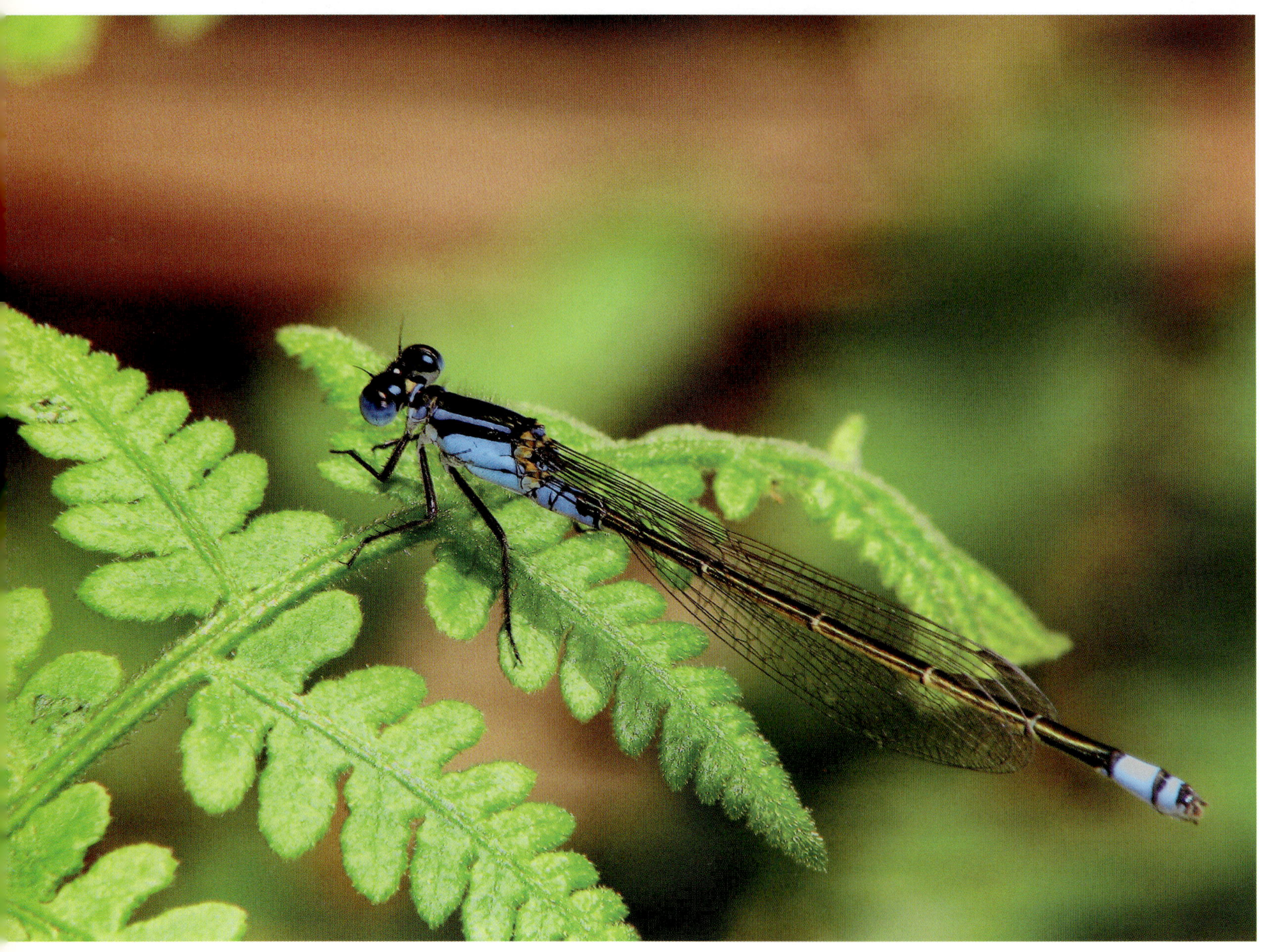

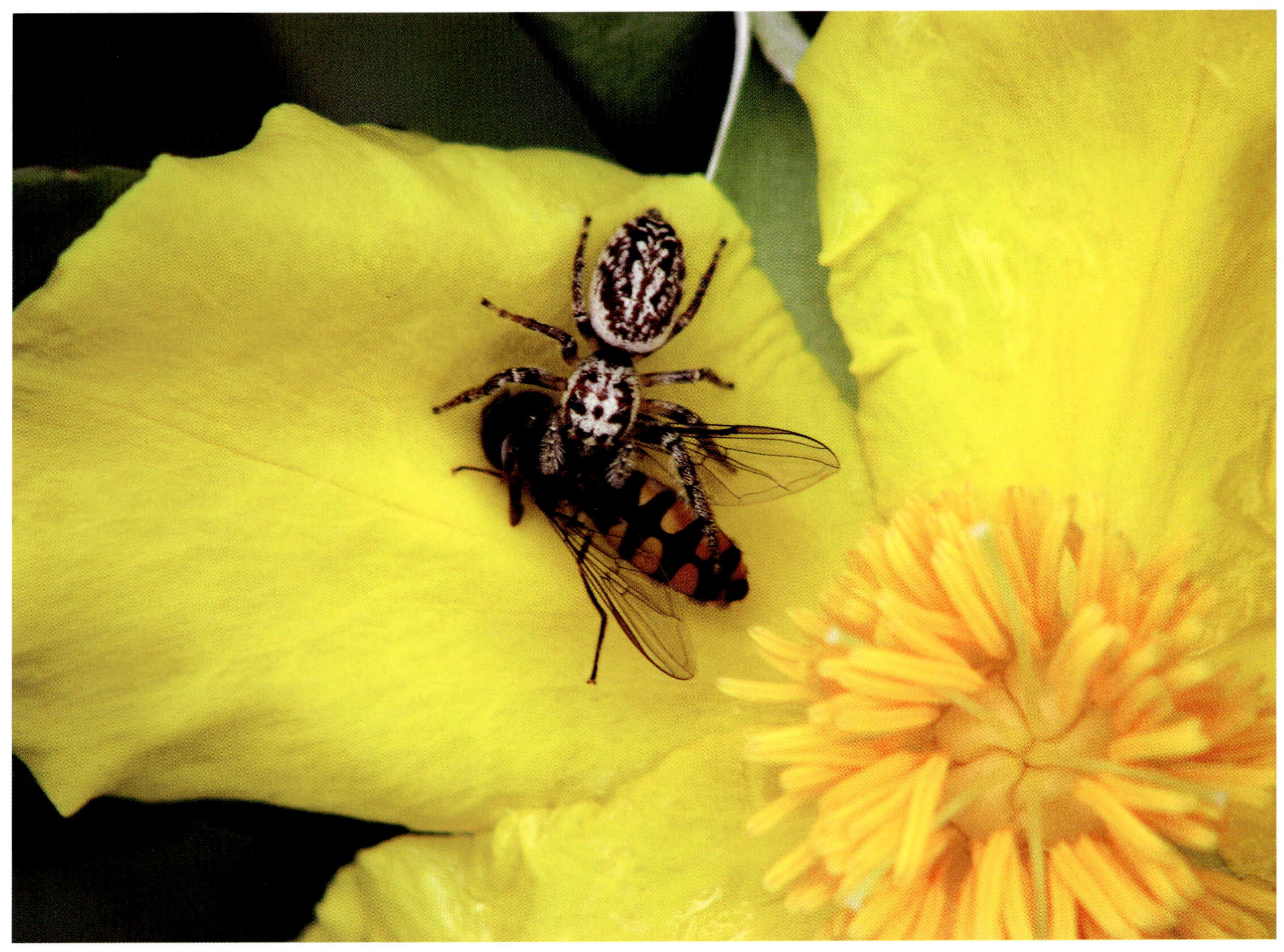

Runner-up, Junior Photography
Common bluetail damselfly
Georgie Ross, Helensburgh, New South Wales

'I was chasing the damselflies to try to get a shot,
then this one perched on a fern, so I snuck up on it
and took this.'
Royal NP, New South Wales

Judges' comment: 'Excellent composition.'

Cannon S31S, 500D diopter, 1/160, f8, ISO 80
2008 10-2 Exhibition

Highly Commended, Junior Photography
Spider with prey on *Hibbertia scandens*
Georgie Ross, Helensburgh, New South Wales

'Everything in my backyard was flowering, so I was
looking for good flowers to photograph. Then I saw
the spider with a hover-fly it had caught.'
Helensburgh, New South Wales

Cannon S31S, 500D diopter, 1/80, f3.5, ISO 80
2008 10-3 Exhibition

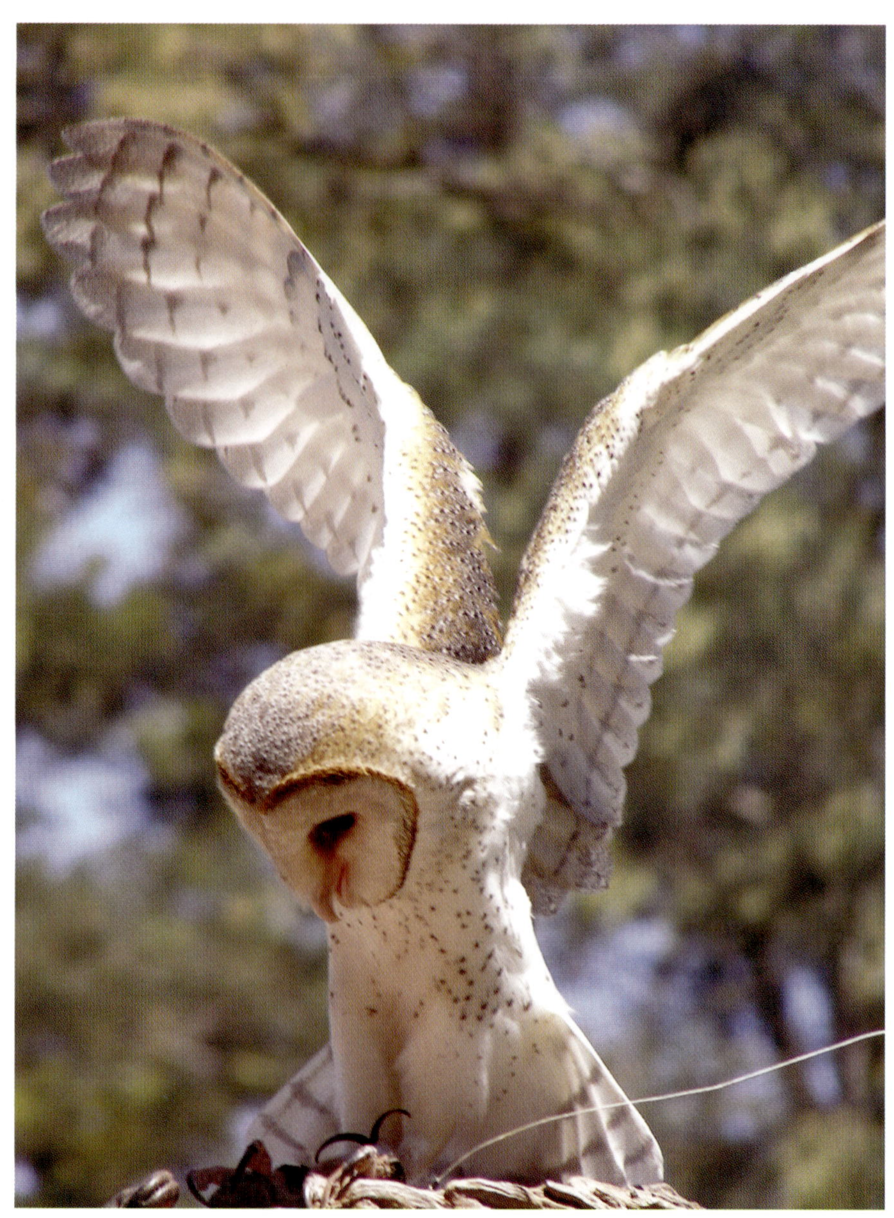

Highly Commended, Junior Photography
Startled owl
Alexander Coletti, East Doncaster, Victoria

'This was taken on my first serious attempt at
wildlife photography. I was invited to join a school
photographic excursion to meet the well renowned
Australian photographer Steve Parish. The day was a
wonderful learning experience.'
Healesville Sanctuary, Victoria

2008 10-5

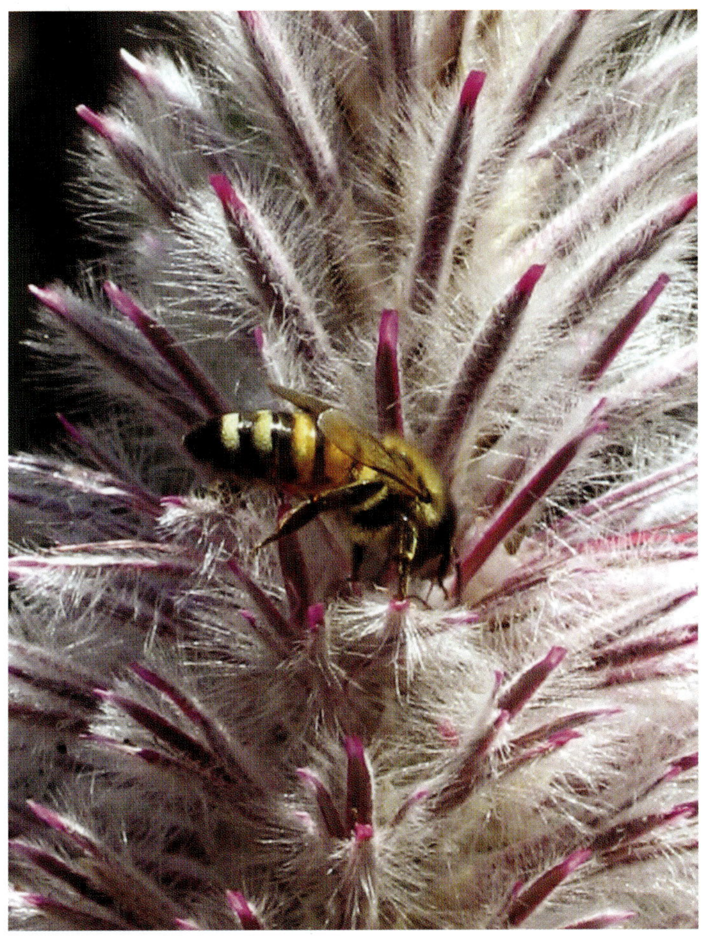

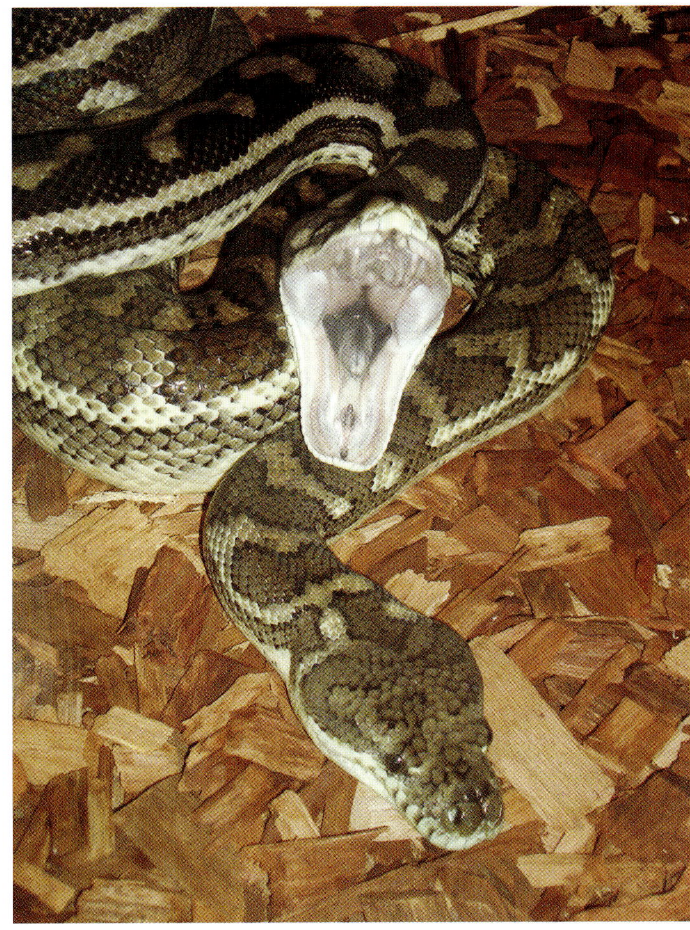

Highly Commended, Junior Photography
Ligurian bee on flower
Luke Secomb, Walkley Heights, South Australia

'This is a pure ligurian bee which is only found on Kangaroo Island. We were taking a tour of the Bush Garden which has many beautiful Australian plants and many bees among the flowers.'
Kangaroo Island, South Australia

Cannon Powershot A550, 23.5mm 1/500, f5.5, ISO 100
2008 10-6

Highly Commended, Junior Photography
Open wide
Megan Beltramelli, Albany Creek, Queensland

'I had my camera poised as I looked into the reptile enclosure and this beautiful carpet python yawned. The fact that there are two in the shot was a surprise.'
Australia Zoo, Queensland

2008 10-4

Digital Photographic Workflow:
Selected Photographers' Comments

Those photographers whose entries were shortlisted for a prize or high commendation in this year's competition were asked, for the benefit of public education, to outline their workflow sequence in Photoshop (or other preferred digital image management software) for their particular shortlisted image or images or, if difficult to recall, their general pattern of workflow.

Allen Peate, ANZANG Nature and Landscape Photographer of the Year – 2008

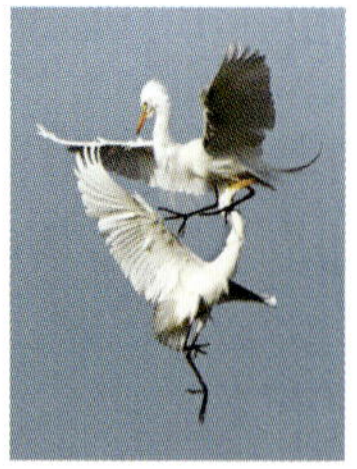

My usual workflow is in Raw to tweak exposure, contrast, saturation and, if necessary, to touch up sharpness. I then go into Photoshop, adjust levels and curves and again sharpness before outputting.

Andy Trowbridge, Portfolio Prize

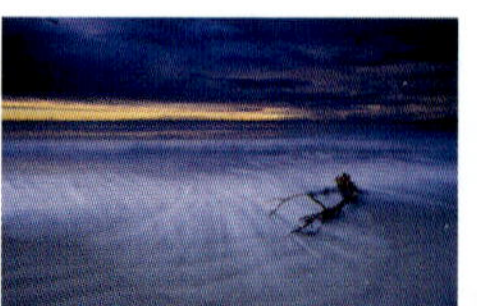

Open Raw Image in Adobe Raw. Make basic colour and contrast adjustment and check image for dust spots. Open image in Photoshop and make final colour and contrast adjustments if needed. Resize files to print dimensions and resolution, sharpen file then print.

Graham Morgan, Winner, Animal Behaviour; Winner, Black and White

Raw capture downloaded via Firewire to Macbook pro then edited in Bridge/ Adobe Camera Raw (as it operates in a 14 bit mode). Files are saved as 16 bit psd files and sharpened in Photoshop. Finished images are saved as high-quality 8 bit jpegs on mirrored hard drives. The black and white conversion was done entirely in Adobe Camera Raw.

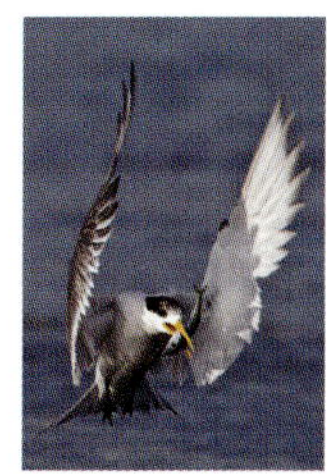

Raymond E. Alley, Runner-up, Animal Behaviour

My workflow starts with checking my gear before every shoot. I always shoot Raw plus camera jpeg. The download is in Adobe Bridge, the images are then rated and the final images are cropped if needed. Colour corrections are made in Adobe Photoshop CS3 and then finally an unsharp mask is applied.

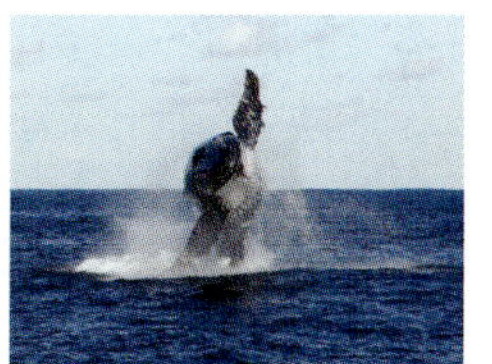

Darran Leal, Runner-up, Animal Portrait

I use Adobe Lightrooom and Photoshop CS3 for my cataloguing, processing and retrieval of images. In the last year Lightroom has become the key tool as I love the fact that it is a very visual program that takes away the complexities often associated with Photoshop. While I do have fun at times exploring creative post-production techniques, most of the images are simply processed with saturation, contrast and sharpening.

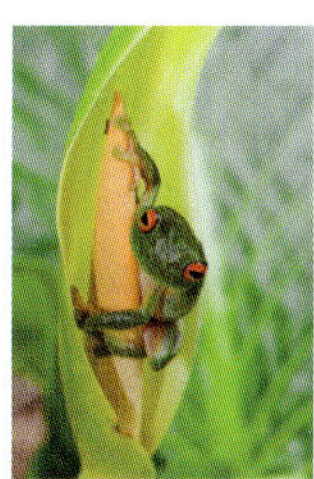

Stanley & Kaisa Breeden, Winner, Botanical Subject

We develop the Raw files in different converters, depending on the image. Here we also eliminate unwanted colour casts. Once in Photoshop we optimise the tonal range and use curves to accentuate textures and detail.

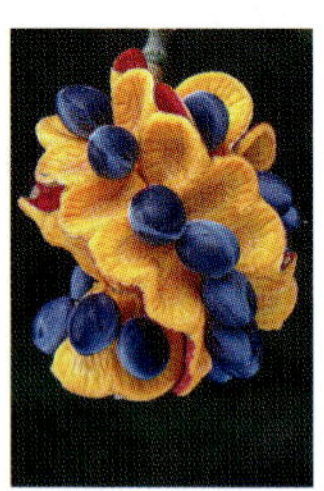

Kate Miners, Runner-up, Botanical Subject

This image has been cropped slightly to create a square format. Using Photoshop I have increased the contrast and saturation slightly.

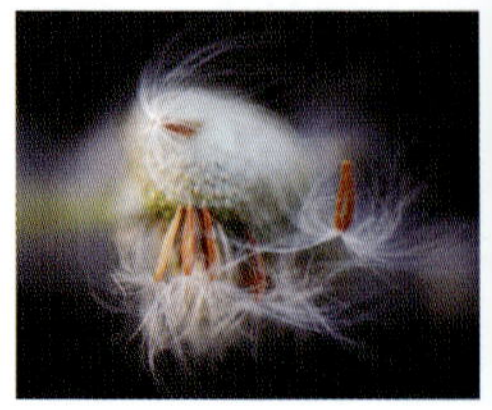

Shannon Conway, Winner, Underwater Subject

I take the RAW image from my camera and convert with Adobe CS3 RAW converter and resize in Photoshop.

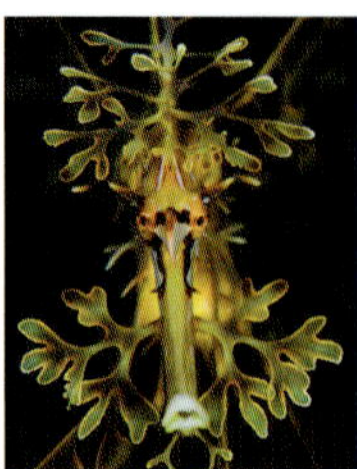

Mark Spencer, Runner-up, Underwater Subject

This image was shot on 35mm Provia 400 film. The slide was scanned and all of my image editing was performed using Adobe Lightroom. The highlights were increased slightly using the 'Exposure' slider to a level that was natural for underwater. The blacks were increased to improve contrast. The midtones ('Clarity' slider) was increased to 40 for extra midtone contrast and for extra detail. There was no adjustment to saturation or 'Vibrance' because the image was already very blue.

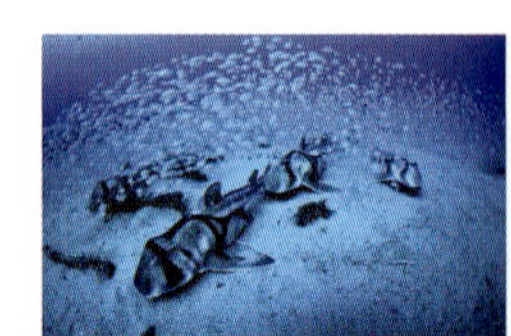

Tony Hopkins, Winner, Wilderness Landscape

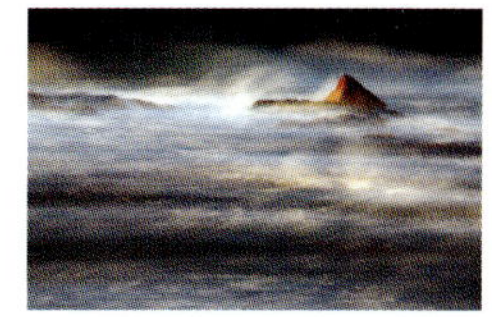

I make minor adjustments in levels, contrast and sharpening.

Nick Edards, Runner-up, Threatened Animals or Plants

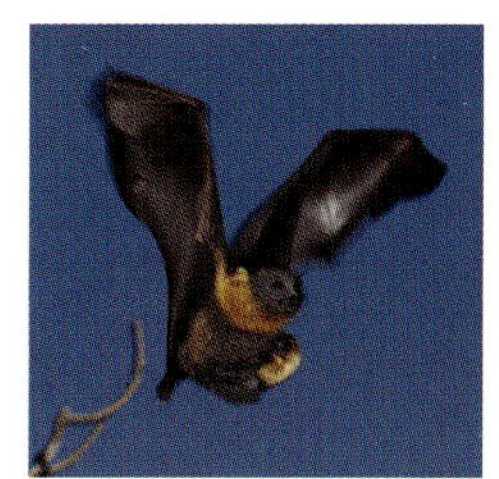

The image was shot in Nikon compressed RAW format then imported into Lightroom where I made some small tone curve adjustments. The original image was cropped and rotated in Lightroom prior to being exported to Photoshop CS3 where Noise Ninja was used to reduce noise and increase sharpness.

Jan Glover, Winner, Interpretive Photography

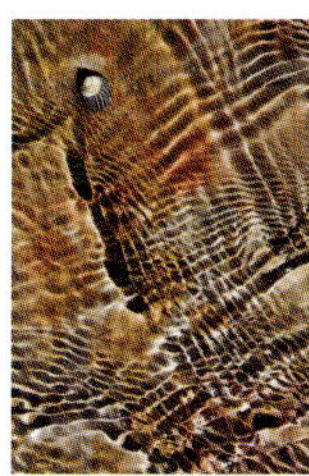

The image was captured in RAW and adjustments made to exposure, contrast, brightness and saturation.

Jessica Drake, Runner-up, Interpretive Photography

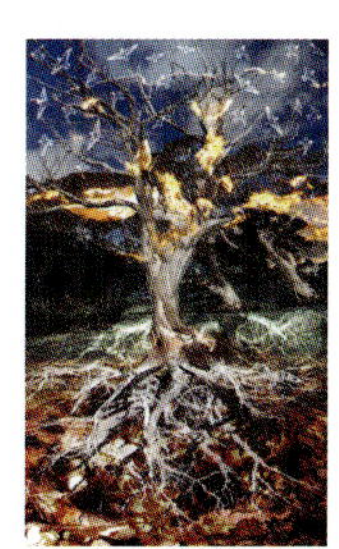

A variety of images were sandwiched together. I started with a grand snow gum in the prime of its life (a centrepiece to the forest behind it), this was overlaid with an image of sunset and clouds which gave the appearance of the tree being on fire yet still alive. The soil was made of several layers of photos of sunlight streaming through leaves, the colours changed to reflect soil and detritus. The roots were constructed of branches cut and pasted from an image of a dying snow gum. The birds were added from another image with the blending mode changed to give them a ghostly appearance.

Olga Barrington, Winner, Our Impact

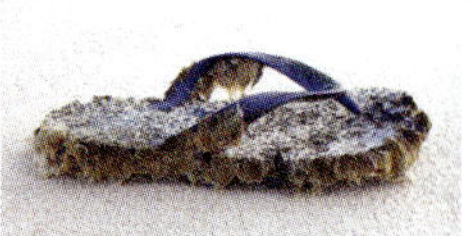

Usually I like to get the best shot in the camera and adjust as little as possible. I am not very good with computers so normally I duplicate the image to make sure I can always go back to the start. I may adjust levels and up the saturation a bit.

Michael Williams, Runner-up, Our Impact

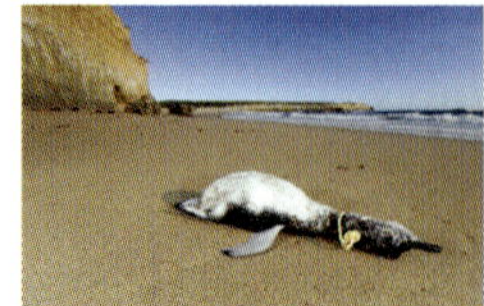

Only basic changes to my images are ever made. All images are taken in RAW format and in opening the file in Photoshop RAW dialog box I then adjust the colour in the calibrate section. I sometime use the vignetting and then sharpen the image and reduce the colour noise. The adjust section is where the last touches are made before closing the dialog box. Any fine adjustments are done in the Photoshop window.

Georgie Ross, Runner-up, Junior Photography

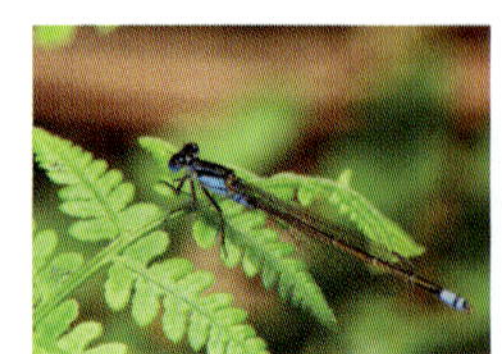

Image files are imported to Photoshop, levels and contrast are adjusted then sharpening before printing.